The Psychology of Social Influence

This is a broadly based and readable account of an increasingly important area within psychology, the study of social influence. One of the book's main strengths lies in its historical perspective, enabling readers properly to understand the foundations of present-day research and to identify the links and contrasts between various past and present traditions in America and Europe. In addition, Geneviève Paicheler shows how cultural and social factors, as well as applied concerns such as advertising and other persuasion techniques, may have determined the specific nature of theoretical and methodological approaches.

By exploring the social context of aspects of influence (suggestion, conformity, innovation), Geneviève Paicheler demonstrates that influence is essentially a socio-cognitive relationship between actor and target, rather than a confrontation between weak and strong personalities. Within this framework she also considers a number of interesting phenomena, such as hypnosis, mass hysteria, etc., that have rarely before been treated under the rubric of social influence.

This original and useful synthesis will interest readers in applied disciplines such as advertising and management and policy studies as much as psychologists, social psychologists and sociologists who want an introduction to the field.

This book is published as part of the joint publishing agreement established in 1977 between the Fondation de la Maison des Sciences de l'Homme and the Press Syndicate of the University of Cambridge. Titles published under this arrangement may appear in any European language or, in the case of volumes of collected essays, in several languages.

New books will appear either as individual titles or in one of the series which the Maison des Sciences de l'Homme and the Cambridge University Press have jointly agreed to publish. All books published jointly by the Maison des Sciences de l'Homme and the Cambridge University Press will be distributed by the Press throughout the world.

Cet ouvrage est publié dans le cadre de l'accord de co-édition passé en 1977 entre la Fondation de la Maison des Sciences de l'Homme et le Press Syndicate de l'Université de Cambridge. Toutes les langues européennes sont admises pour les titres couverts par cet accord, et les ouvrages collectifs peuvent en plusieurs langues.

Les ouvrages paraissent soit isolément, soit dans l'une des séries que la Maison des Sciences de l'Homme et Cambridge University Press ont convenu de publier ensemble. La distribution dans le monde entier des titres ainsi publiés conjointement par les deux établissements est assurée par Cambridge University Press.

The Psychology
of Social Influence

Geneviève Paicheler

Centre National de la Recherche Scientifique, Paris

Translated by Angela St James-Emler and Nicholas Emler

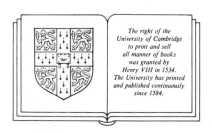

The right of the
University of Cambridge
to print and sell
all manner of books
was granted by
Henry VIII in 1534.
The University has printed
and published continuously
since 1584.

Cambridge University Press

Cambridge
New York *New Rochelle* *Melbourne* *Sydney*

& Editions de la Maison des Sciences de l'Homme

Paris

Published by the Press Syndicate of the University of Cambridge
The Pitt Building, Trumpington Street, Cambridge CB2 1RP
32 East 57th Street, New York, NY10022, USA
10 Stamford Road, Oakleigh, Melbourne 3166, Australia
and Editions Maison des Sciences de l'Homme
54 Boulevard Raspail, 75270 Paris Cedex 06

First published by Maison des Sciences de l'Homme and
Cambridge University Press 1988

Printed in Great Britain at the University Press, Cambridge

British Library cataloguing in publication data

Paicheler, Geneviève
The psychology of social influence.
1. Influence (Psychology) 2. Social interaction
I. Title
302   HM132

Library of Congress cataloguing in publication data

Paicheler, Geneviève, 1947-
The psychology of social influence
Translation of: Psychologie des influences sociales.
Bibliography.
1. Social psychology. I. Title.
[DNLM: 1. Psychology, Social. HM 251 P142p]
HM251.P1713   1988   302   87-21827

ISBN 0 521 30940 9
ISBN 2 7351 0218 1 (France only)

Contents

Introduction

The limits of the social

To consider the problem of influence is to ask about the fashion in which the actions and thoughts of individuals and groups are determined by their environment. It is to explore a fundamental phenomenon of social life: the impressions or changes produced in individuals by their relations with others, whether or not they are conscious of such effects.

A basic question arises out of this introductory statement. Where are the limits of the social to be found? For the most part they are perfectly clear. The social ends where the individual or the personal begins. To cast doubt on this common-sense view is almost invariably to invite incredulity and incomprehension. Matters are further complicated by the fact that 'individual' and 'social' are not simply principles for the categorisation of reality; they are just as much means for ordering reality on a scale of values contrasting the good and the bad.

The good is situated on the side of the individual. The solitary individual, or the individual purified of all social influences is good, creative, rational, autonomous. The social, the cultural, the phenomena of influence, these operate only to stifle this individual, destroying his capacities and crushing his aspirations. 'Society' constitutes a rigid mould, begetting 'cultural preserves' (a term coined by Moreno, 1934) from which we must strive to liberate ourselves if we are to recover our vitality, and the full scope of those inherent potentials that society suppresses in the individual.

In pursuit of this goal over several decades, social psychologists have evolved numerous methods, including paradoxically, group methods, intended to lead the individual to appreciate the extensiveness of social constraints and to free him from their grip. Thus psychodrama, therapeutic groups, and diagnostic groups have been devised to reestablish in the participants that natural spontaneity eliminated by an oppressive society. The individual only achieves the full range of his potential in opposition to society.

Similarly, the child possesses that most treasured capacity, creativity, while society, in making an adult of the child, steadily reduces it to the point where no spark of originality remains.

These assertions are all so thoroughly accepted that they have no capacity to surprise. They *have the flavour of self-evident truths*. Indeed they are regarded as so obvious as to merit little further discussion. We believe, nonetheless, that their weakness lies precisely in their very obviousness. We have known for a long time that if there is anything we should distrust it is precisely those facts which are too self-evident. The danger in the social sciences, particularly in those areas where the man in the street believes he can without hesitation handle complex theoretical arguments, is precisely that facts concerning human behaviour and experience have a self-evident character which can be grasped without ever embarking upon rigorous investigation. Far from helping us, this transparency is an obstacle to a balanced appreciation of social processes, the more especially as an apparently scientific analysis is often no more than a sophisticated mimicry of these misleading manifestations.

The first and elementary precaution consists in questioning and moving beyond the evidence which these processes seem to provide in themselves.

The uniformity of others

Now, if we and those like us seem able to defend our individuality against the totalitarian assaults of the social, what never fails to strike us is the uniformity of others. The conspicuous character of this inclination in others is the essence of stereotypes, those evaluative and perceptual abstractions which allow us so confidently to assert that 'Germans are orderly, obedient and disciplined', the Italians 'garrulous, expansive and sentimental', the Japanese 'impassive and meticulous'... Thus, the most striking thing about social influence is the uniformity it produces...in others.

Certainly, this observation is not original. Travellers and other enlightened spirits have long been astonished by, and inclined to remark upon, the uniformity of opinions and practices in countries and cultures very different from their own; such uniformity seemed especially conspicuous. And besides opinions and practices, this uniformity also typified matters apparently more 'natural', like the body, gestures, and posture.

The social body

As early as 1934, the anthropologist Marcel Mauss had established the importance for the social sciences of a field of research bearing on the techniques of the body, and concerned with sets of actions which have common physiological functions but which vary across culture. He recounts jokingly how the idea had come to him when he was confined to hospital in the United States: 'A kind of revelation came to me in hospital; I was ill in New York. I asked myself where I had seen young ladies walking like the nurses. I had the time to reflect on it and I realised finally that it was at the cinema. On my return to France I noted, particularly in Paris, the frequency of this walk; the young girls were French but they walked in the same fashion. In effect the fashion of the American gait, thanks to the cinema, had arrived in our own country. It was an idea that I could generalise' (Mauss, 1978, p. 368).

And Mauss so generalised this idea that he came, in his illuminating essay on the 'techniques of the body', to the following conclusion: 'In sum, perhaps there does not exist a 'natural' fashion in the adult' (*ibid.*, p. 370). It was a revolutionary conclusion at the time of writing and one whose full richness and implications we have yet to appreciate. It is also a conclusion that continues to meet stiff resistance because it goes against the tenacious evidence of common sense which separates the individual and his body from the social, placing the former on the side of the natural and the good and the latter on the side of destructive and devouring culture.

Following Mauss, Lévi-Strauss deplored the fact that by 1950 so little progress had yet been achieved in the study of body techniques. 'Nevertheless, any ethnologist who has worked in the field knows that the [body's] possibilities are astonishingly variable across countries. The threshold of excitability, the limits of resistance are different in each culture. "Impossible" effort, "intolerable" pain, "unparalleled" pleasure are less a function of particular individuals than of *standards sanctioned by the approval or disapproval of the collective*' (my italics). Hence, man is not a natural product of his body; on the contrary, 'it is man who above all and always makes of his body a product of his techniques and his representations' (Lévi-Strauss in Mauss, 1978, p. xiii).

This body, which carries imprinted within it the marks of historical, cultural and social heritage, at the same time renders them obscure and inaccessible by the very fact that they are constantly present and so lacking in salience. This is why we so readily notice, for example, that styles of movement are so different from our own in other groups and cultures. This observation has resulted in such bland assertions as the claim that 'the African woman moves in an erotic fashion', the perception of a refreshing and liberating eroticism, where our own impoverished Western eroticism is compressed and channelled by an iron corset which deprives us of the opportunity or capacity to move in 'an erotic fashion' ourselves.

We seldom recognise our own uniformity, our own conformity. It is like the air we breathe, just as invisible and indiscernible, and just as indispensable.

If bodies themselves do not mark the limits of the influence towards uniformity exercised by society on individuals, then we must look elsewhere for the boundaries of what is specific to the individual in his opposition to society. Posing the problem thus we find ourselves with the following alternative: either these limits exist or the very attempt to locate them is based on a false assumption.

Basic personality

Perhaps these limits, if indeed there are such, are to be found in the determinants of character or personality. Some are inclined to believe that our character is determined by heavenly bodies, those omnipotent masters of the world and its affairs; the course of our lives is subject to this all-powerful fate and quite independent of our will. Clearly the social has no part in this. Others, though sometimes also the same people as in the preceding case, are certain that hereditary factors or, to be more contemporary, genetic factors are pre-eminent in the formation of personalities. They rely here on an evident fact: children psychologically resemble their parents. A quick-tempered father 'manufactures' quick-tempered children; the intuitive intelligence of a mother will re-emerge in the intellectual capacities of the daughter. There are many such clichés and truisms, and no one regards them as exceptionable. If particular families do indeed constitute the seed-beds of characteristic personalities, nonetheless these and many similar observations find the certainty of their assumptions threatened on all sides. Psychoanalysis has demonstrated the error of this type of simplistic claim, revealing the subtle processes on which the development of individual psychology is founded. And anthropologists have gone into the field imbued with the lessons of psychoanalysis. The 'culturalist' movement has put the emphasis squarely on the predominance of culture in the formation of personality. Anthropologists have demonstrated that each culture produces a kind of 'basic personality type' which constitutes the foundation for the personalities of all its members. Ruth Benedict (1934) among others, has given us wonderful descriptions of idyllic, *Apollonian* cultures in which everyone is gentle, good, cooperative, generous, and of terrifying *Dionysian* cultures in which everyone is aggressive, wicked, selfish and quarrelsome. In the same way, social and professional groups 'manufacture' individuals displaying equally homogeneous modes of thought and behaviour.

Historians have also entered the fray, opening up the history of thought as a major field of inquiry, investigating the evolution of everyday emotions, feelings and inner experiences – intimate relationships, birth, domestic work... Historians also have contributed to our appreciation of the extent to which these matters, embedded in practices, rituals and beliefs, depend more on cultural than on biological factors.

The overwhelming character of society

In emphasising the ascendancy that societies exercise over individuals, right down to the heart of their most trivial activities, we risk creating at the extreme a caricature of individuals as totally controlled by hidden and ubiquitous social systems over which they have no control and in which they have no involvement. Here again is to be found an image in which the social is opposed to the individual. But in this case, the destructive effects of the social are taken to the very limit, annihilating the individual, reducing him to a cog in a machine that is monstrous and remote, uniform and mindless. This is the allegory created by the novelist George Orwell in *1984*. The book derives its impact from the fact that it is not so very far removed from reality. It constitutes no more than a moderate side-step, opening up a social universe that is all the more terrifying to us for being so close to our own. The 'television screen' inquisitor who suppresses deviation even in the home is no more than an extreme metaphor for the systems of control which surround the individual in our society.

> The telescreen received and transmitted simultaneously. Any sound that Winston made, above the level of a very low whisper, would be picked up by it; moreover, so long as he remained within the field of vision which the metal plaque commanded he could be seen as well as heard. There was, of course, no way of knowing whether you were being watched at any given moment. How often, or on what system the Thought Police plugged in on any individual wire was guesswork. It was even conceivable they watched everybody all the time. But at any rate they could plug into your wire whenever they wanted to. You had to live – did live, from habit that became instinct – in the assumption that every sound you made was overheard and, except in darkness, every movement scrutinised. (1949, p. 7)

Necessary influences

Social influence is thus self-evident and all the more obvious when we see it produced in others. It appears as a necessity for others and as alienating for ourselves, and from this arise conceptions which vary according to whether or not the individual is opposed to society. An initial analysis of these conceptions suggests that the phenomenon of influence is common to all human beings. But beyond its self-evident character, we are very rapidly confronted with the complexity of the phenomenon. Language hinders our progress here. The single word *influence* is used to designate a collection of different and indeed contradictory realities; it is used to designate the action as much as its effect, to designate, depending on circumstances, the best or the worst of things. Our task must be to clean out the Augean Stables of this confused semantic universe, to put things in order, to classify the collection of social phenomena and manifestations which the various forms of influence involve.

Beneficial Influence

We are not bound to construe social influence only as an evil force against which 'individuals' must struggle if it is not to engulf them. On the contrary, in many respects it simplifies our lives. It enables us to 'think straight' and to act 'as we should' in most situations. It causes us to be polite, well-behaved, civilised beings, marked by the stamp of culture and society. What was called, in the age of the Enlightenment, 'imitation' is none other than this fundamental aspect of influence. 'Imitation is thus the principal means for the perfection [of man]; it shapes him from birth to death. Without imitation, the advances made by one individual would be lost to all others. It is by this means that children learn our customs and conventions, submit to our practices, and are introduced to our language' (In *Exposé des recherches faites pour l'examen du magnetisme animal*, 1784). Here, society mounts no unconstrained assault on the individual. On the contrary, it wins him over little by little, making of him a socialised being, equipped with its complex heritage; it enhances him and leads him to achieve his true humanity. Man is not degraded if he behaves according to 'the customs and conventions'.

From the beginning of the twentieth century one finds the same positive vision of social influence represented in the social psychology that developed in the United States. J. M. Baldwin maintained that imitation not only possessed a clearly utilitarian character but also contributed to the independence and creativity of individuals. 'Imitation, to the intelligent and earnest imitator, is never slavish, never mere repetition; it is on the contrary, a means to further ends, a method of absorbing what is present in others and of making it over in forms peculiar to one's own temper and valuable to one's own genius' (Baldwin, 1911, p. 22).

Strong suggestion and gentle persuasion

The difficulty in detecting social influence is also the mark of its effectiveness. It impregnates us to such a degree that we identify as emanating from ourselves and our own choices what is in reality the imprint of a group or society. This internalisation of influence is the basis on which social uniformities may be upheld without overt pressure. It eliminates all unduly brutal, and hence dangerous, expressions of conflict. Clearly it is preferable to convince than to repress, to request than to demand.

The power of social influence is more apparent in its commonplace or everyday effects and its ubiquity than in highly dramatic and exceptional cases. But the impact of one being on another, or a group on a single person can take much more violent and cataclysmic forms. The recent discovery in Guyana of the mass suicide of nine hundred persons, members of a sect led by a certain Jim Jones, plunged the public into horror and disbelief. How could this have happened? How were these people able to let themselves be persuaded to drink poison or make their children drink it? How could they have been able, without protest or resistance, to submit to the megalomaniac proposals of such a crazy man, a Blue Beard of modern times who shot himself full of amphetamines? How could they have been capable of abdicating all critical impulses, and sustaining faith in the philosophico-religious concoction which he served to them daily? This kind of destructive influence does not happen overnight; it is created progressively, by successive steps, almost by trial and error. The ratchet is turned ever tighter. Everyone finds themselves enmeshed in an organisational structure and group pressures which they themselves created and which they themselves perpetuate, founded on their faith and their need to adhere to some reassuring, unflawed system for explanation of the world. This type of influence derives from suggestion and it is in hypnosis that it finds its most highly developed form. It is a form of influence difficult to identify until it goes too far.

Here we find outlined two contrasting facets of influence: *gentle persuasion* and *strong suggestion*. Nonetheless, both involve means of control the precise effectiveness of which varies according to circumstances.

Where gentle persuasion is possible, it is always preferable to strong suggestion; any social system is all the more fragile if reliant on repression rather than persuasion, coercion rather than request. 'Gentle persuasion' entails a transformation of power into a multitude of persistent and omnipresent powers. Potent, conspicuous, and far-reaching power is split into a collection of little powers incorporated in each person, controlled and perpetuated by all, and resulting in a tight control of the most minute and the most intimate of activities. It results in a mass of petty fears about not being 'as one should be' or doing 'as one should'. Within such a mesh of pressures, each individual is readily supervised without anyone consciously recognising it. Each one endeavours to be 'the obedient subject, the individual subjected to habits, rules, orders, an authority that is exercised continually around and upon him, and which he must allow to function automatically in him' (Foucault, 1977, p.128-9). This multiplication of authority ensures its effect and the strength of commitment it produces nips all resistance in the bud. Influence thus takes the form of conformity, or normalisation. It reduces the separation between controllable and self-controlled individuals.

The internal eye

In the present day, social influence possesses a special dimension. Each one of us is caught within the play of a set of pressures. At the same time, as more and more sophisticated means of mass communication have developed, as information has multiplied and the means for processing information have been refined, so has the desire for social control strengthened and the search for increasingly effective means of persuasion intensified.

At the end of the eighteenth century, Bentham's conception of an architecture founded on visibility prefigured, reified, and concentrated the desire for 'gentle persuasion' in the shape of a strictly ordered environment. He conceived the 'panopticon'.

> At the periphery, an annular building; at the centre a tower; this tower is pierced with wide windows that open onto the inner side of the ring; the peripheric building is divided into cells, each of which extends the whole width of the building; they have two windows, one on the inside corresponding to the windows of the tower; the other on the outside allows the light to cross the cell from one end to the other. All that is needed, then, is to place a supervisor in a central tower, and to shut up in each cell a madman, a patient, a condemned man, a worker, or a schoolboy. By the effect of back-lighting, one can observe from the tower, standing out precisely against the light, the small captive shadows in the cells of the periphery. They are so many cages or so many small theatres, in which each actor is alone, perfectly individualized and constantly visible. The panoptic mechanism arranges spatial unities that make it possible to see constantly and to recognize immediately. (Foucault, *ibid.*, p.200)

This panoptic tower from which each individual can be surveyed unawares is today effectively replaced by the unremitting attention to which we are all subjected by the press, publicity and television. The individual is always the object, never the subject of an inquiry, and the prisoner of a 'machinery that assures dissymmetry, lack of balance, difference' (*ibid.* p.202).

1984... We have already arrived. In the opinion of an article published in *Le Monde*, on 20 March 1983, it can in truth be said that reality has overtaken Orwell's fiction, certainly in so far as the technical means for making employees more visible are concerned, techniques which make visibility the most inexorable of traps: internal phones, telephone paging, cameras, electronic name tags governing movements within buildings and ensuring strict accounting of working time, rigorously recording and controlling rhythms. In order to survive in the organisation, employees must accommodate their time and space to this system of control without error; they have no option but to consent to this octopus-like system of discipline. One among their number notes: 'People are more and more passive, particularly the young, they are there to work, they participate in their own bondage, *without being particularly aware of it*' (my italics). Here we reach the extremities of those highly insidious and well-integrated forms of influence: *normalisation* and *conformity*.

Adaptations and transformations

Social systems simultaneously destroy and adapt. They destroy in creating the conditions for maintaining uniformity. They adapt in organising and limiting those changes they cannot control. They normalise or impose conformity, but they must also accommodate to innovation. Our problem is to demonstrate the conditions and the processes by which these two varieties of phenomenon together contribute to the functioning of social systems.

What is striking about a mechanistic conception of society is its image of a set of cogs which take as much time to be activated as to be stopped. Such inertial force hinders any attempt at change. On the one side is the habitual, the reassuring, the functioning of a routine which the known brings to the unknown, in which shocks and jolts are minimised. On the other side is the unusual, the unaccustomed, indeed the terrifying, but also change in which one must be prepared to confront the unknown.

Happily there are occasions in the life of a society when another language is heard, turning its back on established rules and institutions, a language which, by its freshness, shatters the routine. It is a language of renovation, a cry of hope that seems, after a long journey, like the long-awaited dawn, a language which redefines priorities, a language which is given reality in action as it enters into the struggle against suffocation and repression.

These two aspects perpetually coexist in systems where forces of homogeneity and of heterogeneity, of stability and change, are combined and confronted.

New minorities

The nineteen seventies made familiar the language of opposition and debate with its abundance of neologisms – 'alternative' society, 'counter' culture, 'new' fathers, 'new' women, etc... The impulse to suppress any hint of change or novelty, however ridiculous, has too often taken precedence over a more disinterested analysis of the phenomena of innovation and their implications. This is the gap we must strive to fill through the analysis of a particular phenomenon, that of the minority. Two complementary aspects of the transformation of social systems require particular attention on our part: minority influence and innovation.

We have seen how visibility constitutes a means of control; to be able to see and to know that one can be seen leads to greater circumspection in behaviour. On the other hand, it can serve as a device for social change. In this case visibility is no longer imposed or submitted to, it is overcome and turned against the system. It is both the prelude to and the condition for change. It is at the very heart of the strategy used by all minority groups seeking to force social change.

Let us take an example. In the last few years France has seen the proliferation of laws and government measures aimed at according to women the prerogatives and rights formerly only accorded to men. Nevertheless, few recall the slogan: 'Even more unknown than the warrior: his wife.'

This slogan marked the first overt demonstration of a tiny group which was later to become known as the 'Movement for the Liberation of Women'. It was 26 August 1970. In the great calm of the holiday period and under the bewildered eyes of tourists visiting the Arc de Triomphe in Paris, a small group of women tried to place on the tomb of the unknown warrior wreaths of flowers with ribbons declaring: 'One man in two is a woman' and 'Even more unknown than the warrior: his wife.' 'Journalists were gathered to cover the event... But before we had a chance to leave our vehicles and move towards the Eternal Flame, the cops appeared and roughly grabbed our wreaths and banners. Before we had realised what was happening, they brutally dragged some of us off' (Tristan and de Pisan, 1977, p. 54). The scene was set, the spectacle commenced: action, reaction, repression. Its consequence was to bring things into the open. 'The next day *France Soir* ran the following headline on its front page: "Feminist demonstrators unable to lay their wreath 'To the Soldier's unknown wife'." For the first time there was talk of the Women's Liberation Movement. We did not give ourselves this name. It was the press who, by analogy with the American "Women's Lib", so baptised us. Feminism was in the process of being born' (*ibid.* p. 54). From the beginning, there was a deliberate and conscious intention among these women to seek publicity, to seek access to the public domain, a basic, primordial quest for *visibility*. 'By laying this wreath, we denounced our oppression in a fashion which was both *spectacular* and humorous. It was necessary to make a *breach in the great wall of silence* about our true condition, reaching the press so that it would echo with our action. It was necessary to let other women know that a handful of women did not agree with the majority about the position of women and that they would continue the struggle' (*ibid*. p. 58, my italics).

After this exemplary act of baptism, the women continued to beat a path to the public arena, using the only means they possessed, vociferous, shock-provoking minority action. Another objective emerged, an urgent requirement for all women, in particular for those who had abortions secretly and in the face of risks which were as much penal as hygienic: repeal of the law of 1920 forbidding all abortion other than the strictly therapeutic, a truly murderous and retrograde law. This law was ruthlessly protected and defended by every reactionary element obstinately ignoring the degree to which it was distorted and infringed; it was a law which weighed with all its force on the least advantaged women in society. It was necessary to break the silence and hypocrisy by some outrageous action. Thus came the publication in *Le Nouvel Observateur* of the 'Proclamation of the 343 harlots'.

> One million women have an abortion each year in France. They have it done in conditions which are dangerous by reason of the secrecy to which they are condemned, although this operation, carried out under medical control, is the simplest possible. Silence is imposed on these millions of women. I declare myself to be one of them. I declare that I have had an abortion.

There followed the signatures of 343 women, stars from the world of entertainment, women from intellectual circles, ordinary women, who had the audacity to brave the taboo and to transform the hidden search for individual solutions into a collective protest, and who were all by this act liable to prosecution and judicial sanctions.

> Incontestably, *Le Nouvel Observateur* was the first newspaper to understand that the struggle for abortion and contraception was a political battle, the only one willing to make the proclamation one of a number that would become historic. But it was inevitable that differences would arise between the requirements of a newspaper necessarily integrated into a system whose laws we disapproved of and ourselves, a handful of women who wished to breach the walls of political expediency by revolt. The ups and downs of our collaboration with *Le Nouvel Observateur* were of minor importance, given that we achieved publication of all the signatures, famous or otherwise, quite an achievement in

a press where one is normally obliged to use the exclusive channel of 'personalities' to get a hearing. And then *Le Nouvel Observateur* gave us an uncensored page to present our own explosive point of view on maternity. Personally I considered this a great step forward ... On the first page of *Le Monde* on 5 April 1971, the following headline could be found: 'A date', and on two inside pages followed all the signatures to the proclamation and commentaries... The tangible results of our action were paraded in all the newspapers. *The women's movement publicly existed and could not be ignored.* (*ibid.* pp. 68-9; my italics)

Three years later, after many more ups and downs, the influence of a movement that was in such a minority at the outset was assured and, following several days of stormy and passionate debate in the National Assembly, the Minister of Health, Simone Weil, secured a vote for a liberalised abortion law. This protest action, at the beginning the action of a minority but subsequently increasingly organised, had shaken and finally forced the position of the majority government of the period.

The views and the actions of feminist groups, initiated at the beginning of the seventies, had started a movement, had served to arouse people, had made possible the spread of ideas and behaviour, even to those men and women who spurned feminism and without them being aware of the profound changes this had introduced into their lives. From small beginnings in the early seventies, feminism now seems well established. It has at least prevailed over the ministerial portfolio. Now it is more a matter of ensuring that claims are sustained. For several years, however, the objective was to draw attention to or bring to light the flagrant failings of the established order, to create the possibility and the conditions for social change.

The action of the minority involved simultaneous pursuit of several aims. It provoked public debate. It brought into question in public what had been hidden. By clarifying what was at stake and where the opposition lay, it created a movement toward engagement. The minority rejected the mundane and routine ways of operating. Its members constructed an autonomy which allowed them to master their own destiny through the production of an analysis and critique which others could also grasp.

In specifying the nature of minority influence and the processes which constitute it, we are led to compare it with majority influence. This allows us to define the second axis of our investigation: *majority influence–minority influence* or, in other terms, *conformity/normalisation–innovation.* Relating minority and majority influence does not mean contrasting them point by point, construing one as the inverse or negative of the other, the other, procedures which might lead to a consideration of the one in terms of the other. These are two phenomena which operate in quite different ways, producing contrary effects in social systems.

Public and private

Research on reliable means of persuasion leads to questions about their nature and their effectiveness, about the depth and the durability of the changes they induce. This was one of the first questions to be raised in social psychology. It is an issue which permeates all research on influence. How can individuals or groups be made to change, under what circumstances, by playing on what motives, and with what results? Such are the questions which all analysts of social influence have asked, and to which each in his turn has supplied the parts of an answer, contributing to an increasingly comprehensive perspective on these phenomena.

To ask about the nature and the effectiveness of means of persuasion leads in particular to questions about the permanence of the changes they produce. Two broad categories of response to influence are possible: acceptance and resistance. If resistance occurs, we need to know how great it is, what are its causes and what is its object. It is also necessary to know whether it is general or overt. Does it, even without the subjects' knowledge, open up breaches through which change may overtake them? Resistance can take the form of either an unconditional or a partial rejection of influence.

To influence, in contrast, is to cause changes. All influence implies a modification of the groups or individuals influenced. Demonstrating the existence of such does not of itself allow any conclusions about its depth or its stability; it does not establish whether change has occurred at the level of what is said or at the level of what is thought, or whether yielding to the influence entails any substantial revision in systems of thought or representation.

We happen to wear certain clothes, not because we find them aesthetic or suitable, but because they are in fashion. We feel relieved at no longer having to wear them when the fashion passes, though while it remains à la mode we cannot imagine wearing anything else. For example, a degree of comfort previously only dreamt of was realised at the beginning of this century under the influence of fashion designers like Poiret and Chanel who did away with stifling whalebone corsets and replaced them with skirts and petticoats, to create a supple and less physically constraining fashion. In the same way, there often exists a contradiction between our public words and deeds and our 'inner convictions'.

This contradiction is just as apparent when influence is accepted as when it is rejected. Thus, we hesitate to wear certain clothes which please us and which we find suitable because we judge them to be 'too much the new fashion'. Several months later, when the fashion is established, we don them without the slightest apprehension. This time-lag between *the public level* and *the private level* constitutes the third axis of our investigation.

To begin with, influence was only conceived and studied as an overt experience, expressing a complete agreement between actions and inner convictions. In order to grasp the true extent and complexity of influence it has been necessary to refer to progressively more subtle processes which are either latent initially or which remain latent because they remain beyond the reach of consciousness. This public–private dimension of analysis is in turn related to the depth or superficiality of influence effects. Publicly manifested influence may be either superficial or profound. Influence confined to the private domain is always profound, an influence of which the subject himself may not be aware, surreptitiously directing his modes of action and his understanding of reality.

To be systematic, we should say that our first two axes of study – gentle persuasion/strong suggestion and conformity/innovation – place the emphasis on process, the course of influence rather than the effects or results of influence. Here again we must be aware of the trap contained in the word 'influence' which at the same time designates the intention to influence, reactions to influence, and the fluid space between the two, surrounding the complex course of influence. We must, however, be content with the term language provides, even though it is imprecise. 'Influence' designates two complementary aspects of the same phenomenon. Our third analytic axis – private–public – is itself more related to the effects of influence.

Influences and representations

A fourth and final analytic axis completes the picture, touching again on processes rather than effects. It will deal with the links which unite influence with *meaning*, that is to say, with systems of signification, with social codes, with the representations contained in social systems which make possible the exercise of forms of influence specific to particular circumstances. Influence never occurs within a social vacuum; it is always part of a historical context, always embedded in social relationships, both a ritual and a symbol. 'Social reality' is indissolubly linked to social meanings; it has no existence outside the intellectual means possessed by a group for its understanding.

Take the case of Potlatch, so well described by Marcel Mauss (1978). It involves a ceremony of conspicuous consumption in which those who wish to remain chiefs are required, in a costly competitive rite, to consume, burn or give away a considerable amount of goods. Some see in this a device for the distribution of resources, a means of economic exchange, others a scandalous squandering, an intolerable waste. But for those who practise it, it is a sacred and unchangeable ritual, integrated into a language and set of symbolic practices centred on power, gift-giving, and obligation, undertaken only by those who are truly worthy to be chiefs and recipro-cate the gift.

Interpretive frameworks

Reality is not transparent. It does not present itself directly to the interpreter. The decoding of all reality occurs in terms of interpretive frames and conversely these frameworks constitute reality.

A priori, social reality is at once decoded and constructed in terms of interpretive frames derived from social groups. The latter are related to and interrelated within the practices, rituals and conditions of existence of these social groups and their human, ecological and economic environments. The complexity of these systems of meaning produces configurations in which contradictions do occur.

Further, the reproduction of social reality occurs in each of the individuals constituting the group in which it is expressed; it is embodied in their modes of thought and in their habitual behaviour. It is constantly validated, the forms of decoding are daily reaffirmed. Change becomes possible only when there is some consciousness of a gap between reality and the communal interpretation.

In our own society, in which we are like fish in water unaware of this ubiquitous substance so necessary to their survival, we have difficulty in recognising and questioning our own ways of constructing reality, all the more as they rapidly become intricate and contradictory. It is obviously easier for us to dwell on those societies distant from our own, societies which are both more simple and clearly different. This is why the work of anthropology is so valuable to us.

In his extensive study of Baruya society in New Guinea, Godelier (1983) examined the dominant relationship of men with respect to women. Such domination is universal, certainly; what varies is the universe of meanings within which this fact is located, the discourse which gives it meaning and sets it up as a rule shared by women as much as by men. It is particularly conspicuous in Baruya society, which practises a radical cleavage between men and women, upheld in daily as well as symbolic and sacred practices and in myths.

Three centuries ago, La Boétie (1976) raised the problem of 'voluntary servitude'; he asked why it is that subservient individuals do not revolt against leaders who exercise a 'tyrannical' oppression over them. In the same fashion one may ask why women do not revolt, all the more so when their domination seems so burdensome. However, this is only a naive way of posing the inverse problem: why is it that the more completely they are subordinated the less they revolt? Godelier among others has provided us with the beginnings of a convincing answer. The anthropologist asks what the links are between the ideal and the real, demonstrating the point at which the real is sustained by the ideal, by rites and myths or, to put it more simply, by what occurs in people's heads.

> Let us pause for a moment at what a symbolic practice is in general terms. It is a means of causing ideas in the world of thought to pass into the world of the body or into nature, and at the same time of changing them into social relations or social materials: talk and symbolic gestures transform ideas into a directly visible material and social reality. But it would be false to imagine that for the Baruya their symbols and rituals are only recreations or representations of fundamental realities which act upon them in a manner that is normally invisible. For them, symbols are not simply signs, they are the means of acting directly upon these basic but invisible realities. Their symbolic practices are more than acts, because they reproduce these invisible realities and at the same time make them serve their own social order. It is this belief in the concrete effectiveness of symbolic practices which ensures that to display some-thing symbolically is, for them, to demonstrate it, because it is to act and produce results which are verifiable and verified every day in a multitude of indications of the superiority of men over women. Now, this belief is shared by the two sexes and it is this sharing of representations which constitutes the principal force, silent and invisi-ble, behind masculine domination. (Godelier, 1983, pp. 347-8)

This 'power of ideas' is something altogether concrete, materially incorporated in social life. It is not an element which comes to be added on to the 'objective conditions of life', independent of the modes of under-standing of those who live it. From this are derived Godelier's two formulae which, in their abbreviated form, perfectly summarise the degree of importance that systems of meaning have in social life. 'The imaginary partakes of the real and...it is socially as real as the other elements of social life' (*ibid*, p. 348) and '...humans...not only live in society but produce a society to live in' (*ibid*, p. 358).

Meaning and influence
Having sketched out the way in which we define social meaning, let us

move on to the links uniting influence and meaning. It will be necessary for us to demonstrate the paradoxical relation between the two: influence is exercised within the framework of, and is channelled through, pre-existing social meanings. These determine the visibility of influence. Influence is thus all the more effective if it is in accord with the social norms and representations within which it is integrated. And it is all the more difficult for influence to diverge from them. Therein lies both its strength and its weakness. This is why uniformities are so solid, so difficult to shake. Now, to initiate a process of innovation, relations of influence have to become integrated within a new universe of meaning, a universe they also help create and sustain. The scope, the stability, indeed the very possibility of influence all depend upon integration with or creation of social representations. The step from deviance to innovation is difficult but cannot be skipped. And stepping from the one to the other depends upon that set of social meanings which determines rejection or acceptance of influence, and upon the effectiveness of those means of coercion established to exclude the abnormal.

Conformity bias

To increase the clarity and accessibility of our approach to the study of social influence, we must relate it finally to a debate which reaches beyond social psychology as such and spans the entire social sciences. Our intention is to encompass within the same inquiry both uniformity and innovation without, it should be stressed, assimilating either one to the other. At the theoretical level we believe an equal place must be accorded to both stability and social change, if processes of social influence are to be understood as a whole. Now, the tradition of social psychological research developed in the United States, and since the fifties largely adopted in Europe, places exclusive emphasis on the maintenance of uniformities, whether in terms of theory or in terms of practical applications.

Theorists have frequently been well aware of this restricted approach and have even reacted critically. Thus, according to Merton (1961), 'The great concern of functionalist sociologists and anthropologists with problems of "social order" and with the "maintenance" of social systems has generally focussed their scientific attention on the study of processes whereby a social system is largely preserved intact' (p. 122).

Social psychology is itself to a large degree a discipline concerned with the reproduction of social uniformities. Morton Deutsch, one of its more prestigious representatives, has both underlined and deplored this:

Suppose that as social scientists we are consultants to the poor and weak rather than the rich and strong... Let me note that this would be an unusual and new position for most of us. If we have given any advice at all, it has been to those in high power. The unwilling consequence of this one-sided consultant role has been that we have too often assumed that the social pathology has been in the ghetto rather than in those who have built the walls to surround it, that the 'disadvantaged' are the ones who need to be changed rather than the people and the institutions who have kept the disadvantaged in a submerged position. It is more important that educational institutions, the political and economic systems be changed so that they will permit those groups who are now largely excluded from important positions in decision making to share power than to try to inculcate new attitudes and skills in those who are excluded.' (1983, p. 248)

This laudable declaration of intent has remained a pious vow for the majority of social psychologists. Their perspective remains that of the dominant majority. Critiques of the same kind appear periodically without producing any significant change either at the more general level of society or within the discipline. Consequently, confronted with a public who are only willing to give any credit to majority views, the idea of minority influence has often been poorly understood, sometimes barely tolerated, and at best watered down.

In order to fill this void, we offer a general approach to social influence, integrating the most recent developments from this area of study and from this vast and ubiquitous field of events.

1 Suggestion: a mental alchemy

'Even those things which the stricter humanism of the last century would
not tolerate have now slipped surreptitiously into the noise of the fair.'
Thomas Mann, Address to the Germans (1930)

A strange epidemic

Between 21 March and 3 April 1983, a mysterious epidemic swept
through the town of Djenine in Trans-Jordan. The individuals affected –
mainly adolescents – presented serious problems: headaches, dizzy spells,
fainting fits, photophobia, difficulties with vision, stomach pains, neural-
gia, respiratory difficulties. This collection of symptoms represented a
baffling picture in clinical terms. The hospitals were overwhelmed by the
influx of the sick, and uncertainty and panic spread throughout the
population. The Palestine Liberation Organisation accused the Israeli
authorities of wanting to poison or sterilise the Palestinian female population. The hatred of the Israeli occupation, the frustration and powerless-
ness it created, found here an extreme and dramatic expression.

Two American doctors from the Centre for the Study of Diseases at
Atlanta were called in as consultants in this affair by the Israeli Ministry of
Health. They studied and analysed the medical records and evidence, they
immersed themselves in clinical, epidemiological, toxicological and ecological inquiries. The results revealed not a single anomaly. At the same time,
the medical experts could find no common factor in the clinical antece-
dents of the patients. There was not the least clinically convincing
indication of the presence of any environmental poison.

'We have reached the conclusion', the doctors stated, 'that this epidemic
of serious illnesses has been released by *anxiety*. The fact that the illness
has then continued to spread is due to *"psychogenic factors"* , that is to say
to mental factors' (my italics).

Anxiety is thus revealed as the basic cause. This modern concept,
immediately both vague and all-encompassing, has already served to
explain all manner of things, so why should it not shed light on this strange
epidemic? If psychogenic factors are also involved, everything becomes
clear...

This admission of impotence by the medical experts indicates in the first place that we have passed from the realm of medicine to that of social psychology. For we must understand and explain how anxiety can lie at the origin of such real illnesses and how these illnesses of the mind are spread by a kind of social virus involving *psychogenic factors*.

Thus, an entire population displays a a deep-rooted belief which is constantly reinforced by the ebb and flow of rumour but also by the 'real' and tangible existence of quite conclusive symptoms. The difficult, indeed insoluble, problem here is to know where reality begins and to understand what the tests prove. Social reality is surely contained as much in the symptoms as in what everyone says about them. This is not a matter of imaginary sickness or shamming but of genuine illnesses which spread according to the indisputable rules of contagion. The embarrassment of the doctors from Atlanta, and the vagueness of their conclusions does indeed alert us that this was not just a matter of medicine but also one of social psychology, and particularly the potent phenomena of influence.

On the basis of this initial example, we may pose a first postulate concerning the propagation of social influence: the reality social groups give to their systems of beliefs, even though these are seldom either material or tangible, is sufficiently solid to be proof against all tests, the more so as the logic of these systems of beliefs incorporates various indisputable social facts.

Collective error

Three centuries ago no one spoke of social contagion in such terms as 'anxiety' or 'psychogenic factors'. But the concepts did already exist. Thus people spoke of 'sickness of the mind' or of 'diseases of the imagination'. These were the terms in which the phenomena of demonic possession were discussed by learned men – magistrates, doctors, philosophers – and by 'commissions of inquiry' around 1692, the year of Colbert's edict forbidding all prosecution of witchcraft within the territory of France.

Now, it was precisely three centuries ago that there occurred a decisive shift in mentalities and practices, characterised by a fundamental transformation in processes of influence. Within the space of a hundred years, society passed, though not altogether painlessly, from an all-encompassing representation of life and the order of things in which God and the devil were engaged in an incessant and bitter struggle, with good always finally triumphing over evil, to a rejection of supernatural phenomena with man regarded as the master of his actions, capable of exercising free will. The turning point of this transformation was a trial, one which caused a great scandal, contributing substantially to the doubts which had begun to grow concerning belief in the devil. This was the trial of Loudun.

True, there are considerable differences between the epidemic among adolescents in Djenine and the possession of the Ursulines of Loudun, but fundamentally they involved the same kind of phenomena and the same type of reaction. A decisively rational response was given to a fundamentally irrational occurrence which derived its potency from a logic of irrationality and from apparently indisputable bodily signs. Rightly, the doctors from Atlanta offered vague conclusions which rejected any intentionality or calculated staging. There was no deliberate attempt to deceive or mystify but rather an adherence in 'body and soul' to a communal conviction, in a highly effective process of influence.

By centring our attention on the social and mental universe of witchcraft and upon its transformation, we confront the issue of *communal error*, one of the greatest delusions of history which enveloped an entire population for several centuries within a single and unified framework of thought. Simultaneously we enter directly into a debate which illustrates the complexity of social influence.

Let us start by outlining the basic characteristics of this mental universe, described in the following terms by the historian Mandrou:

> Three elements constitute the essential content of the mental system that legitimised witch-hunts: a Christian belief based at once on ecclesiastical tradition and on the innumerable examples provided by a relentless case-law; direct experience, available to everyone, of a judicial procedure which implied a ready consensus of all the participants – judges, witnesses and accused; finally and above all, sentences and confessions, burnings at the stake, fines and confiscations, representing the judgment of God and man, provided the clearest evidence of the crime. All these virtually univocal components played their part in this tradition, ensuring its strength: they were the basis in actual experience for innumerable accounts... (1968, p. 75)

Experience of the devil

Witchcraft, that 'crime of sacrilegious high-treason', was based on a set of beliefs well known to all, from the most backward peasant to members of the royal court. The devil clearly existed, just like God. The evidence of numerous witnesses concurred on the universal presence of Satan. He was a 'Prince of Darkness', a black man mounted on a black horse making nocturnal visits to his victims, sometimes violating them or promising them great riches, pots of gold, and occasionally even giving them these things. But at the break of day these riches would be transformed into nothingness, or else into base objects – dry leaves, stones, dung. When his victims were at his mercy, he would lift them on to his horse and take them to the witches' Sabbath. In a clearing at the top of a mountain, and always at night, a motley collection of people, usually naked, would vie with one another in fornication, as they were led through every debauchery and perversion in celebration of black masses, masses that were inverted and blasphemous. In an evil pact, he would delegate his malevolent and supernatural powers to his disciples who could be recognised by a mark that he made on their bodies, an area that would then become insensitive to pain.

This oral tradition is reflected in and draws upon an extensive juridical and theological literature. During the sixteenth century, the fame of two works, *La démonomanie des sorciers* by Bodin and *Malleus maleficarum* by Sprenger and Kramer, spread throughout Europe. They were translated into numerous languages and reissued several times. The universe of demonical beliefs also drew support from passages of holy scripture, relying as much on the Old as on the New Testament.

Witchcraft was thus nourished on this mutually supporting bundle of evidence, knowledge and practices. For a considerable period it was also sustained by sentences, by case-law, and by confessions, which all confirmed the truth of these beliefs. The unfortunate victims were brought by suspicion, by *common reputation*, and by denunciations before judges and executioners, finding themselves presumed guilty. This presumption was quickly confirmed by various tests based on an implacable logic. Inch by square inch, the bodies of victims were probed, pricked, and scratched to discover the supposed insensitive areas. If they were not discovered then it was the devil himself who was thwarting the judges and doctors in their investigations by making the victims cry out even when they felt no pain. But the water test was infallible. If, with hands and feet tied, the accused floated it was clear proof that she had concluded a pact with the devil that made her unsinkable. If she sank, it was because the devil had used this trick to show her innocence. If the accused persisted in denials, if she did not confess, then to make her confess she would be promised release and then put to terrible tortures, interrogated on questions both ordinary and extraordinary. By the time they reached this final stage, most of the victims had confessed, exactly in the terms expected of them, these expectations being clearly conveyed through highly leading questions. They confessed because they preferred a quick and certain death to long drawn-out torture which in any case would only end with their death.

They confessed all the more readily because they feared for the salvation of their souls, for throughout the duration of a trial of unceasing tortures and interrogations in which judges and doctors remained united in certainty of their guilt, they themselves no longer knew if they were innocent or of what they were innocent. They were harassed, confused, paralysed with fear by the prospect both of an imminent death and of the loss of their immortal soul. They themselves shared in the same oral tradition as their judges and executioners. And all these confessions were just so many additional proofs which further reinforced these beliefs. Finally, the verdicts and judgments, which so effectively confirm their own validity, provided an ultimate and definitive affirmation of this system of beliefs, so perfectly organised in its logic and so thoroughly confirmed by practice.

Today, we no longer believe (or hardly) in the devil or witches. We find our evils elsewhere. Indeed, we are now inclined to pass the same kind of peremptory judgment on witchcraft as did Voltaire in his *Philosophical dictionary*: 'It has been said that more than one hundred thousand supposed witches were put to death in Europe. Only philosophy finally cured men of this abominable chimera and taught judges that there was no point in burning imbeciles.' We are now able to see this system of beliefs as a collection of grotesque superstitions, a 'gross, simplistic, and terribly effective Manicheism' (Mandrou, 1968, p. 76).

In the course of this brief examination, we have encountered the principal elements of the 'communal delusion' which was witchcraft, a communal delusion which functioned as such for centuries. More than a hundred years of argument, of bold initiatives, of innovations, of disputes with magistrates, theologians, and doctors, were necessary to put an end to it, or at least to have judicial procedures against the manifestations of witchcraft officially banished.

More than a system of beliefs, faith in the existence of witchcraft was a system of explanation of the world, a way of *knowing* the world, all the better established because it relied upon a system of validation that rested internally on the logical interrelation of its propositions, and externally on, among other things, its social and judicial effectiveness.

Thus we have in the first place a set of beliefs which functions perfectly, both at the level of the logic of ideas – basic premises – and at the factual level. This set of beliefs involves a generalised and tremendously potent system of influence based on 'inquiry', on the quasi-rational quest of scholarship, and on the irrational phenomena of contagion and suggestion.

At the dawn of the century of Enlightenment, radicals were calling this system of beliefs into question, employing a set of refutations emphasising rationality. Against devastating and epidemic processes of influence were ranged more subtle and moderate means. These refutations were to be repeated three times and in similar terms in the centuries that followed.

The scandal of possession

The infamous trial of Loudun was one of the precipitating events in the re-examination of the traditional mentality and practices of society relating to witchcraft. By the end of this trial, doubts which had previously only been expressed here and there, silently and privately, for example in the works of Montaigne, burst into the light of day. Such doubts were voiced first by an elite who formed an 'active minority', the Parliament and the magistrates of Paris, and then gradually by a majority of the population.

The trial of Loudun, well known to everyone in the period, was a resounding scandal. A witness recounts, in 1643, how 'the story of the Ursulines of Loudun, possessed by what the wisest had seen, is so well-known in every part, that there is no need to write of it'. It has, moreover, remained celebrated right down to the present, inspiring a novel, by Aldous Huxley, and two films.

In 1632, Mother Jeanne of the Angels and the Ursulines over whom she had charge showed obvious signs of diabolic possession. The Ursulines were young girls of good family, offspring of the minor aristocracy. One of them was a relative of Cardinal Richelieu, a detail which was not without importance in what was to follow.

This affair was also the occasion which introduced the term *possession* to describe that set of phenomena in which human beings are inhabited, and orchestrated by, supernatural and evil beings.

Possession marked the most extreme degree of influence possible. What 'animated' the body of the possessed was no longer his or her conscience but the spirit of another which spoke through his or her mouth, acted through his or her body. In our culture, from the Middle Ages down to the present, possession has always been regarded as something evil or diabolical.

Before an audience that became more and more numerous and impressionable, and with obvious satisfaction, the Ursulines and their Mother Superior made the fact of their demonic possession abundantly clear: exhibiting convulsions, prostrations, frenetic attacks in which they would wail and roll around on the ground, uttering obscenities and writhing in quite outrageous fashion. The Ursulines were thus 'possessed'. Who was the diabolic intermediary, the redoubtable suborner of these innocent, pious victims? They had no trouble in identifying him to the vindictive public and the authorities. All asserted that the instrument of Satan was Urbain Grandier, the curé of Sainte-Croix-de-Loudun. He was a renowned priest, educated, well known and liked in the town. But his reputation was somewhat besmirched. He had on occasion abused his position as confessor and had not displayed an entirely irreproachable chastity. He had made no secret of it; he himself had written an indictment of the celibacy of the priesthood. Endless intrigues were plotted against him and finally they triumphed.

One year before the beginning of the Possession, in 1631, and to his misfortune, he refused a request from Mother Jeanne of the Angels to direct the consciences of the Ursulines. The Mother Superior then contacted a sworn enemy of his. The first signs of possession appeared soon after. Almost immediately, he was accused of witchcraft. Indignant, he appealed to the ecclesiastical hierarchy, securing the intervention of the Archbishop of Bordeaux and achieving a temporary peace.

But the accusations persisted and a veritable machination was set in motion against him, thanks to the support of Cardinal Richelieu himself. The town of Loudun fell within the legal jurisdiction of the Parliament of Paris, which displayed some reticence in putting on a witchcraft trial. Then exceptional jurisdiction was granted, on appeal to the Parliament of Bordeaux, which took up the mission of acquainting itself with this affair and prosecuting Grandier. He was immediately incarcerated at Angers. The inquiry went on for several months, not a single charge being proven against him. He was then moved to Loudun where the inquiry speeded up, and all the while the extravagant behaviour of the Ursulines grew. He was submitted to incessant interrogation. Scenes of possession and exorcism continued without a break in the churches of the town, before an ever-increasing crowd, providing the proof of his guilt. 'By the sheer force of violent demonstration, the possessed were able to incite genuine collective emotion; onlookers gaped in astonishment but also shuddered with dread and pity for these wild unfortunates' (Mandrou, 1968, p. 213).

Grandier denied everything, even under torture. He sent a plea for mercy to the king in which he set down with great logic the flagrant irregularities of his trial and the inadequacies of the inquiry. It was in vain. He was promptly condemned and burned at the stake in front of a crowd of six thousand.

With good demonic logic, the death of Satan's accomplice should have put an end to the possession of the Ursulines. Far from it. They then accused Grandier's friends. The 'histrionic mystique' – to adopt the expression of one witness – practised by Mother Jeanne of the Angels and the Ursulines continued until the death of the Mother Superior. She seemed to have acquired a taste for it, as she wrote in her autobiography: 'The devil often tricked me with a little pleasure which I felt over the actions and other extraordinary things that he produced in my body. I took great pleasure in hearing these things spoken of and I felt good in appearing more worked up than the others, which gave such great force to these evil spirits.'

For many long years following the trial, Loudun was the centre of an extraordinary spectacle:

> Exorcisms continued everywhere through 1636 and 1637, this accumulation of additional evidence never ceasing to excite curiosity. Each nun had a distinct style, whether it be mimicry, or unexpected vomiting. The people of the world constantly appeared at the doors of the convents, they flocked to the public exorcisms, and lamented over those cases developing in the calm of the convent interior. These 'crying, wailing girls, rolling in the dirt, making faces,' or else 'talking, laughing, singing, raising their hands and voices,' and people coming and going, running from one to another, 'sighing to one, mocking another, singing to yet others' continued to provide an extraordinary spectacle. (cited in Mandrou, 1968, p. 274)

The first rational rejoinder

In the face of these excessive outbursts and in a society where libertines were more and more numerous, scepticism and irony grew beside the doubts. The scandal provoked an extensive debate, a wide reaching re-examination of beliefs and a decisive growth in awareness which presaged a profound revolution in thinking. Scepticism was rife among courtiers close to the king but also among eminent churchmen who styled possession as 'the divination of bohemians' and tracked down the deceit in the doings of the Ursulines, having no hesitation in exposing the clumsy deceptions of these young women. Through their mouths, the all-powerful demons expressed themselves in dog Latin and gave very little sign of intelligence though much of bad faith in the face of theological questions, while 'Satan's' characteristics were revealed to include an intellect as formidable as it was evil.

Magistrates became more and more reluctant to pursue accusations of witchcraft, doctors refused to let themselves be embroiled in 'this ridiculous opinion, which has no foundation beyond a popular delusion'. What had been 'collective error' became popular ignorance. Doctors located possession at the boundary between normality and pathology, defining it as 'hysteromania', 'erotomania', 'melancholic delirium' or 'disease of the imagination'. Three centuries before the Atlanta doctors, they had identified and based their case upon those infamous 'psychogenic factors'.

Theologians and jurists were equally involved in this vast exercise of re-examination. In 1671, P. Lalemant, Chancellor of the University of Paris, demonstrated the irresponsibility of witches. Commenting in a truly social psychological fashion upon the process of witchcraft, he wrote: 'We find that in those provinces of France where no one speaks of witches and no one cares about them, they are seldom ever found. This makes us realise that there are diseases of the imagination which are as contagious as those of the body, that the most ridiculous stupidities are found in the minds to which they are proportional; in a word, that the best means for exterminating witches is to turn them to ridicule or to hold them up to contempt...' (cited in Mandrou, 1968, p. 455). Thus he emphasised the phenomena of suggestion and the circularity between the legal procedure and the offence on which it fed.

Philosophers also contributed to this debate. In 'The search for truth', in 1676, Malebranche remarks 'I know well that some people will find it repetitive for me to attribute most witchcraft to the power of imagination.' For him also, witchcraft was a circular process based on a reality defined by social consensus. It was self-reinforcing, finding its own justification through the proliferation of accusations. The remedy was quite simple: to achieve the disappearance of witches, it is sufficient not to prosecute them, for otherwise, he said, 'communal persuasion is strengthened, and witches are multiplied by the imagination'.

All of this intellectual ferment, all this debate, the audacious and innovative refusal by the progressive Parliament of Paris to prosecute witches led to the promulgation, in 1682, of a general ordinance by Colbert forbidding all witchcraft prosecutions.

The eighteenth century had indeed been the stage for a veritable ideological revolution, a radical social change. This is why belief in witchcraft as much as its change takes us to the heart of a fundamental investigation of social influence. Should it be understood as a set of external and irrepressible forces exercised upon the individual or as the outcome of a reasoned and concerted acceptance by each one?

Mandrou's comment on this change is clearly framed in historical and (social) psychological terms. 'The abundant polemical literature published around the great trials, just like the treatise on demonology, adequately proves that this awareness overtook the magistrature, involving it in a larger debate in which magistrates discussed with theologians and doctors to "enlighten" religion and decide on *new norms*' (Mandrou, 1968, p. 554, my italics).

An exploration of this slow mutation allows some definition of what should be understood by the Progress of the Enlightenment; it was not just scientific progress, the truth of the Sciences, which cast its spell on the eighteenth century, not just a debate of ideas to which each great philosophy brought its contribution, discussing and overtaking its predecessors, but a greater awareness which cast doubt on the forms of

thinking and consciousness, the deep-rooted mental structures, constituted by visions of a world inherited from the distant past and accepted
by particular groups, indeed by an entire society. (Mandrou, 1968, p.
560)

Sleight of hand – magnetic passes

About one hundred years after the Edict of Colbert, in the middle of the
period of the Enlightenment, witchcraft was defined in the encyclopedia as
follows: 'Evil, shameful or ridiculous activity, foolishly attributed by
superstition to the invocation or the power of demons'. Superstition
seemed to be long dead and with it the long procession of possessions and
exorcisms. But then the contagion flared up again in a quite dazzling
fashion. It gave rise to a new concept: suggestion, which was to shed
further light on the strange effects of the spread of influence.

A powerful fluid
Frédéric-Anton Mesmer came to live in Paris in 1778. It was due to him
that a new scandal came to pass. The doctrine of a magnetic fluid that he
preached was itself not entirely new. The Freemasons had been convinced
of the existence and action of a universal fluid, the means by which the
reciprocal influence of the stars and matter was accomplished. This fluid is
by no means tangential to our discussion; indeed it takes us to the very
heart of the concept of influence, to its very origins. Etymologically,
influence refers to a *fluid*, a flux to which is attributed a secret and
mysterious effect on the destiny of men and matter. This fluid is supposed
to emanate from 'heavenly bodies'. The concept has been expanded so that
the fluid is no longer something of exclusively cosmic origin, but can issue
forth from other individuals. Thus the notion has become banal; in coming
to refer to the effects exercised voluntarily by one person or group upon
the thoughts, wishes or actions of others, it has lost its fluid origins, its
supernatural aspect.

Mesmer claimed to have discovered the existence of a magnetic fluid
which made possible a new form of therapeutic practice. This fluid was the
basic vehicle for a universal principle of functioning: 'Animal Magnetism'.
Mesmer originally labelled it 'animal gravity'. It was certain to hold the
key to a reformulation and extension of Newton's Law of Gravity.
Manipulation of this fluid would have therapeutic effects. The illnesses
which Mesmer undertook to treat were those arising from imbalances in
the distribution of magnetic fluid: nervous attacks, convulsive attacks and
other 'illnesses of the mind' or 'diseases of the imagination'. He founded

the practice of magnetising in which the magnetiser was the great manipulator of fluid. However, this manipulation also depended on total *consent* and complete submission on the part of the magnetisee to the magnetiser. Here again, the commitment of both to the same system of beliefs is fundamental. The magnetiser makes 'magnetic passes' over the body of the magnetisee. These passes induce convulsive attacks which continue until the magnetisee feels some improvement. It works to such good effect that he requests more and the 'treatment' sometimes continues for years at a time.

This treatment was nevertheless surprising because it involved no speech; its effect was based on a bodily struggle between an all-powerful therapist and a submissive and consenting subject. Mesmer preached this denial of language; he argued that it clears the cure and is also proof of the existence of this magnetic fluid which interpenetrates objects and bodies. 'As it seems to me that every time we have an idea, we immediately and without thinking translate it into the language with which we are familiar, I formed the resolve to emancipate myself from this enslavement' (Mesmer, 1971, p. 100). In this way Mesmer sought access to a part of the universal truth of nature, divesting himself of the distortions imposed by language. The ransom paid for access to such dizzying truth would be madness for any who ventured there without the support of an omnipotent guide. The fluid could not be manipulated to good effect except via the fusion between magnetiser and magnetisee, taking the latter back to a primitive state of basic impotence in relation to an unconditional power. 'By forbidding "verbal dialogue", he constrains the patient to a profoundly regressed state in which only "somatic dialogue" is authorised. He manipulates the patient, he leads him to a pre-verbal state, he dominates him' (Chertok and de Saussure, 1973, p. 20).

The practice of manipulating magnetic fluid spread, making a number of disciples and converts, and became a drawing-room entertainment. It was a spectacle much to the taste of an idle and blasé aristocracy in search of strong sensations and experiences. And there was much to see around the celebrated magnetic tub, a wooden receptacle filled with scrap iron and filings supposed to gather the famous fluid. The trances spread from one to another. It worked well and occasionally even beneficially.

Second rational rejoinder

Nonetheless, it created a scandal. A commission of experts was appointed by the king and it condemned the practice in the name of science and reason. 'It was a scandal for Europe to see an entire people, enlightened by all the sciences and all the arts, a people among whom philosophy had made some of its greatest progress, forget the lesson of Descartes who was its initiator' (*Exposé des recherches faites pour l'examen du magnétisme animal*, 1784). Following systematic investigation, which involved some genuinely social psychological methods of experimentation, the experts produced a report denouncing animal magnetism, not without humour, as a staged masquerade, an orchestrated swindle. 'Such a spectacle seems to take us back to the time and the reign of Fairyland; this dominion exercised over so many individuals, the man who controls it, the wand which serves as his instrument, in effect it all resembles the enchantment of our fables. It is such fairy tales put into action.' Employing strict logic, and using systematic experimental methods, the authors concluded that there was no magnetic fluid, only the *influence* of the *imagination*; here again we encounter those infamous *psychogenic factors*. 'Animal magnetism', concludes the report, 'will not be totally useless to the philosophy which condemns it. Rather it is an observation to be added to the history of errors of the human mind, and a great experiment in the power of the imagination.' For us it is also an example of the power and effectiveness of commitment to a shared system of beliefs.

In a second but secret report, magnetism was condemned in the interests of public order and out of a concern for public morals. Involving the highly charged relation between a man and – as was most frequently the case – an exceptionally suggestible woman, and contact with particularly sensitive parts of the body, the breasts and abdomen, the activities in question were not always platonic and in their scope for abuse offended against public morality. 'The extended proximity, the inevitable physical contact, the individual warmth communicated, and the mutual glances are the universal paths of Nature and the means which she has always prepared for carrying out a complete communication of feelings and sensations... It is not suprising that the senses are aroused.'

The fashion for magnetism again revealed the wild and fanciful desire to transgress, under limited and protected conditions, the most clearly established standards. The demonic belief according to which numerous women claimed to have been violated by the devil, and to have participated in orgiastic sabbaths and black masses, reemerges as Magnetism (or magnetic belief) in which women have fainting fits or fall into trances under the sway of the magnetiser. Irrationality is menacing because it is a sign of uncontrolled powers which carry within themselves anarchy and rebellion. Far better to tame the forces of influence by submitting them to the control of reason.

Royal condemnation did not prevent the magnetisers pursuing their therapeutic work (Darnton, 1977; Hoffeld, 1980). But little by little the fluid was transformed. From the magnetic principle evolved the spiritual principle. Here the stress is on the relationship between therapist and patient; this was to mark the transition from magnetism to hypnotic suggestion. Immmediately, a row flared up between the fluidists and the anti-fluidists. Braid, the Abbé Faria, abandoned animal magnetism in favour of hypnotism. No more bodily struggle, no more magnetic passes; instead the subject fixates on a bright object and becomes susceptible to suggestion, unconsciously executing orders received. Thus began the era of hypnotism's great popularity.

Spirals of reason and unreason

From hell to the asylum

Over the course of the nineteenth century, we observe a gradual rationalisation of illness and madness. At the beginning of the century, Pinel, not content to free the insane from their chains, also undertook a systematic observation of mental illnesses with a view to naming, pigeonholing and grouping their symptoms and thence formalising an explanatory theory. His disciple, Esquirol, undertook the extension of these clinical observations and the refining and complementing of his classification.

> To refer to Pinel and Esquirol means first to combine approaches. And then to define entities. In contrast to a religious or literary vocabulary which had always labelled disturbances of the mind and of behaviour in their own way, there appeared a new language which either astonished or amused the honest man: monomania or partial madness, circular madness or duplicated madness, persecution delirium, lucid madness or reasoning madness, nervasthenia (later neurasthenia), nervous diathesis (later neurosis), etc... (Léonard, 1981, p. 164)

Esquirol described the clinical forms of numerous mental illnesses. Of interest to us here, he described a form of 'monomania' which he termed 'demonomania'. The phenomena of possession entered smoothly into the category of psychiatric diseases. Parallel to this, treatment of illness in general and mental illness in particular passed from the hands of the theologian into those of the doctor, to the greater glory of reason, or so it seemed initially. But things were far from being so simple. As much in the clinical descriptions as in the treatments, the dialectical relation of reason and unreason persisted. The passage of illness from the supernatural to the natural domain was not after all entirely smooth.

For the Christian, since Saint Augustine and thus since the fourth century, health had been considered a sign of divine protection. All illness carried the mark of the devil and this demonic presence could be extirpated from the affected body only by a miracle. But some illnesses were more demonic than others. The devil seemed to have a predilection for nervous illnesses, those which had links with sexuality, the evocation of which carried undeniably within it the mark of the Prince of Darkness. And it was without dispute that these manifestations were most visible and most shocking among women. They were also the most understandable. Since antiquity, upward displacement of the uterus among women – hysteria – had been most frequently described in terms of deprivation of sexual pleasure accompanied by various disturbances and by disorders of behaviour.

This somatic interpretation became transformed into collusion with the devil. The sickness was no longer the result of an organic dysfunction but of an evil pact. The woman, this *'vas impuritatis'*, this soiled receptacle of temptations, was preordained to this alliance with Satan, an alliance confirmed by the sexual tone of delerium, the hallucinations of rape by 'incubi', the inclination to invent stories, reinforced by the suggestive power of beliefs in which everyone shared. The Middle Ages, as much as the Renaissance, was to be the setting for the spread of the demonic practices and witchcraft whose logic and method of discovery we analysed above.

Among enlightened circles it became good form thereafter to talk of sickness of the mind or diseases of the imagination, of melacholy and hysteria, in describing these bizarre afflictions. But there was no known remedy for these 'vapours' of the uterus which clouded judgment, these demonstrative and fractious illnesses, except marriage, fumigation and... horse riding.

In 1758, J. Raulin, one of Louis XV's doctors, cast doubt on the idea that 'vaporous afflictions' were due to emanations from the uterus and stressed instead the suggestive origins of hysterical attacks. 'These illnesses, and others of the same nature in which women invent, exaggerate or repeat all the various absurdities of which a depraved imagination is capable, are sometimes epidemic and contagious' (cited in Veith, 1973, p. 169). He also considered the fact that 'men are not exempt from the effects of the imagination', but this claim was not taken up until much later, at the end of the nineteenth century, while fascination with female hysteria remained strong.

Mesmer tried in his turn to put an end to the attacks suffered by his subjects, integrating the new concepts of physics into a bogus therapeutic procedure. Rejection of Mesmer's thesis marked a further step in the rationalisation of hysteria, though its achievement was neither rapid nor smooth. Belief in a magnetic fluid persisted for a long time in scientific circles. The 'great' Charcot himself tried hard to modify lateralisation of hysterical paralyses with the aid of magnets. As for Binet and Fere (1885), they also used magnets to control the magnetic forces present in 'psychic polarisation'. Nevertheless, the thread which led us from possession to suggestion takes us towards an increasingly psychological description of the phenomena concerned.

The transformations of demonomania

One of the most significant episodes in the mutation of theological description into psychiatric description again involves possession. The relevant events occurred at Morzine between 1857 and 1873, and are well described by C. L. Maire (1981). What is remarkable in these cases of possession is the total loss of credibility of both religious and anti-religious arguments and the psychiatrisation of those involved in these arguments. These cases are equally notable for the fact that the possessed progressively adapted themselves to a medical discourse, in so far as they were aware of it, and to the expectations of the doctors. 'Demonomania' gave way little by little to 'erotomania'.

But let us go back to 'demonomania', that 'neurotic' affliction which in the middle of the nineteenth century Esquirol honoured with a detailed description and a category all to itself in the taxonomy of psychiatric disorders. It was described as a 'variety of religious melancholia', caused by 'ignorance, prejudice and weakness of the human mind', and was based on 'false ideas about religion and a shocking deprivation of morals'. The antidote was 'enlightenment through education and instruction' (cited in Maire, 1981, p. 50).

For the *Larousse du XIXème siècle*, which appeared in 1870 and devoted a long article to demonomania, these illnesses affect feeble minds and, among these, female ones for preference. Responsibility for this was laid at the feet of the obscurantism of the clerical mentality. Esquirol explains for us why women in particular are affected by demonomania. 'Woman is nervous to a higher degree, she is more dependent on her imagination, more vulnerable to the effects of fear and dread, more open to religious ideas, more inclined to the supernatural, more subject to melancholy' (cited in Maire, 1981, p. 53).

At Morzine, one of the last strongholds of the offensive of demonic illness, two asylum doctors succeeded in putting an end to disorders which were as much social and mental. The first diagnosed 'pretence possession of fanatics' and 'Mesmeric trickery'. The second, equally sceptical regarding these 'charlatan tactics', identified an 'epidemic of hysterical demonomania', because this was very contagious. The church authorities had to give way in the face of political and medical pressures acting in concert, encroaching into private life and breaking up families.

Here again, attention centred on the women. No one was prepared to

33

concede that the men could be affected as well. In the latter case the problem was more likely to be alcoholism, mania or epilepsy. Their delirium of possession was used to mislead the doctors.

The psychiatric classification of disorders advanced. Demonomania now appeared to be no more than a particular form of hysteria. This latter, large and ill-defined category, was envisaged less and less as an illness of the uterus and conceived increasingly as an illness of the brain, indeed of the mind, and hence as a deviation from normal psychological processes such as persuasion. The possessed of Morzine were no longer able to make any impression by invoking the devil. They had to find something else; this turned out to be the very same thing that the doctors were suggesting to them, namely erotomania. In the final analysis, the idea was the same as always: the fantasy of unbridled, insatiable and unquenched feminine sexuality, but no longer based on an uncontrollable demonic power. In this way it was possible to devalue the victims of the illness. The final medical reports accorded the Morzine possessed precious little dignity, describing them as 'hallucinating imbeciles', 'superstitious old women', 'deceivers' etc...

With difficulty doctors had arrived at a definition of hysteria and its symptoms but they did not know either how 'it could be caught' because 'it is contagious' or how it could be cured.

Disorders of imitation

Charcot displayed considerable eclecticism when it came to therapeutic methods. He drew on every possible technique to treat the hysteric's refractory illness. He assembled a remarkable apparatus of constraint called the 'ovary compressor'. This large leather and metal belt fitted with nuts and bolts was intended to forestall serious attacks. We may imagine that it was not totally ineffective. He used magnets to control magnetic forces. Finally and most important, following Braid's work on 'nervous sleep', he used and abused hypnosis.

If truth must be told, this impassive, cold, even harsh doctor, this great master never undertook the hypnosis of patients himself. He assigned this subordinate task to his assistants. Undoubtedly this was why patients responded to his expectations in a manner which was as uniform as it was surprising. Charcot became convinced that the tendency to hypnosis, or hypnotism, was a fundamental indication of hysteria. Bernheim strenuously challenged this notion, being certain that the hypnotic state did no more than exaggerate a suggestibility that is present in everyone and only exacerbated in hysterics.

The links between hysteria, suggestion and imitation were increasingly clarified. But, more fascinated by the manifestations of hysteria than by the elucidation of its mechanisms, Charcot was responsible for obscuring a potentially illuminating phenomenon. The decrepit state of the Salpêtrière buildings necessitated housing the hysterics with epileptics. It was thus that 'epileptic hysteria' was born, that is to say the 'severe' hysteria described by Charcot with its 'great arc' created by a permanent contraction of the patient's body, a veritable masterpiece of psychiatric nosography.

At the end of his life, Charcot modified his erroneous conceptions of hysteria. In 1892, in an article on 'faith healing', the faith that cures, he emphasised the direct links with suggestion:

> To summarise, I believe that, for it to be able to work, faith healing requires special subjects and special illnesses, those which are amenable to the influence which the mind has over the body. Hysterics possess a mental state eminently favourable to the development of Faith Healing, for it is essential that they are suggestible, whether suggestion is exercised by external influences or more especially if they contain within themselves powerful elements of auto-suggestion. (cited in Veith, 1973, p. 241)

In the same spirit his disciple Babinsky (1909) proposed that the term hysteria be replaced by 'pithiatisme', curable homeopathically by persuasion.

To the degree that the explanation of the mechanisms of hysteria abandoned a somatic locus or the domain of the supernatural, and emphasised instead exaggeration of a psychological principle, the disorder tended to be assimilated to suggestion. Paradoxically, the hysteria – femininity – influence linkage became stronger at the same time that the uterine location was abandoned in favour of disorders of the mind. In effect, the womb was previously regarded as contained within women but also independent of them, an animal within an animal which Rabelais, for one, evoked in comical fashion. Thus women were not held totally responsible for their escapades. At the end of the nineteenth century, matters converged to define a female principle in psychological life characterised by obscurantism, inconsistency, and weakness. It was contrasted with a masculine principle, conceived as the basis for a strong self and an enlightened individuality. This dichotomy also served to describe social life. Moscovici (1985) nicely demonstrates the central role of the linkage mob–women–madness in the theories of Le Bon.

During the whole of the nineteenth century, mental specialists were employed in perfecting the spectacle of hysteria. Achieving a veritable psychiatric work of art, they furnished an instructive model for the new-born social psychology, the model of hypnotic suggestion. It is now time to present this model in more detail.

Hypnotic fascination

An astonishing spectacle

Hypnosis, practised at Nancy under the direction of Liebault and Bernheim, and at the Salpétrière in Paris under Charcot, experienced a considerable vogue. It seemed especially effective in the treatment of 'nervous' disorders, hysteria in particular. Its practice became a theatrical spectacle which fascinated both the popular and the learned imagination. The public flocked to hypnotic sessions, as it had flocked to the churches of Loudun, to see the contortions of the possessed, by this time defined by the doctor Guy Patin as *hysterics*.

Every hypnotic session had two aspects, one involving an affective relation, the other a physical manipulation. The first consisted of a relationship of absolute confidence and absolute submission of the hypnotised subject with respect to the hypnotist. The physical change took the form of a restriction of vision and sensation. This sensory deprivation limited contact with the external world. The consequence was that it made the subject fall into a hypnotic state of active dreaming; subjects were plunged into a trance. They would obey absolutely any order given to them, carrying out any actions they were asked to perform without any awareness of what they did or said. In the hands of the hypnotist, they became automatons, raising their arms, walking, shouting, laughing or crying without understanding or knowing why.

Beyond good and evil

The effects of hypnosis were absolutely astonishing. A coin placed on the skin could, under the effect of suggestion, induce not just a sensation of burning but a blister. Such effects were limitless. 'Suicides' could be induced by hypnotic influence. Of course, they were not real but the hypnotised subject did not know this. Thus a harmless beverage administered as 'poison' under hypnosis resulted in these would-be suicides contorting themselves with agony and experiencing severe stomach pains.

Suggestion was capable of precipitating the most timid or honest of individuals into theft, as happened at Nancy where hypnotists experimented on unfortunate hypnotic subjects who were then sometimes rediscovered later in custody. They could also be pushed to assassination. To prove it, a number of astonishingly realistic, and sometimes quite perverse, mock poisonings and deaths were staged. However, the loss of all sense of morality under hypnosis was a subject of great controversy between the Salpétrière and the Nancy School, the latter attempting to generate evidence in support of this contention and against the conviction of Charcot and his disciples who believed suggestion was incapable of suppressing the moral sense.

> Doctor Liégeois offered Tristan a white powder of whose nature the latter was ignorant... 'Pay careful attention to what I am going to ask you,' declared the hypnotist. 'You will shortly return to the home of your aunt, Madame Virtuel, present here. You will take a cup of water. Into this you will empty the arsenic which you will then carefully dissolve. Then you will offer this poisoned drink to your aunt.' Tristan agreed to Liégeois's demand and the latter then brought him out of the hypnotic trance. The young man took his leave of the doctor and departed quite naturally with his aunt. That evening, the aunt sent the following message to Liégeois: 'Madame Virtuel has the honour of informing you that the experiment succeeded perfectly,' her nephew having indeed served her the poison. 'As for the criminal,' wrote Liégeois, 'he remembered nothing and it took great difficulty to persuade him that he had in fact tried to poison an aunt for whom he had a deep affection. Automatism had been complete. (Revue de l'hypnotisme in *ORNICAR*, 1975, p. 34)

Freud, who paid visits to the two famous schools of hypnotism, remained sceptical of the method which he quickly abandoned in order, like his friend Breuer and his famous patient Anna O. who was impervious to hypnosis, to devote himself to 'the talking cure'. In *Group psychology and the analysis of the ego*, the founder of psychoanalysis expressed the 'muffled hostility' which he felt towards this 'tyranny of suggestion'. 'When a patient who showed himself unamenable was met with the shout: "What are you doing? *Vous vous contre-suggestionez!*" I said to myself that this was an evident injustice and an act of violence. For the man certainly had a right to counter-suggestions if people were trying to subdue him with suggestions. Later on my resistance took the direction of protesting against the view that suggestion, which explained everything, was itself to be exempt from explanation' (1955, p. 89).

The effects obtained under hypnosis were the quintessential achievement of all the forms of influence observed in a society. How often has one observed a person repeating words or gestures a long time after they had seen or heard them and without intending to or even realising that they were doing it, or adopting ideas which someone had inculcated in them without their awareness. These effects reveal that many thoughts and actions which seem deliberate and conscious, which appear to result from an internal decision, are in fact the automatic executions of external orders. The hypnotist's practice reaches beyond personal conscience, violating the domain of reason and overt feeling, achieving access to a domain of psychic unconsciousness.

Social somnambulism

Hypnotic suggestion came to furnish a conceptual framework for the first social psychological theorists, Le Bon and Tarde, shaping their conceptions of social life. Social life was characterised in terms of irrationality. For Le Bon (1896), rationality was located only in the individual, the person who thinks, judges, decides, and exercises his freewill. The individual in a crowd finds himself in a degraded state of consciousness. In groups, individuals regress towards primitive states, descending several degrees on the 'scale of civilisation'. The behaviour of an adult and responsible man becomes more like that of a woman, a child, an animal, a sick person, a primitive; it is characterised by impulsiveness, irritability, instability, credulity. It becomes insensitive to appeals to reason and reacts uncontrollably to suggestions amplified by the collective situation, which serves as a kind of echo chamber.

> In [the case of the individual in a crowd], as in the case of the hypnotised subject, at the same time that certain faculties are destroyed, others may be brought to a high degree of exaltation. Under the influence of a suggestion he will undertake the accomplishment of certain acts with irresistible impetuosity. This impetuosity is the more irresistible in the case of crowds than in that of the hypnotised subject from the fact that, the suggestion being the same for all the individuals of the crowd, it gains in strength by reciprocity. (p. 35)

The individual's controls are overcome by forces of greater power, transforming crowds into alarming hordes, prey to uncontrolled emotions.

> The individual forming part of a crowd acquires, solely from numerical considerations, a sentiment of invincible power which allows him to yield to instincts which, had he been alone, he would perforce have kept under restraint. He will be the less disposed to check himself from the consideration that, a crowd being anonymous, and in consequence irresponsible, the sentiment of responsibility which always controls individuals disappears entirely. (p. 33)

Contagion is possible because of a reciprocal suggestion accompanied by a loss of any sense of responsibility and the normal intellectual capacities that the isolated individual possesses. Suggestion ensures fusion of the individual into the mass.

he obeys all the suggestions of the operator...and commits acts in utter contradiction with his character and habits. The most careful observations seem to prove that an individual immersed for some time in a crowd in action soon finds himself – either in consequence of the magnetic influence given out by the crowd, or for some other cause of which we are ignorant – in a special state, which much remembles the state of fascination in which the hypnotised individual finds himself in the hands of the hypnotist. (p. 34)

For the psychology of the crowd, as Le Bon conceived it, hypnosis is the principal model for social actions and reactions. The leader unleashes these chain-reactions and exploits them; he is the epicentre from which the initial shock wave spreads out through the community.

For Tarde (1890) likewise, individuals are plunged into a hypnotic state every time they find themselves together. One result of this state is that it leads them to copy the behaviours and the ideas of an individual taken as a model; it thus facilitates the creation of social uniformities. Through imitation, everything which is individual becomes social, everything which is different becomes alike. But what was conceived in the Age of Enlightenment as 'the primary means for the perfectibility of man', involves for Tarde the degradation of conscience. It is suggestion which explains the radical transformation brought about by imitation. Social life results in an alteration of consciousness and is based on suggestions transmitted from person to person, making social man a veritable sleep-walker. 'The social state, like the hypnotic state, is nothing but a form of dream, an enforced dream and a dream in action. To have only suggested ideas and to believe them spontaneous, such is the illusion of the sleepwalker and equally of the social man' (p. 83). The author goes on to argue that magnetism is the source of all faith and obedience and that all social life results from a 'cascade of successive and connected magnetisations' (p. 92). Furthermore, it is restrained here because 'society is imitation, it is a form of somnambulism' (p. 95).

There is a certain irony in the fact that, in an epoch in which parliamentary democracy seemed finally to have carried the day against despotism in all its forms, the thoroughly pessimistic social conceptions of these two authors should have achieved such success. It was a premonition of things to come.

If for Le Bon this success was largely, and to his eternal disappointment, outside the universities, he nonetheless attracted the admiration of Mussolini and influenced the *political thinking* of Hitler.

His teaching only succeeded in giving grist to their mill, in lending comfort to their dismal philosophy. Clearly they would have relished such propositions as the following: 'a crowd perpetually hovering on the borderland of unconsciousness, readily yielding to all suggestions, having all the violence of feeling peculiar to beings who cannot appeal to the influence of reason, deprived of all critical faculty, cannot be otherwise than excessively credulous' (p. 45). Quite evidently in their oratory they put into practice Le Bon's precious lessons:

> Affirmation pure and simple, kept free of all reasoning and all proof, is one of the surest means of making an idea penetrate into the mind of crowds. The conciser an affirmation is, the more destitute of every appearance of proof and demonstration, the more weight it carries... Affirmation, however, has no real influence unless it be constantly repeated, and as far as possible in the same terms... The thing affirmed comes by repetition to fix itself in the mind in such a way that it is accepted in the end as a demonstrated truth. (pp. 141-2)

The contempt for the masses evident in these positions derived from a fierce anti-egalitarianism. But Le Bon was not content to espouse them in the solitude of his writer's study, deprecating crowds and reflecting with disgust upon the revolutionary mobs of 1789, 1830, 1848 ('the howling, swarming, miserable mob which invaded the Tuileries during the revolution of 1848...' p. 73), or the Commune, closer to his own time. In a less well-known but equally significant manner he indulged a rather inglorious craniological battle to establish *scientifically* the intellectual inferiority of women. He was by no means the only one to attempt this and the theme would be repeated many times. But what is remarkable is his extreme virulence and the transparency of his intentions.

> This inferiority is too evident to be disputed for a moment, and there is barely anything to discuss except its degree. Every psychologist who has studied the intelligence of women, whether among novelists or poets, recognises today that they represent the most inferior forms of human evolution and are much closer to children and savages than to adult, civilised man. They are foremost in instability and inconsistency, in absence of reflection and logic, the incapacity to reason or let themselves be influenced by reason, lack of foresight and the habit of having nothing but the instinct of the moment as a guide. (Le Bon, 1879; cited in Gould, 1983, p. 110)

This description of women is altogether similar to his descriptions of crowds. Is this to say that woman is the essence of the crowd? Descending on the scale of civilisation, individuals in crowds become more like women. Moreover, the 'feminine' essence of crowds is asserted; they are fickle, emotional, easily influenced, changeable, with short memories and weak wills.

So far as women were concerned, at least Le Bon made no attempt to hide his deeper motives. These were overtly political, concerned with ensuring the maintenance of a social order in which he occupied a privileged position.

> The day when, scorning the inferior occupations which nature has given her, the woman quits her home and comes to participate in our struggles, on that day a social revolution will commence in which everything will disappear that today constitutes the sacred ties of the family, [a revolution] of which the future will say that there has never been one more disastrous. (Cited in Gould, 1983, p.111)

From collective to rational individual

From Mesmer to Le Bon and Tarde, influence is supposed to be exercised beyond consciousness or reason. It reveals a superhuman capacity for communication which is not mediated by language and which transcends time and space. The individual is nothing but the passive receptacle of a universal principle of energy. What characterises this type of influence is that its source evades control by any individual, while its effect is unidirectional and irresistible. Thus it links into a common view of influence as designating a set of forces operating against autonomy, the individual, the personality, and free will, forces which escape logic or desire, which enfeeble or annihilate the self.

Influence 'works' because, as in witchcraft, and as in magnetism, the influencer and the one influenced share the same code, are committed to the same beliefs, possess the same faith. Simultaneously, this state of irrepressible influence is satisfying because, despising the limits of language and possibility, it allows eruption of the unspeakable, the breaking through of desires and impulses. If social life is founded on the emergence of trance states, no one can be truly guilty or responsible.

This conception fosters a profound contempt for collective life, but also considerable fear because nothing can restrain or limit the effects of any union between altered states of consciousness. In fact, blind compliance does not create a conscious and consenting sociality but an archaic gregariousness combined with servile submission.

In reaction, the elaboration of a reasoned Christian faith and the establishment of a rational philosophy led to rejection of those irrational phenomena that led up to the promulgation of Colbert's ordinance. The result was innovation, modernism, the march of progress, triumphing over backward mentalities. Witchcraft was no longer condemned; it no longer threatened public order though the scandalous character of the trials did trouble society. In the face of growing doubt an entire vision of the world collapsed.

When Mesmeric practices were banned a century later, it was also because these threatened public order. The ambiguous bodily contacts which accompanied these practices were leading astray young ladies of good family and women of the better classes. Backs had to be turned on such dissolute behaviour. It was a fashionable diversion, hardly a therapy, and neither individual nor universal. But situations in which apparently normal individuals were prey to the most uncontrollable outbursts and passions were not to be tolerated in a century in which the philosophy of the Enlightenment preached the progress of the sciences, the triumph of reason and individual self-control.

Social somnambulism, however, was not to cause a scandal. Instead it was to be warmly welcomed in intellectual circles. The psychology of crowds experienced considerable success, particularly outside academic circles and with the practitioners of fascism. Such inglorious affiliations it came to share with a set of contemporary and concordant theories, social Darwinism and eugenics among others. Initially these ideas were very well received in the United States, but they rapidly ran into direct opposition, an opposition again based in rationality. In France itself, where these ideas were born, they created a furore but then fell into disuse without ever creating an autonomous social psychology in the universities. Following a long eclipse, social psychology was only reborn in the fifties and was then defined only in relation to American work.

We see here the reciprocal development of two contrasting conceptions of social influence. On the one hand is an irrational conception in which influence is a quasi-supernatural, irresistible process, independent of the subject's will. This influence is a manifestation at once of a force difficult to counter and a counter-force difficult to quell. It is based on an absolute power that denies the subject and a massive counter-force that is difficult to contain or overcome. To play on this type of influence is a little like choosing to manipulate a powder keg. It is a powerful weapon, but one which can explode in the user's hands. This influence is impossible to modify or control, all the more so given that it operates at a pre-conscious level. Contagion and suggestion can render the masses docile, but they can also arouse rebellion in the mob. This was one of the great fears of one Gustav Le Bon.

For Tarde and Le Bon, influence seemed to constitute the principal 'contribution' of society to the individual being, a contribution alienating to all. The 'solitary' individual is rational and becomes irrational under the influence of his fellows. The collective individual is located in the debased mass, an undifferentiated social ectoplasm, and he is bound to be reduced to its mercy, subjugated, put in awe, his rights taken over.

In contrast, the rational position which came to be elaborated in the United States put its faith in man, in his free-will and in his volition. A rational being is also a reasonable being. This is the basis of all enlightened power, all democracy. This positive conception of social life rests on consensus, the agreement of all, and on consent. Individual control in concert with a moderate consensus comes to constitute the basis for harmonious social functioning. This operates in terms of commitment to a community and a common identity, and to an enthusiastic and idealistic vision of society. It is this which, in the most ancient democracy of the modern world, ensures the gradual passage from strong suggestion to gentle persuasion.

2 The symphony of the New World

'Here individuals of all nations are melted into a new race of men.'
J. Hector St John de Crevecoeur, Letter from an American farmer, 1782

'The question is, said Humpty Dumpty, which is to be the master – that is all.'

Lewis Carroll, *Through the looking glass*

Suggestion and democracy

Lost in oblivion

Few authors have been lucky enough to achieve the resounding success experienced by Le Bon. His *Lois psychologiques de l'évolution des peuples*, first published in 1894, has been reissued seventeen times and translated into sixteen languages. His greatest success, *La psychologie des foules*, dating from 1895, had been reprinted forty-five times by 1963 (it was translated into English in 1896 and reviewed in the *American Journal of Sociology* as soon as it appeared) and translated into sixteen other languages. Such wide dissemination should have brought considerable renown to its author. He should also have been given detailed coverage in all the social psychology texts. But this was not the case, save for a few scattered allusions and the occasional acknowledgement and save for the resurrection of a few of his ideas but taken out of context so as to appear as extreme generalities. Thus in 1968, in the very weighty and thorough *Handbook of social psychology*, edited by Lindsey and Aronson, Milgram and Toch say of *La psychologie des foules*, 'There is scarcely a discussion in his book that is not reflected in the experimental social psychology of this century... And it is not merely a highly general discussion that Le Bon provides, but a rich storehouse of imaginative, testable hypotheses' (p. 534).

One is never a prophet in his own land. The judgment accorded to Le Bon by Stoezel in *The international encyclopedia of the social sciences* is much more acerbic: 'Ironically, the fame of some men is based on their mistakes and thereby confronts the critics with a dilemma: either to blame such a man for the very things that made him popular or to praise him for contributions that would not have existed were it not for the mistakes' (In D. Sills, 1968, p. 84).

However, the mantle of oblivion that has descended over Le Bon's work must be viewed in relation to his enormous success. Was it simply a matter of the way in which his theories were used or instead was it more to do with the way they were 'twisted' by fascist doctrines and practices? Sternhell (1978) offers the following hypothesis regarding the fate of *La psychologie des foules*.

> And yet, the silence which descended around it following the death of its author, in December 1931, was total. Certainly, the hostility of the university had some part in this, but also and more important were his fascist sympathies, his apology for Mussolini, as well as the eulogy which the Duce had given his work. Again the fact that innumerable formulations in *Mein Kampf* seem to have been directly drawn from the pages of Le Bon certainly has much to do with this voluntary disregard. (p. 148)

The reticence one finds among the first writers on social psychology in America is notable. At a time when the recently created American universities had begun to take off, and when the social sciences very rapidly benefited from specific and preferential attention, Paris still remained the centre of intellectual life. So it is surprising to find, going through three of the first American textbooks on social psychology, those of Cooley (1902), Baldwin (1911) and Ross (1908), that Le Bon is cited just once in Ross's *Social psychology*, though some of the chapters come very close to Le Bon's conceptions.

Tarde fared rather better. Ross has twelve citations of his book *Les lois de l'imitation* and two of *La logique sociale*. Athough Baldwin places imitation at the very heart of his argument, he only cites Tarde twice, while Cooley mentions him just once. These three authors nonetheless seem perfectly familiar with the contemporary currents of French work and mention several works and articles published in that language. What is even more surprising is that the concepts, ideas, and hypotheses had themselves crossed the Atlantic; there was talk of the crowd, of suggestion and imitation, with occasional references to Tarde's work but only rarely mention of the work of Le Bon on these questions, even though we know that its importance was undeniable at this time. It appeared from the evidence that the conceptions and theories developed on the other side of the Atlantic at the beginning of the twentieth century were, beyond a few polite allusions, in complete opposition to those of Le Bon and rather reticent regarding those of Tarde.

Against democracy

Let us try to elucidate the reasons for this. The hypothesis that we shall endeavour to demonstrate is as follows: the anti-democratic character of Le Bon's and Tarde's thesis is in complete opposition to the 'foundation myths' of the American society to which our three authors so completely belong. At a deeper level they could neither concede nor truly understand these theses.

There is a sentence in Le Bon (1894) which perfectly sums up his political thinking: '[man] has seen that what he called liberty was only ignorance of the forces which enslaved him and that in the mesh of necessities which directs him the natural condition of all beings is to be enslaved' (p. 154). The first assertion, then, is that man is enslaved, enslaved by forces beyond him, enslaved by involuntary psychological conditions, enslaved by the immutable laws of psychology, and enslaved *last but not least* by his biological origins. Le Bon, moreover, was not content to write about it; he experimented and measured and if he demonstrated some restraint in his purely discursive writings, then all prudence flew out of the window where he was able to draw upon the *scientific* quality of a series of *objective* measures. We have already made reference to his 'Anatomical and mathematical studies of the laws of variation of cranial volume and their relations with intelligence' (1879), and to his peremptory claims about the inferiority of women. The human being is the plaything of his biology, his anatomy and his unconscious.

After the fashion of all other theories, those of Le Bon and Tarde were not conceived *sua sponte*. They belong in a particular context. It is clear that they militate in favour of a particular political position. They represent a reaction against the triumphant scientism of the end of the nineteenth century, an exaltation of irrationality in which feelings and instincts dominate. They are profoundly tainted with anti-intellectualism. In the final analysis, they embody a rejection of the liberal values extolled in the eighteenth century, a challenge to the philosophy of the Enlightenment and the bases of democracy, in terms refuting rationalism and individualism. Human behaviour is no longer founded on rational choices but determined by immutable forces over which one has no control.

Retrograde evolutionism

These theoretical conceptions are also profoundly impregnated with the great theory in vogue at that time, commonly referred to as social Darwinism, although the applications of Darwin's discovery in social analyses generally went well beyond the English biologist's intentions. Spencer applied the laws of selection to social structure. The first formulations of his evolutionary theory predated Darwin's revolutionary biological theory. But after the publication of *The origin of species* in 1859, Spencer was able to derive from it an increase in the scientific status of his own position, validating his concepts and systems of explanation on the basis of these profoundly influential developments in biological theory.

Having achieved this, he then went beyond the limits which Darwin had applied to his own theories.

Despite the influential weight of all eugenics which was inevitably inferred from the established action of artificial or natural selection, and despite the clear reticence and hesitancy in the text of *The descent of man* itself, Darwinian anthropology...excluded not only from its spirit but also from its writings, any ethic founded on approval of the hierarchical and eliminatory effects of natural selection at the heart of *civilised human groups*. (Tort, 1983, p. 403. My italics; even a moderate commitment to evolutionism could lead to the exclusion of some human groups from 'civilisation'.)

In the constant struggles for which society is the theatre the survival of the fittest and the hegemony of the strongest is what is at stake. The hierarchy is justified and sustained by a natural order; it was in this context that were elaborated at the end of the nineteenth century some highly significant and consequential social theories and practices which still continue to play a part today. Sternhell (1978) touches on the nature of the French intellectual climate of this period:

Darwin's disciples, as much vulgarisers as far-reaching thinkers, gave credibility to the notion that the master's theories were universally valid; they applied to man just as much as to his environment. Thus conceptions such as the principle of evolution or that of natural selection were widely used in history and politics, just as they were in literature. The immediate effect of the impact of social Darwinism was to deprive the human being of sacred status and to identify social life with psychic life. For Darwinism, as society is an organism subject to the same laws as living organisms, human reality is no more than an incessant struggle the natural consequence of which is, to employ Spencer's apt phrase, the survival of the fittest. The world belongs to the strongest; it is a question here of a scientifically established natural law, which in consequence provides it with an absolute justification. Thus, political Darwinism very rapidly derived from this an identification of evolution with progress, that is to say, a confounding of the most physically fit with the best. Applied to society, Darwin's hypotheses cease to constitute a scientific theory and become a philosophy, almost a religion. The Darwinian revolution profoundly impregnated the intellectual atmosphere of the second half of the century; it nourished very varied forms of nationalism and imperialism, though all were characterised by their brutality and aggression, their cult of strength and their taste for force and, it goes without saying, their deep aversion for democracy. (p. 147)

47

This account leaves out all the more liberal aspects of Spencer's theory, which although clearly in contradiction with his description of survival in society, represents the other essential, though less well known, side of his thinking; in effect, he extols the equality of those who have succeeded in overcoming the implacable laws of selection.

The Protestant ethic and the spirit of America

It is quite clear from this brief analysis that the conceptions of Tarde and Le Bon are fundamentally opposed to the 'foundation myths' of America. These foundation myths draw simultaneously and sometimes in a quite contradictory way upon the philosophy of the Enlightenment and the religious ethic of the first inhabitants of the New World: a puritan ethic of Protestant sects which collectively contributed to the American national ideology.

In order to understand the reception accorded to Tarde's and Le Bon's theories in the United States, and the way they were modified there, it would seem to be necessary to understand this ideology.

In the eyes of the first immigrants to New England, America was in a real as much as a figurative sense a 'promised land'. It was a virgin land of inexhaustible riches, a land of unlimited scale which required only to be cultivated to bring forth its wealth. Because this land was conceived as a new Eden, a new Jerusalem, it was the land of the elect, placed by God at the disposition of those on whom His grace was conferred. To this gift from God, proof of His favour, man must respond unstintingly with his labour, and by keeping to the straight and narrow road of probity and perseverance.

Thus, the American ideology is based on a puritanical ideology rather more than on the heritage of the Enlightenment.

> The universalist and liberal ideology of the Enlightenment is, in the heritage which the American revolution has contributed to history, the least disputed but also the most deceptive aspect of revolutionary thought. For, if the values of the new nation are based on the Enlightenment, their universalism was that of the white and Christian West, their liberalism allowed an unhindered path to individual initiative, which is to say, the imposition on the entire nation of the ideology of those who took themselves to be its champions and who belonged to the political and social elite. (Marienstras, 1976, pp. 33-4)

This prosperous and generous American land was an indisputable proof of divine providence. The Lord had placed it at the disposition of His elected people, who would accomplish this sacred purpose through the execution of material tasks. 'Elected by God, after the manner of members of the puritan sect, the American nation embarked upon a great and providential design. The benefits it has derived from the creation of colonies and from the battles which led to its independence are the signs that it is destined by God for an exceptional mission' (*ibid.* p. 99). The fundamental principles of this morality were summarised in an article by Jonathan Mason, 'Patriotism and virtue' (1780; cited in Marienstras, p. 99):

> Let our minds be impregnated with the sacred principle according to which, so long as patriotism is our guide, and our laws are conceived with wisdom and executed with firmness, so long as labour, frugality and temperance are held in esteem and the happiness of our society rests upon a civic spirit and love of virtue, peace and abundance will unite individuals, our community will prosper, our land will be the land of liberty, and America a sanctuary for the oppressed.

This land placed its first agricultural colonists (*yeomen*) and small entrepreneurs in a condition of equal rights; thanks to the natural resources and by dint of their personal virtue and efforts, all could partake of its riches.

This equality is the corollary of the individualism that forms the basis of the puritan ethic. Man is alone in his dialogue with God. His salvation depends only on himself, on the self-control he exercises and his own irreproachable conduct and sobriety. According to Weber (1930), Calvinism places man in a situation of individualism stripped of any illusions. He depends on himself and only on himself, without embellishment or misplaced sentimentality. 'Combined with the harsh doctrine of the absolute transcendentality of God and the corruption of everything pertaining to the flesh, this inner isolation of the individual contains on the one hand the reason for the entirely negative attitude of Puritanism to all the sensuous and emotional elements in culture and religion' (p. 105).

Only the moral qualities of man can contribute to his good fortune and well being. They are the consequences of efforts necessary to attain the universe of the elect, while the obsessive anguish of Calvinists concerns the outcome of this election.

The language of the founding fathers stressed equality, which in turn implied the absence of class struggle and the illusion of consensus. However, this basic egalitarianism rapidly and *entirely naturally* came up against its limits regarding excluded individuals. Were the Indians and the blacks, excluded from the Christian community, also men? The question was posed quite seriously. In effect, how could the fact be accommodated that according to the Holy Scriptures Adam and Eve were the ancestors of *all* humans? In contrast to the thesis of a single race which upheld this idea but assumed the *degeneracy* of blacks, emerged a multi-racial view postulating multiple Adams. But this thesis was poorly received because it was stricly speaking inconsistent with Biblical claims. What was nevertheless certain was that these impious, lazy and lustful beings were excluded from God's grand design. Egalitarianism was nonetheless not unduly embarrassed by this contradiction.

In addition, in puritan sects the service of God was executed through membership of communities protected by the ethical qualities of their members. Alert to deviations and keeping their members on the straight and narrow, the shared path, they helped to perpetuate and ensure continuing respect for their moral values, providing warnings of and eliminating any signs of deviance.

Among the *yeomen*, the puritan entrepreneurs, members of egalitarian communities and American citizens, there was no conflict. The nation was a body of freely contracting citizens, united, as the Declaration of Independence proclaimed, by consensus. 'To guarantee these rights, men institute governments which derive their just power from the consent of the governed.' The condition for this justice and this consent is the negation of differences or diversity among citizens. 'Neither economic contrasts nor cultural diversity, nor juridical differences are regarded as important. Only unity counts, based not only on law and patriotic sentiment, but also on a deep communion between citizens' (Marienstras, 1976, p. 301).

Everything is bound together by an unshakeable logic. This puritan tradition, transmitted and developed through a long and dogged educational process, contributed to reinforcing the conditions for the success of industrial capitalism. Weber (1964) has masterfully demonstrated how in this ethic the pursuit of profit becomes a moral obligation that must be fulfilled to please God. Simultaneously, by incorporating Spencerian evolutionism, it becomes the sign of more successful adaptation, poverty constituting the 'natural' wastage of society. 'The capacity to concentrate one's thought as well as the fact of considering one's work a "moral obligation" is here to be found associated with a spirit of strict economy, knowing how to calculate the possibility of higher gains and with a mastery of the self, a sobriety which considerably increases the yield' (p. 64).

Over the years, at the same time as mass industrialisation was occurring and the capitalisation of the land and means of production was developing, the myth and reality of a nation of individuals in free competition was to some extent eroded. But both myth and reality persisted because they upheld fundamental ethical necessities which hid their backwardness or isolation from the domain of exceptions even if these tended to become the rule. 'Individualism, equal opportunity and self-sufficient communities might undergo deep alterations, but belief in American destiny and the virtue of democracy persisted' (Weisberger, 1969, p. 9).

The dawn of American social psychology

Triple paternity

At the time when American social psychology was formed, the foundation myths had already been subjected to a considerable battering by reality. But, like most myths, they are highly durable; some modification and even contortion was necessary but their reign continued. In any event, these myths clearly impinged upon the precursors of social psychology.

Their writings are all characterised by an essentially discursive style. Their demonstrations rest upon historical, literary, philosophical and religious examples. There is no trace in their work of the application of any rigorous methodology. This is hardly surprising; social psychology only gradually became an independent discipline. The boundaries between social sciences, arbitrary though they may be, were still a long way from being established. Certain concepts were illustrated by limited observations. For example, to study imitation, Cooley undertook a somewhat impressionistic observation of two children. Generally, what emerges from these works is a humanist vision profoundly impregnated with a puritan ethic. These founding fathers conducted themselves as moralists, approving or disapproving of various features of their society, specifying directives for action.

Our intention within the framework of this presentation is not to provide an exhaustive analysis of the content of these works. Let us note merely that the most detailed text is also the oldest. *Human nature and the social order* by Cooley provides an incisive analysis of the relationship between individual behaviour and social behaviour which is not only unsurpassed even today but also reflects entirely modern preoccupations with the cognitive aspects of social behaviour. It is surprising to find that no contemporary social psychology refers to it and that the author's highly profound and original observations have fallen into the most complete oblivion.

What is of interest to us here is to determine how the notions developed by Tarde and by Le Bon are incorporated in these works and how they approach the phenomena of influence under the two headings of conformity and suggestion.

Choice and suggestion

Cooley's (1902) principal objective is to limit the scope of suggestion by contrasting it with the possibility of choice. It is evident that Cooley had read Le Bon but disapproved of his analysis. Now, this notion of choice is fundamental in American ideology, as much on the level of secular as of sacred activity.

Suggestion is an influence which functions in the manner of a reflex, mechanically, 'without calling out that higher selective activity of the mind implied in choice or will' (p. 51). It refers to simple thought or mental action excluding choice. However, the author defends the thesis that there is no radical contradiction between suggestion and choice, but a difference of degree. 'We speak of suggestion as mechanical, but it seems probable that all psychical life is selective, or, in some sense, choosing, and that the rudiments of consciousness and will may be discerned or inferred in the simplest reaction of the lowest living creature' (p. 53). For Cooley suggestion is involved mainly in simple social situations, while reactions to the complexity of the social environment require choice.

> When life is simple, thought and action are comparatively mechanical or suggestive; the higher consciousness is not aroused, the reflective will has little or nothing to do; the captain stays below and inferior officers work the ship. But when life is diverse, thought is so likewise and the mind must achieve the higher synthesis or suffer that sense of division which is its peculiar pain. In short the question of suggestion and choice is only another view of the question of uniformity and complexity in social relations. (p. 54)

Cooley adds that the choice is not determined by individual will alone; it is also the reflection or expression of the environment and the social conditions within which the individual operates; he is a social actor controlled 'through his own will and not in spite of it' (p. 56).

At the same time, Cooley is sceptical regarding a purely mechanical imitation insensitive to social influence. On the basis of his observations of two of his children, he came to the conclusion that imitation is a complex process entailing a substantial amount of information and necessitating elaborate intellectual activity and 'mental effort'. 'A novel imitation is not at all mechanical, but a strenuous voluntary activity, accompanied by effort and followed by pleasure in success' (p. 61).

The place accorded to instincts in social life by Cooley, and to processes which do not require any deep elaboration is ultimately very limited. 'Suggestion has little part in the mature life of a *rational* being and though the control of involuntary impulses is recognised in tricks of speech and manner, in fads, fashions and the like, it is not perceived to touch the more important points of conduct' (p. 66).

Furthermore, it is possible in a complex and diversified society to choose among the suggestions encountered there. 'Where suggestions are numerous and conflicting, we feel the need to choose; to make these choices is the function of will and the result of them is a step in the progress of life, an act of freedom or creation' (p. 68).

On the basis of these conceptions, Cooley was only able to regard suggestion in the context of crowds as a transitory, quasi-abnormal phenomenon, which he compared with secondary states, the ecstatic states provoked by prolonged dancing, flagellation and shouting. But these states are exceptional and limited. Following this plea for reason and against the less elaborate mental states, what is one to make of the sentence which closes the chapter on 'choice and suggestion' in Cooley's book: 'Rationality in the sense of a patient and open-minded attempt to think out the general problem of life is, and perhaps always must be confined to a small minority even of the most intelligent population' (p. 80)?

Choice and free will are eminently desirable faculties, *but not for everyone*. The majority does not have the capacity. It remains to discover *who* among them are capable, which are these populations that are the most intelligent. On this particular point Cooley is in accord with Spencerian evolutionism: it is only when a society attains the most elevated evolutionary level that it becomes a society of voluntary cooperation, substituting contract for constraint, reciprocal dependence for subordination. All men are equal but some are more equal than others, particularly in this beautiful America.

Creative imitation

From his preface onwards, Baldwin (1911) takes up the thesis of social Darwinism. Society as a whole is conceived as an organism subject to the laws of competition and natural selection. He develops these evolutionary conceptions extensively and then makes a fierce plea for eugenics. There is little doubt that Baldwin was a man of his time.

In contrast to Tarde, to whom he acknowledges enormous gratitude on several occasions, Baldwin develops a very positive conception of imitation.

> By imitation, [the man] gets the feel of things that others do, and so learns to value the safe and sane; by imitation he tries on the varied ways of doing things and so learns his own capacities and limitations; by imitation he actually acquires the stored up riches of the social movements of history; by imitation he learns to use the tools of culture, speech, writing, manual skills, so that through the independent use of these tools he may become a more competent and fruitful individual; finally, it is by imitation that he succeeds in being original and inventive. (p. 21)

Imitation is not copying or servile compliance.

Baldwin refutes the idea that mechanical imitation and compulsive suggestion are at the root of social functioning, *especially* in those societies that are most advanced in terms of 'racial evolution'.

> The reign of suggestion and contagion, and with it the rule of tradition, with its compulsion, do not result in those forms of organisation which show progress. Individual advancement in the more complicated relations of life, and the formation of institutions of social utility, both require inventive thought on the part of single man and the adoption of this thought on the part of society. (p. 55)

He also spoke always on behalf of the most advanced civilisations and races, and, for these, thought, originality, invention have come to supplant the 'instincts' that are the lot of subordinate peoples.

Robust individuality: the prophylaxis of suggestion

Though expressing his debt to Tarde, Ross (1908) draws extensively for the concepts used in *Social psychology*, written in 1908, both upon Tarde and on Le Bon, but mentions the latter only once and in an incidental fashion. Nonetheless, it would be wrong to assume that Ross's interests were stimulated by Le Bon. At the same time that Le Bon's book was translated into English, in 1896, Ross's 'Social control' was published in the *American Journal of Sociology*; it included a chapter on suggestion as an aspect of social influence. It seems likely that the two authors were drawing on the same sources.

Employing a number of historical and anthropological examples, and seeking the basis for his argument in American culture, Ross was entirely of Le Bon's opinion concerning the analysis of suggestion and crowd phenomena. In the same way, he postulated the existence of a group mind or 'mob mind'. The term 'mob', substituted for that of 'crowd' takes on a pejorative meaning here; it refers to the populace or the throng. (The English subtitle of Le Bon's *Psychologie des foules* is *A study of the popular mind*.)

In a rather pragmatic fashion, Ross inquires into the conditions that would favour the emergence of a 'robust individuality' to counteract the mental contagion to which 'inferior' individuals are vulnerable. He suggests a veritable 'prophylaxis', appropriate to developing 'immunity against illness, sin and poverty' (p. 84). He recommends quite arbitrarily what he has himself benefited from: a Presbyterian upbringing, in the country, by a justice of the peace; a superior education, a deep knowledge of the body, the mind and society, familiarity with the classical authors and wholesome teachers and avoidance of the sensational press; the practice of sports, life in the country, a secure basis in the home and a united family, 'associated with a lively sense of obligation in relation to the community' (p. 88). The time spent outside the family circle, frequenting cafes and 'plazas' would be liable to make the Latins more sensitive to suggestion. Furthermore, propriety is prophylactic in the same way that participation in voluntary associations gives the English or 'the Anglo-Saxon race' its 'widely acknowledged political sense' (p. 98). 'Self-mastery, a sense of honor, self-respect and faith in a religion of life and work is more individualising than faith in a contemplative religion of devotion' (p. 91).

Like Tarde, Ross regarded imitation as one of the springs of social life and one of the carriers of the uniformities peculiar to a society. He provides a highly meticulous description of all the types and conditions of imitation. However, he introduces a category of rational imitation which he links to creation and invention and which always remains 'the prerogative of a small number of people'. Rational imitation lies at the origin of practical as much as intellectual progress. It is also presented as the basis of all scientific activity. 'The intensive growth of rational imitation means the entrance of science with its verifiable statements into realms ruled hitherto by authority, tradition or convention' (p. 293).

On the verge of conformity

Besides suggestion and imitation, we find in these first American works on social psychology the establishment of concepts dealing with conformity, uniformity and submission to group pressure. And it is really this that represents their original contribution in relation to the French work.

Cooley (1902) develops a mixed conception of conformity. As well as being intentional it is a 'passive' form of action, 'aiming to keep rather than to excel, and concerning itself for the most part with what is outward and formal' (p. 293). The need to conform arises from avoidance of the inconveniences of non-conformity and from attribution to others of an unfavourable image of ourselves. Not to conform is to risk being unloved because 'it would seem that the expression of non-conformity is a native impulse and that tolerance always requires some moral exertion' (p. 294).

Nonetheless, conformity remains the rule and non-conformity the exception. The former has certain advantages; it economises on effort and protects against madness. If it sometimes happens that individuals are levelled down, they are more often levelled up.

It is certain that Cooley's sympathies are really with non-conformity, regarded as so much more arduous and conferring a much higher value. 'There is joy in the sense of self assertion; it is sweet to do one's own things. To brave the disapproval of men is tonic; it is like climbing along a mountain path in the teeth of the wind' (p. 298). The passion for differentiation is not given to everyone; it signifies self-confidence, discipline, endurance, perseverance, qualities which form the basis of the powers of superior peoples and 'races'. 'How much of Anglo-Saxon history is rooted in the intrinsic cantankerousness of the race! It is largely this that makes the world-winning pioneer, who keeps pushing on because he wants a place all to himself, and hates to be bothered by other people over whom he has no control' (p. 299). Here again we see outlined these superior races carving out a choice location in the promised land placed by God at the disposal of His elect.

Furthermore, those who assert themselves, who are enterprising are the pioneers and heroes, the kind of people who launch off to conquer the North Pole. They do not just renew social structure, their action gives it a life without which it would perish. Thus one has no difficulty in understanding the endorsement given to successful businessmen in both their actions and their ethics; everything is ordered for the best for them in the best of all possible worlds.

The example here of non-conformity comes from above. As a means of self-affirmation, non-conformity, when it is justified, excuses errors and aberrations and accords a conquering power by force of arms.

> The men we admire most, including those we look upon as peculiarly good, are invariably men of notable self-assertion. Thus Martin Luther, to take a conspicuous instance, was a man of the most intense self-feeling, resentful of opposition, dogmatic, with an absolute confidence in his infallibility, practically speaking, of his own judgment. This is a trait belonging to nearly all great leaders, and a main cause of their success. That what distinguishes Luther from the vulgarly ambitious and aggressive people we know is not the qualities of his self-feeling but the fact that it was identified in his imagination and endeavours with sentiments and purposes that we look upon as noble, progressive or right. (p. 212)

Non-conformity leads to social change or progress as a result of the clear-sightedness and resolution of exceptional individuals.

However, as far as Cooley is concerned there is little doubt that these are exceptions. Individuals generally are unable to evade social influence. Non-conformity itself is a form of conformity to external groups; in Thoreau's utopian image, it is marching to the sound of a different drummer. But the possibility does exist for individuals to choose the drums to whose beat they wish to march. No matter what the rhythm, it should then be followed. 'The group to which we give allegiance, and to whose standards we try to conform, is determined by our own selective affinity, choosing among all the personal influences accessible to us; and so far as we select with any independence of our palpable companions, we have the appearance of non-conformity' (p. 301). Non-conformity, when not that of great men, can only be a facade.

Conformity and non-conformity can coexist; one corresponds to an economy of means, the other to investment and effort. This is why Cooley gives the following advice, which sounds like a commandment: 'Assert your individuality in matters which you deem important, conform in those you deem unimportant' (p. 304). Conformity, then, is apparent in times of stability and uniformity, non-conformity in times of change.

The fatalism of the multitude

Ross, for his part, stresses a process which has gradually come to monopolise the attention of American social psychologists: the dependence of the individual in relation to the majority. For him this is one of the fundamental consequences of the functioning of democracies. He is completely in accord with Tocqueville who asserts that in such a regime the individual is happy to be regarded as the equal of his peers but simultaneously is oppressed by the multitude of his fellows.

> Not only is common opinion the only guide which private judgment retains amongst a democratic people, but amongst such a people it possesses a power infinitely beyond what it has elsewhere. At periods of equality men have no faith in one another, by reason of their common resemblance; but this very resemblance gives them almost unbounded confidence in the judgment of the public; for it would not seem probable, as they are all endowed with equal means of judging, but that the greater truth should go with the greater number.
>
> When the inhabitant of a democratic country compares himself individually with all those about him, he feels with pride that he is the equal of any one of them; but when he comes to survey the totality of his fellows, and to place himself in contrast to so huge a body, he is instantly overwhelmed by the sense of his own insignificance and weakness.
>
> The same equality which renders him independent of each of his fellow-citizens, taken severally, exposes him alone and unprotected to the influence of the greater number. (Tocqueville, 1961, vol. ii, pp. 10-11)

Ross notes this psychological process, labelling it *conventionality*, but his description is not exempt from a pejorative value judgment. This process of uniformity is also one of alienation of the individual; it operates to limit his choices; it undermines the individuality that would otherwise enable him to control his own destiny, or reject undesirable contingencies and select the good ones, or construct a strong and solid ego dedicated to mastery of the self and respect for fundamental values. So, here the majority or the opinion of the greater number lays siege to the individual, reducing him to its mercy to such a degree that he is bereft of the capacity to react, much less to resist. The term Ross employs to designate this implacable process is particularly significant: he adopts Bryce's expression, *the fatalism of the multitude.*

> Out of the mingled feelings that the multitude will prevail and that the multitude, because it will prevail, must be right, there flows a self-distrust, a despondency, a disposition to fall into line, to acquiesce in the dominant, to submit thought as well as action to the encompassing power of numbers... This tendency to acquiesce...and...submission, this sense of the insignificance of individual effort, this belief that the affairs of men are swayed by large forces whose movement may be studied but cannot be turned, I have ventured to call the fatalism of the multitude. (Ross, 1908, p. 191)

What Bryce and Ross demonstrate and what seems to them inexplicable is that dependence in relation to the majority does not rest on any clear or overt repression, but on what they called a 'moral force', or what we might call in more contemporary language, ideological mechanisms. Consequently, what is off-putting for these authors – and for many who followed them – is that this force cannot be interpreted in terms of directly observable facts, but that it must be assumed on the basis of these facts. Nonetheless, these authors have no doubt about the potency of this force. 'It is true that the force to which the citizen of the vast democracy submits is a moral force... But it is a moral force acting on so vast a scale, and from causes often so obscure, that its effect on the mind of the individual may well be compared with that which religions or scientific fatalism create' (*ibid.*, p. 191).

All things considered, this democratic regime is a long way from offering only advantages. It gives preference to the opinions of the greater number in every domain and not infrequently these are erroneous or maladaptive. The majority comes to flatten everything, including perhaps the worst, but particularly the best, the initiatives and ideas that derive from an elite minority.

> Some argue that democracy means the ascendancy of majorities not in government alone, but in all spheres of opinion and feeling; that, while it lifts up the many, it saps the independence and self-confidence of the exceptional man, and that by discrediting, even overawing and silencing

the elite few, it condemns society at last to conformity, mediocracy and stagnation. This indictment, were it true, would be crushing, for in a highly dynamic society, unguided majorities are apt to be wrong... In an advancing society, there will be, in the earlier stages of every discussion, a minority that is nearer right than any majority. This is not to say that in any particular division of opinion the smaller number is more likely to be right than the greater. The presumption is with it only when it includes the elite. (*ibid.*, p. 192)

The solution to this democratic dilemma is simple, though it brings into question the very essence of democracy. The people must put all their confidence in the *experts*, and acknowledge their superiority as guides. Simultaneously, democracy can only be achieved on the basis of a paradox which Ross finds in Tarde and then adopts himself. Social and political equality must be established first of all on a small scale at the top of society. Through imitation of the higher classes this equality will then become conceivable and even possible in other social classes. Here again, as in Cooley's work, we find that there are some men more equal than others, but with this subsidiary claim: democracy is not good for everyone, only for the best among us. These ideas become altogether more understandable when seen in terms of the socio-historical context of the period. This dilemma concerning democracy involved the entire United States, resulting in people adopting passionately committed positions expressing every form of contempt and fear of immigrant invasion.

The twilight of the first founding fathers

For the first attempts at theorising which took influence as their object of study, the links between individual and society or the social group were defined sociologically. There was, however, one exception. The application of a theory of instincts based on biology and psychology gave rise in 1908 to the publication of MacDougall's book, *An introduction to social psychology*. Instincts here were conceived as the bases not only of individual conduct but also of social life. This naturalist interpretation of social life as based on universal impulses left very little room for interaction or social influence. Despite the immense success of this work, MacDougall's theoretical conceptions fell into disuse, reduced to counts and taxonomies that prompted sterile polemics, incapable of lending any force to the creation of an autonomous social psychology (see Krantz and Allen, 1976).

Similarly, the writings of Cooley, Baldwin and Ross are surprisingly seldom cited in contemporary social psychological works and not at all in textbooks or specialised studies dealing with influence. It is interesting to

note in this respect the three page summary that Jones and Gerard give of
the history of social psychology (1967, pp. 2-3). They do, though, have the
merit of making some allusion to its history. Necessarily schematic and
even caricatured it may be, but their abridged history is nonetheless
enlightening about the myths concerning the origins of social psychology.
It appears that in 1924 F. H. Allport, drawing on theories of conditioning,
created the necessary link between a naturalistic and instinctive social
psychology 'à la MacDougall' and sociological social psychology 'à la
Ross'.

It goes without saying that the emergence of a social psychology with its
own problematics and practices was much more complex. My aim here is
not to attempt a complete historical reconstruction of this discipline as a
whole but rather to identify the appearance and transformation of the
concept of social influence. As the latter has been both central to, and to a
considerable degree constitutive of, the discipline, there has been a
constant necessity to locate the emergence of social psychology within
both its historical and scientific context.

At the beginning it was necessary for social psychology to constitute
itself as an objective, academic discipline, capable of practical application.
Social psychology was not alone in this; it was part of a more general
context of specialisation and indeed professionalisation within the social
sciences as a whole. At the end of the nineteenth and beginning of the
twentieth century, social psychology, like economics and sociology, had to
separate itself from those amiable, discursive sciences associated with
moral philosophy. It was necessary for it to create a network of academic
associations, university chairs, journals, and *last but not least* it had to find
funds to conduct research and thus to generate a demand for its services.
To acquire this credibility, it therefore had to construct specific research
objectives. Such conditions were gradually fulfilled.

From social protection to social science

Social psychology was preceded in this development by sociology. The
latter, under Cooley's inspiration, distinguished itself on the one hand
from biology, setting itself apart from evolutionism, and on the other hand
from economics (see Reiss, 1968); Cooley and Ross were both economists
before turning to sociology. Social psychology also had to abandon the
humanitarian and philanthropic tradition which still, for example, per-
vaded the writings – and the lives – of Ross and Cooley.

Philanthropy, the childhood illness of the social sciences
In 1865 the American Social Science Association was established. Fi-
nanced by philanthropists, its role was to assemble information and create

techniques that could improve the social conditions of the least-advantaged members of society. Immigration, particularly from Ireland, together with industrialisation, were producing categories of Americans who were disadvantaged and for whom the standard charitable solutions proved insufficient. The members of the ASSA rejected any idea that the disadvantaged were themselves responsible for their suffering.

The goal of this association was to promote reform. One circular produced by the ASSA stated:

> Our attention has lately been called to the importance of some organisations in the United States, both local and national, whose object will be the discussion of the questions relating to the sanitary conditions of the people, the relief, employment and education of the poor, the prevention of crime, the amelioration of the insane, and the numerous matters of statistical and philanthropic interest which are included under the general head of 'Social Science'. (quoted in Furner, 1975, p. 12; see also Haskell, 1976)

The development of these Social Sciences was envisaged as the basis of a quiet social revolution which would create a 'paradise on earth', an 'enchanted land'.

Many remained unconvinced by these charitable aims; the sceptics were to be found as much among the rather conservative patrons as among the founders and staff of the universities which were by then in existence. Considerable ambiguity was engendered by linking the terms 'social' and 'science', and was indeed exaggerated by the inclusion within the very heart of this unique association, of more or less enlightened 'amateurs' as well as those who had recently achieved the title of 'professionals'. The ASSA thus rapidly became the setting for a struggle from which the academics emerged as the victors, to the detriment of charity. For them, understanding of a society required a scientific study of social phenomena. The corollary to this was the specialisation and professionalisation of university researchers in the social sciences. In fact, ten years after its creation, these professionals had begun to take over the ASSA, which now had almost four hundred members. Their attention was directed more toward academic investigation than to the solution of social problems, to helping society. 'As professionalisation proceeded, most academic social scientists stopped asking ethical questions. Instead they turned their attention to carefully controlled empirical investigations of problems that were normally defined by the state of knowledge in their fields rather than by the state of society' (Furner, 1975, p. 8).

The ASSA began to experience violent attacks from all quarters. It was accused of conducting philanthropy rather than science. 'As long as the term "social science" is employed to characterise the heterogeneous and discordant opinions of unscientific men upon the most intricate and refractory problems of civilised life, it will be discredited in its true application' (Youmans, 1875, pp. 365-6). It was necessary to move on to more serious matters; terms were being brought into disrepute by people wallowing in the naive belief that social knowledge could improve the human condition. In 1874 an editorial in *Popular Science Monthly* noted, 'Of pure investigation of the strict and passionless study of society from a scientific point of view, we hear but very little' (quoted in Furner, 1975, p. 32). This editorial was written by Youmans, a friend and convinced disciple of Spencer.

The professionalisation of social wisdom

The result of such complaints was not long in coming. In 1880, the ASSA became a *genuine* scientific society so as to deepen the knowledge that might bolster its wavering authority. Two movements were then initiated; first it dedicated itself to higher education and second it sought to serve as an organ of consultation in relation to government. But the ASSA had problems in surviving the growing specialisation of the different social sciences which were creating their own independent associations and means for the diffusion of knowledge. The difficulty in defining a unitary, synthesising, and operational, social science only increased until the ASSA finally succumbed in 1909. With it disappeared for a considerable time any hope of a pluralist, open social science in the United States.

The sanctions and pressures towards uniformity became increasingly strong against those favouring a quiet social revolution to improve the human condition. The question was posed quite directly: 'Why should an institution pay a professor to teach social doctrines which are contrary to the consensus of opinions of the faculty, the supporters of the institution and the general community?' (in *Public Opinion*, Nov. 1895). Social science chose sides. In the end, the practitioners of *pure* social sciences came to side with the establishment.

Ross, who had abandoned economics for sociology, got involved in a heated conflict with Ms Jane Stanford, who had founded the university of that name in memory of her son. Ross paid the price; these contests that were to occur so regularly between liberal university faculty members and their tyrannical paymasters were generally unequal. The professionals wanted to safeguard their independence and to specify and protect their prerogative to define their own fields of investigation. But they did not always have the means to do so.

Thus, Ross, as well as Cooley and Baldwin, and despite his openly racist opinions based on the assumption of Aryan racial supremacy – views that were very common at the time and voiced more unashamedly than today – belonged to the second generation of these as yet rather undifferentiated 'social scientists', champions of a humanitarian vision of social science.

Their theoretical preoccupations also included themes that are inherent in the issue of social influence – suggestion, imitation, uniformity, conformity, non-conformity. Nonetheless, these three authors were forgotten by those social psychologists who later came to study social influence. Thus their social psychology, closely linked to sociology, philosophy, and history, temperate and introspective, was not to experience any further development in this form. Instead it became isolated from the subsequent development of social psychology and no one referred to them again.

The facts and psychological science

We should elucidate the reasons for this eclipse. To this end we need to understand how social psychology came to be established as a discipline that was far more independent of sociology than of psychology. Social psychology was created out of a two-fold development of external and internal validation, the former preceding the latter.

In contrast to the tradition inherited from moral philosophy and social science, it was defined as a pragmatic discipline. To achieve credibility, it was necessary to rely not on vague theories or opinions but on *facts*. It was in vain that Cooley (1902), aware of this objection, reiterated on several occasions that social ideas are the *solid facts of society*, that the ideas people carry in their heads are social products. One could not see or touch or measure *social ideas*; hence they could not be regarded as operationalisable concepts. What psychology and social psychology were expected to study were the consequences of ideas, namely facts and forms of action. These constitute *objects*, which become *objectives*, and from this objectivity derives effective *action*! But at the beginning great things were not expected of social psychology. It had first of all to prove itself and generate a demand, matters to which the commercial travellers of the university world began to apply themselves on behalf of this new-born discipline.

Practical problems

If in the United States at the beginning of the twentieth century no one could see what purpose could be served by a 'social psychology', social problems themselves were still very much in evidence. In the same period we observe an unprecedented and constantly accelerating technological creativity, establishing industry and mass production which, to find markets, had to generate mass consumption. These industries needed to be administered and work needed to be organised in a 'scientific fashion', as recommended in 1911 by Taylor, and by Ford advocating the creation of production lines.

In order to extend mass production it was necessary to create a new man, 'man as consumer' who must be induced via more or less covert means to buy. Needs might be aroused and instincts pandered to through suggestion (see Kuna, 1976), but also conformity might be induced by playing on imitation. What disciplines would come to the rescue of advertisers and give them recommendations for action or enlighten them as to the determinants of behaviour? Psychology and then social psychology found ready employment here.

During the same period, America was receiving immigrants from every corner of the globe. In 1880 they were coming primarily from Northern Europe, from Britain, Ireland, Germany, Holland, and Scandinavia. After 1896, they were coming mainly from South and Central Europe, from Austria, Hungary, Rumania, Italy, Greece, Turkey, Poland, and Russia. The number of new arrivals increased every year, from 250,000 in 1865 to 800,000 in 1882 and one million in 1905. In 1907, the record year for immigration, almost 1,300,000 people arrived in the United States. The influx of these populations stimulated an outburst of racist theories and practices: the immigrants were a 'degenerative' menace to the race; they were 'Mediterraneans' and not 'Aryans', 'brachycephalic' and not the 'dolichocephalics' necessary to qualify as one of the elite of humanity. Certainly, these immigrants were poor and often they were Catholics, Jews or Moslems, and for the most part illiterate. The impression Americans formed of these dregs of humanity challenged the myth of the *melting pot* and led to restrictions on immigration.

The boats deposited their miserable human cargoes on Ellis Island, opposite New York. Here the new arrivals, steerage passengers, were interrogated, subjected to medical examinations and even, around 1910, given tests. Smart young university staff were giving intelligence tests to people who had never held a pen before and who had just disembarked exhausted and frightened. And back to Europe were sent the 'mentally defective', the prostitutes, the sick, the socialists and the anarchists. The threat of this mass of mildly retarded defectives or 'morons'[1] flooding 'America the good' became intolerable to decent people as well as the men of politics and the psychological experts from whom their mental deficien-

---

[1] This term designating the mildly retarded was introduced by H. H. Goddard who illustrated it around 1910 with studies on intelligence based on eugenic and racial concepts. This is brilliantly and humorously described by Gould (1983). That fear and hatred of immigration was one of the means by which the social sciences became disseminated among the American public, principally via studies of intelligence, is argued by Satariano (1979).

deficiency and degeneracy could not be hidden. Something had to be done. Legislation was introduced in 1924 in the form of the National Origins Act, limiting immigration and establishing strict quotas on the number of entrants from the countries of South and East Europe.

Evidently these immigrants posed 'social' problems. They needed to be employed, educated and integrated, in a word *Americanised*. Up until the First World War the employment of these immigrants posed no problems, at least for industrialists. Around 1870 the United States had three million unemployed and unemployment remained considerable until the end of the century. It was easy to throw out recalcitrant workers and suppress collective revolts, when necessary using federal troops and armed militia.

Control of the workers

Before the First World War things became much more complicated, at least for the employers of labour. Those who happened to be apt at resolving employment problems and at directing their ranks of workers with their 'sound good sense' rapidly found themselves confronted with a problem of over-employment, with high turn-over and considerable instability in the work force. In 1913, 50,000 workers quit their jobs in the Ford factories, factories employing in the region of 14,000 workers in total! In an attempt to resolve this problem Ford introduced a great innovation; he reduced the working day to eight hours and offered pay of $5.00 per day instead of $2.30, claiming later that it was 'the best investment I ever made'.

At the same time interest in application of the 'human sciences' to industry began to emerge. Ford created a 'department of sociology' which was soon employing one hundred 'investigators' and then three hundred 'counsellors', their title having been changed. Their task was to inquire, in the police sense of the word, into the lives of the workers, to determine their moral standards, the stability of their family lives and the tidiness of their homes, and to supervise their leisure activities and their religious observances. Thus, in one of the first openings between the business world and the world of the social sciences, the latter was given the job of stool pigeon. This was already a long way from the philanthropic preoccupations of the first researchers in the social sciences, though there was something reminiscent here of these earlier concerns because, in the nature of things, the industrialists had to allow changes that led to improvements in conditions of life. The extreme reticence of the owners of business enterprises with respect to Taylorism and the scientific organisation of work and, more generally all those who sought to intervene between them and the employees they controlled with an iron hand, gave way under the pressure of events. The annexation of the social sciences proved to be effective; at Ford and elsewhere, new social arrangements did lead to a reduction in turnover within the work force.

However, at the same time the number of strikes grew from year to year. Unionisation grew apace and the bosses were eventually obliged to come to terms with the powerful American Federation of Labor. Its leader, Gompers, agreed to keep the strikes in check in exchange for material improvements (see Stark, 1980). The 'bread and butter' union, as it became known, wanted 'a larger slice of the cake'. The industrialists' position was under siege, their absolute power broken. They became prey to fears of the 'red menace', of socialists and anarchists as their position became more precarious. Their practical problem could be simply stated: how to supervise and control the workers.

The renaissance of social psychology

This vast social programme – increasing production, encouraging consumption, controlling the workers, Americanising the immigrants – attracted the involvement of psychologists who could not at this stage be defined as 'social' psychologists. They came from universities, torn between the need to create and meet a demand and the fear of getting their hands dirty by abandoning the world of speculation and pure research. These academics led double lives, one of academic work and the other of application, seeking to avoid the disdain of their fellows or, even worse, the loss of their university posts for, according to Titchener 'any such activity could humiliate their associates and lower the dignity of the chosen profession' (quoted in Baritz, 1965, p. 28).

Certainly social psychology did not spring fully armed from the head of Jupiter. In a period when the boundaries between the different social sciences were still very unstable, social psychology was not to be born out of sociology with which it has always maintained rather passionate love-hate relations, the latter sentiment generally prevailing. Instead it was born parthenogenetically out of psychology. Moreover this has been claimed as its only legitimate consanguinity: 'Social psychology is above all else a branch of general psychology. Its center of emphasis is the same: human nature as localised in the person' (G. Allport, 1968, p. 4). It is still this consanguinity that legitimises social psychology as a science dignified by the title, a science of measurement.

Just as it was necessary for us to retrace the origins of American sociology in order to understand why social psychology did not emerge out of sociology, a social science that was still somewhat unscientific, so we must now retrace the origins of modern psychology in order to understand how social psychology progressively emerged from it.

The era of measurement mania

At the end of the last century, psychology itself had to mark off its identity from that of moral philosophy, a quiet and benign discipline which held that introspection would reveal the universal laws of human behaviour. The objective of psychologists was to construct a valid, reliable and pragmatic science.

The objectivity that would guarantee their status as scientists was to be based on *measurement*. Measurement was already well established in psychology at the beginning of the twentieth century. In 1879, Wilhelm Wundt, the founding father of experimental psychology, set up a psychological laboratory in Leipzig. He was interested in psychophysics, in sensations, perceptions and reaction times. He measured the responses of experimental subjects to controlled stimuli, using statistical tables and mathematical averages.

At the same time, Sir Francis Galton, a cousin of Darwin and gifted amateur, inaugurated statistical procedures and involved himself in the study of individual differences, occasionally of very odd kinds; he observed the women he met on his walks in terms of their beauty and then submitted these observations to statistical analyses. As a result of some meteorological research Galton won renown through the discovery of 'anticyclones' which he was also responsible for naming. He then turned his attention to the human sciences; possibly he was vexed by the difficulties involved in manipulating the weather... He applied statistical methods to hereditary theories, founding eugenics, in order, so Jean Rostand wrote, 'to limit the multiplication of the unfit and to improve the race'. He also constructed a series of tests measuring reaction time, perceptions of colour differences, and auditory, visual, tactile and olfactory acuity (see Buss, 1976).

The first American academic psychologist, James MacKeen Cattell, served as a link between these two figures, Wundt and Galton. He gained his doctorate at Leipzig where he became an assistant to Wundt. Later he worked with Galton before returning to the United States where he gave, in 1887, the first course on statistical psychology at the University of Pennsylvania. He was interested primarily in individual differences, using measurement techniques borrowed from his two illustrious mentors, and on the basis of his investigations was responsible for founding individual psychology. The empirical demonstration of individual differences opened up a debate on the origins of individual variability. Was this variability the consequence of nature or of culture? Was it alterable or immutable?

Applications: false starts

These debates were in no sense purely academic. Very rapidly psychology became a discipline of action, of management of human potential. It was desirable to know if it was possible to change people and, if the answer was positive, to determine the means by which this could be accomplished, by working on instincts and impulses, on irrationality or rationality and self-control.

The first request for application addressed to psychology arose out of advertising, which was explicitly concerned with influence and persuasion. In 1895, *Printer's Ink*, the advertising profession's own journal, wrote that psychology could provide valuable material for advertisers. Walter Dill Scott, a lecturer in psychology at Northwestern University, got involved in this question of applied psychology, writing *The theory of advertising* in 1902. However, this book found little favour with the professionals who discovered in it no more than a collection of banalities and repetitions of conclusions they had already come to unaided. But Scott was not to be discouraged. He went on to publish *The psychology of advertising* in 1908 and *Influencing men in business* in 1911. The books contained a mixture of evidence, impressive abstractions and trivial details. Influenced by MacDougall, he based his approach on a conception of human behaviour as dominated by the instincts. But speculation regarding instincts bogged down and led astray the new born discipline of social psychology.

> Despite the immeasurable energy, thought and time psychologists lavished on this attempt to cross the threshold into the wonderful world of certain knowledge, they did not succeed. For the sandy foundation of the whole instinct theory was the recognition of specific instincts, the search for which proved to be fatal... Throughout the 1920s one psychologist after another abandoned this approach until by the end of that decade social psychologists were shorn of instincts and without theoretical base. (Baritz, 1965, pp. 25-6)

The great adventure of intelligence testing

During this same period the science of intelligence was making progress in Europe, having abandoned the convolutions of phrenology. Between 1904 and his death in 1911, Binet, director of the Laboratoire de Psychologie at the Sorbonne, put together a battery of tests for measuring intelligence. Despite his own warnings – he firmly believed that intelligence was not an innate given and he believed in the perfectibility of intelligence – his research and his instruments were greeted with the greatest possible enthusiasm by the hereditarians in the United States to whom Goddard introduced Binet's test in 1908. Even before America became involved in the First World War, the use of instruments for measuring intelligence was well established. Amongst other things it made it possible to identify the mildly retarded – in particular that insidious category, *morons* – in the population, so that on the one hand they could be directed to, and confined to, work suited to their limited competence and on the other so that their reproduction could be controlled if not prevented entirely. Finally, it enabled the repatriation of a growing number of immigrants on the grounds of mental deficiency.

But the scepticism of the public, as well as that of the business establishment was still considerable, for according to the Goddard – Binet test the mayor of Chicago himself was below the threshold for mental debility. The affair created a considerable stir, not only at the Congress of the American Psychological Association which was held in Chicago in 1915, but in the national press through which it reverberated. The *Chicago Herald* of 29 December 1915, devoted a long article to it under the headline 'Experts resort to a practical joke to attack mental tests' and the sub-heading 'Hear how Binet – Simon method classed mayor and other officals as "morons."' (quoted in Chase, 1977, p. 241). But the public was much less indignant when these tests classified immigrants in the same way.

The great leap forward
The entry of the United States into the First World War was finally to provide the measurers of intelligence with a field of investigation on an undreamt-of scale. In this great leap forward for their discipline psychologists were finally able to apply the full scope of their talents.

Matters did not proceed entirely unhindered. Yerkes and his team had to show considerable perseverance and determination. But in the end they succeeded in administering intelligence tests to 1,700,000 recruits! Harlow in his article on 'Yerkes' in the *International encyclopedia of the social sciences* describes this considerable achievement:

> Once they had overcome military and civilian resistance to the test, they trained officers and enlisted men in its administration, and tested more than 1.7 million soldiers in 35 army camps. The programme ended abruptly with the Armistice but the test had proved its usefulness, assuring psychology a fixed place in the military establishment. Moreover, the results constituted the largest intelligence test sample to that date and provided further impetus to the development of group tests. (In Sills, 1968, p. 588)

Apart from the unintentional humour with regard to the end of this experiment, it is certain that it greatly contributed to the improvement of a tool and especially to making it more widely known through its application in the field.

The Yerkes team did certainly encounter a number of difficulties. Yerkes had to devote a great deal of energy to convincing both his colleagues and government officials to carry out this experiment. Even then not all the difficulties were entirely ironed out. The army establishment was highly suspicious of callow youths, promoted to officers without any military training, who sought on the basis of a hour of tests, often administered under dubious conditions, to dictate their decisions regarding men with whom they were in daily contact. One may suppose that they did not think much of the data and they did not always simplify the psychologist-testers' task.[2] All the same, the tests served to filter the entrants into the officer schools. They also served to exclude the conscription of a considerable number of men judged, in terms of their mental age, not worth the expenditure of either equipment or training.

These tests, which, according to Yerkes, contributed to victory, were supposed to have saved a great deal of time in enabling men to be assigned rapidly to those positions most suited to their talents. More than ever the stress was placed on individual differences, on the classification of individuals and the rationality and economy of the means which made it possible.

Walter Dill Scott, returning from his earlier writing on advertising, threw himself enthusiastically into the adventure of measuring aptitudes. He developed a variety of methods for the assessment of personality characteristics. He directed the Committee for the Classification of Personnel, which received a million dollars from the Secretary of State for War, a sign of the administration's growing interest in methods of evaluation. This interest was developing throughout the American nation as a whole, and was responsible for attracting psychologists into industry and industry towards psychologists. There was no longer any doubt that psychology could be useful.

After the war, in Philadelphia in 1919, Scott founded his own consulting firm for industry, the Scott Company. In 1921, James MacKeen Cattell, the pioneer of the study of individual differences created the Psychological Corporation, employing the services of a host of eminent academics, including Bingham and MacDougall, who had by then moved to the United States, Scott, who brought with him his own company, Tichener, the disciple of Wundt, who had in the past been repelled by the prospect of dirtying his hands with applied psychology, Terman, Watson, one of the founders of behaviourism, and Yerkes, to mention but a few of the more celebrated participants (see Sokal, 1981). This institution for the

[2] Gould (1983) reports in this respect exchanges of correspondence that were quite unambiguous. This significant episode in the evolution of psychology is also described by Samelson,(1977).

promotion of psychology had as its mission not research but communication, the task of informing the public and particularly convincing industrialists of the utility of psychology. It was increasingly successful in this. After a few years the personnel of the company consisted of 125 full-time employees and 250 part-timers while the corporation's annual turnover exceeded a million dollars.

Industrialists expected miracles and marvels of tests, these objective methods which defined individuals in such precise numerical terms. Doubtless they expected a great deal more than the tests were able to provide. But the message had sunk in; they had been convinced that they needed psychology. There is hardly any doubt that they expected psychology to supply the means for controlling human activity and to provide the means for producing conformity under conditions where they were going to be defining the rules. By controlling men and directing their actions they intended to treat human material as industrial resources, rationalising the process, reducing the costs incurred in exploiting it, and obtaining the maximum effects with the greatest economy of means.

The act of confirmation of social psychology

Having finally attained the rank of a true science, this reborn social psychology did not pretend to any other objectives than those expected of it by industry. Its profession of faith can be found in the editorial of the very first edition of the *Journal of Abnormal and Social Psychology*, in April 1921. This issue marked the transformation of the old *Journal of Abnormal Psychology* through its integration with a new discipline, social psychology. We now know what should be understood by abnormal psychology; it includes everything that for whatever reason is located at the margins of evaluation methods, hardly a minor matter. As for social psychology, it is science with a 'wide range of practical applications'. Its 'point of departure is the individual' and his personality; secondly, it is concerned with the interaction between the individual and the group, and with 'the adjustment of the human being to his social environment'.

Its practical applications are unequivocal. 'The most important of these is the problem of socialisation, in a broad sense, *the fitting of the behavior of the individual to the social order*. Socialisation involves likewise a reconstruction or reorganisation of the social order so that it shall be better fitted to the individual' (p. 4; my italics). This was an enormous programme and we may suppose that it was often easier to put pressure on individuals than to modify their environment, as revealed among other things by one of the examples cited in the editorial, the movement towards Americanisation.

The issue of influence receives special mention, with respect to its 'importance for governing', which confirms us once again in our view that this issue has been one of the cornerstones of social psychology.

From behaviour to the social individual

While social psychology tried to achieve a better reconciliation between validity and application, psychology was marking out its field of investigation through the development of basic experimental research methods. Eventually casting off all links with the rather doubtful methods of introspection, it endeavoured to base the study of psychological phenomena on observable, verifiable data. From 1913 Watson's behavioural theories were beginning to provide an objective basis for the study of human psychology.

Furthermore, the plasticity of behaviour demonstrated by learning theories allowed the human psyche to be regarded as malleable, if not perfectible, material. Revived by research on intelligence but undermined by disappointments arising from its lack of rigour, hereditary theories found themselves seriously challenged. The control that must be exercised over individuals was no longer an external control involving selection from an unchanging base, but an internal control through adaptation of behaviour and therefore individual psychology to external circumstances.

The social wing of psychology

Behaviourism finally came to provide social psychology with a solid theoretical basis. It was introduced not just into the measurement field, which was only to be expected, but particularly into the field of experimentation and the collection of objective, quantifiable and reproducible facts. F. H. Allport, unanimously regarded as the founding father of scientific social psychology, established its basis. In 1924, after carrying out a number of experimental studies, he published his famous *Social psychology*, which is still frequently cited today, sometimes in a quite grandiloquent fashion. 'Not only did Allport's book help to create the field, but its continuing contribution in the form of theory and research marked the major avenues along which social psychology was to travel through its youth and early maturity.'[3] So many people have been engulfed in these paths that one must fear the congestion and even paralysis it has caused.

Allport's principal contributions were on the one hand to define social influence as a field of investigation based on the collection of individual

[3] Katz, D., article on 'Allport' in the *International encyclopedia of the social sciences*, ed. D. Sills, 1968, p. 271. One can also find a particularly eulogistic analysis of Allport's founding role in Post (1980).

data, and on the other to create a relation between the behavioural and social sciences.

In the preface to *Social psychology*, Allport adopts as his mission the distancing of social psychology from sociology and its reconciliation with psychology. The desire to distance himself from the conceptions of figures like Cooley, Ross and Baldwin is clear. In this sense, Allport's attempt was certainly innovative. It was extending a trend that seemed increasingly unavoidable.

Bringing social psychology closer to psychology meant drawing closer to an experimental science of behaviour. It also meant preserving the social psychology of social influence within the confines of individual mechanisms functioning in terms of the classical model of stimulus – response relations between individual and environment. 'Social behaviour comprises the stimulations and reactions arising between an individual and the *social portion* of his environment, that is between the individual and his fellows... *The significance of social behaviour is exactly the same as that of non-social*' (F. H. Allport, 1924, p. 3; my italics). This final assertion has weighed very heavily on social psychology. We are also surely indebted – if not grateful – to Allport for the iron blinkers of which social psychology is still having difficulty ridding itself. As if his claim was still insufficiently clear in behavioural terms, Allport persisted in stamping it in more general terms. 'There is no psychology of groups which is not essentially and entirely a psychology of individuals. Social psychology must not be placed in contradiction to the psychology of the individual. *It is a part of the psychology of the individual*' (p. 3; my italics).

Allport's repetitive, almost redundant insistence on this point was intended to destroy what he called the *fallacy* of collective consciousness and to make of individual reactions and their aggregation the essence of a social psychology that would be an individual psychology first.

> Collective consciousness and behaviour are simply the aggregation of those states and reactions of individuals which, owing to similarity of constitution, training and common stimulations, are possessed of a similar character... [Collective mind] is a convenient designation for certain universal types of reactions which interest political leaders because they represent points of contact between thousands of *separate individuals*, and therefore serve as a means of acquiring widespread control. (p. 6)

Allport believed that the fundamental explanatory mechanisms of conduct resided in the individual. Reasoning in terms of group consciousness is therefore an ascientific trap. Behavioural reaction is everything; consciousness is an epiphenomenon, indeed an illusion. 'The influence of

73

one individual upon another is always a matter of behaviour. One person stimulates and the other reacts; in this process we have the essence of social psychology. The means, however, by which one person stimulates another are always some external sign of action, never consciousness' (p. 11).

As we have seen, the theories of Le Bon and Tarde were unable to traverse the Atlantic without encountering more or less violent reactions. In 1924, Allport hoped to put a final end to their concept of 'group consciousness'. To this end he was quite prepared to deny the very idea of *social* influence. In a style that was more scientist than scientific, he drew upon advances in neurophysiology to refute the concept of group consciousness.

> The most flagrant form of the group fallacy is the notion of 'group consciousness'. It has long been observed that persons in an excited mob seem to lose control of themselves and be swept along by tempestuous emotions and impelling ideas. The objection to this view is fairly obvious. Psychologists agree in regarding consciousness as dependent upon the functioning of neural structure. Nervous systems are possessed by individuals, but there is no nervous system to the crowd. (p. 12)

It follows that the actions of a crowd are nothing but the sum of the actions of each individual taken separately. To explain behaviour in a crowd, one needs to make no reference to suggestion or to imitation. 'By the similarity of human nature, the individuals of the crowd are all set to react to their common object in the same manner quite apart from any social influence. Stimulations from one another release and augment these responses; but they do not originate them' (p. 299).

Suggestion can only be an aspect of individuality because, in reaction to it, each one can only reveal the same potential for submission. In Allport's conception, the individual-group contradiction also disappears in the sense that the group can be no more than the sum of individualities. This type of rationality takes individuality to the extremes. This individualism leads to the view that social influence is primarily the modification of individual action in the presence of others. Allport's own experiments were concerned with demonstrating this. Various types of individual behaviour – learning, task completion, reaction time, etc. – were elicited in the presence of others. These studies demonstrated the elimination of extreme behaviours and a tendency to conform. 'Early training of social contact has bred in us the avoidance of extremes of all sorts, whether of clothing, of manners or of belief. This tendency is so *fundamental* that we are seldom conscious of it... To think or to judge with others is to submit oneself unconsciously to their standards' (p. 278). To conceive of a co-presence from which all interaction is excluded, as a source of conformity-inducing influence well illustrates the fact that social control is integrated within the individual. 'The mechanism of control lies within the individual' (p. 392).

Internalised control

With Allport we reach the end and the apotheosis of a long evolution. Social control becomes the control of the individual over himself. In this way, each is indebted to the community for his singularity and difference. A subtle and unconscious form of coercion is established. C. Wright Mills (1953) identifies the consequences for social psychology of this development. 'Many whips are inside men, who do not know how they got there, or indeed that they are there. In the movement from authority to manipulation, power shifts from the visible to the invisible, from the known to the anonymous...exploitation becomes less material and more psychological' (p. 110).

Instead of a visible and harsh authority, it was possible to establish more insidious means of influence, separating individuals and inculcating in them a consenting self-control. It was possible for the means of influence to achieve such authority and universality because they were located within a propitious historical and ideological context. Moreover, social psychologists were so totally immersed in this ideology rather than subjugated by it that, far from defending themselves against it, they actively worked in its favour. And the influence imposed upon them and that they recommended to others was that of a uniformity-producing conformity. Morton Deutsch has on occasions deplored this trend, as we saw in the introduction. Baritz drew attention to this bias as early as 1965 but he was whistling in the wind.

> There is no doubt that individuals have internalised the pressures towards social control. It no longer needs to be imposed. It can be encouraged to come from within... A major characteristic of twentieth century manipulation has been that it blinds the victim to the fact of manipulation. Because so many industrial social psychologists have been willing to serve power instead of mind, they have themselves been a case study in manipulation by consent. (p. 210)

From the beginning of the century, advertisers have understood the effectiveness of conformity-inducing influence...just as social psychologists have. Certainly they were initially fascinated by suggestion. But in preference to mental alchemy they inclined towards the biochemistry of conformity and normalisation as means of directing and controlling consumers' desires. Bernays (1928), a nephew of Freud, excelled in the control of these desires. 'If we understand the mechanisms and motives involved in the functioning of the group mind, it should be possible to control and enroll the masses according to our own will and without them being conscious of the fact' (Quoted in Ewen, 1977, p. 91). What an ambition!

Peculiarity and Americanisation

The claims of advertisers were thus already inclined to put the reader ill at ease and direct his critical faculties against himself, dreading that others might recognise his peculiarity. Non-conformity, deriving from individual ill-will, was regarded as a sign of subversion. Let us give a couple of examples. The first is taken from an advertisement in a *Ladies' Home Journal* from 1920. 'You would be astonished to learn how many times in a single day your nails are looked at. Behind each glance is a judgment of you... In fact, there are people who are in the habit of judging new acquaintances on this basis...' (quoted in Ewen, 1977, p. 51). The second describes what happens to the individual who fails to follow the requirements that fashion dictates.

> He will be subjected to scornful glances, perplexed looks and uninviting reactions. People will find him bizarre. He will be judged feeble-minded and possibly undesirable. If he persists (in violating the rules of consumption) and he is employed, he will be fired! He will lose his clients if he is a salesman, his electors if he is a politician, his clientele if he is a doctor or lawyer. All his friends will abandon him. (Nystrom, 1928, quoted in Ewen, 1977, p. 101).

Advertising puts the emphasis on conformity, that is on the homogenisation of consumption aimed at 'rendering the reader shameful of his origins and of behavioural reflexes which betray his foreign origins. By deviating from the norm, one runs the risk of a deserved ostracism' (Ewen, 1977, p. 55).

Americanisation thus involves the emergence of the same desires, consumption of the same products and therefore the abandoning of cultural practices indigenous to immigrants. Frances A. Kellor, director of the Foreign Language Press Association of America, lacked neither clarity nor a clear conscience in her political proposals. In 1915 she wrote, 'Advertising on a national scale, this is the great means of Americanising. The ideas and institutions of America, law, order, and prosperity have still not been sold to all our immigrants, and American products and styles of life still haven't been bought by those who live in this country but were not born here' (quoted in Ewen, p. 74). Homogenisation, the obliteration of differences through adoption of common behaviour and the elimination of peculiarities, these were the aims of politicians, of industrialists and advertisers. One cannot fail to be struck by the congruence and indeed identity of these objectives with the theories and practices of the social psychology that emerged in the same era.

We have sought to disentangle the threads of intellectual and technologial knowledge that proliferated in the United States from the beginning of the twentieth century. This knowledge may have converged, diverged or intermingled but it was all involved in the overall scheme of a society characterised by an undeniably massive consensus.

We have seen how an infallible logical system gradually became established in which the individual practice of conformity became a necessity. Meticulous techniques were established to measure, classify, index, order and homogenise.

> The most striking thing is to observe the degree to which these techniques operated together from 1910, and were shown to be interchangeable, complementary and capable of being superimposed on one another. We do not wish to be either unjust or guilty of caricature. But this similarity of dates, this multivalency of localities, this movement of men indicates something entirely different from a series of unrelated events (Castel, Castel & Lovell, 1979, p. 68)

The common objective of this endless arsenal of techniques was to individualise, to attribute to individuals specific innate or acquired capacities. As Foucault shows in *Discipline and punishment*, it was a matter of applying the principle of individualising patterns. The meticulous rationality revealed in these techniques weaves a powerful spider's web, subtle and ubiquitous.

Conformity and normalisation function as principles of coercion which the individual adopts as his own in order to avoid the risk of appearing different.

> In a sense, the power of normalization imposes homogeneity; but it individualizes by making it possible to measure gaps, to determine levels, to fix specialities and to render the differences useful by fitting them one to another. It is easy to understand how the power of the norm functions within a system of formal equality since, with a homogeneity that is the rule, the norm introduces as a useful imperative and as a result of measurement, all the shading of individual differences. (Foucault, 1977, p. 184)

The individualised pattern and the system of formal equality occur entirely naturally in a democratic system based on conformity and its corollary, consensus. It is not our intention here to develop this point aD Foucault

77

Foucault has demonstrated it in the context of the France of the nineteenth century, but all the authors to whom we have referred, from Allport, through Bernays, Nystrom and the others to Kellor are convinced of it and emphasise it explicitly.

An optimistic and rational humanism

We should consider one of the fundamental critiques of the theory of suggestion by a social psychologist whose fame is still considerable today, Solomon Asch (1952). Strangely, his fame does not rest on the coherence or depth of his theoretical claims, which for the most part are forgotten today, but almost entirely upon an experimental result that was obtained incidentally. This finding was entirely at odds with his theoretical conceptions but it shed light on social behaviour in a rather pessimistic way.

Asch was an immigrant who had been able to flee from Germany and gain admission to the United States. Trained in Gestalt theory, he became interested in social influence in his adopted country with the aim of reaching a better understanding of the rapid spread of Fascism. Nazism had revealed that social influence could assume terrifying proportions. 'It is difficult to avoid noting how readily people come to acquiesce in beliefs and doctrines that run contrary to their needs and interests and how easily they can be induced to support policies and entrust their fate to a leadership whose objectives they do not grasp' (p. 398).

But he felt there were grounds for hope, for thinking that influence would not necessarily gain the ascendancy over suggestion and that even in extreme cases the individual would be able to retain some capacity to resist, at least if he recognised that the object of influence was fallacious. Asch's flight across the Atlantic reflected his absolute rejection of the Fascist system. He wanted to demonstrate the triumph of reason over the devil, over the outbreak of the forces of obscurantism.

But he felt also that the only theories available were too weak and undeveloped, insufficiently powerful to counterbalance the *doctrine* of suggestion that still prevailed. We should pause for a moment at the use of the word *doctrine*; a doctrine in contrast to a theory, requires a complete and unconditional commitment. If one wants to remain within its framework one must forego any critical analysis whatsoever. And the doctrine of suggestion had for a long time governed the formulation of problems, the investigative procedures adopted, and the interpretation of results in the realm of social influence.

Asch did not ignore the fact that the doctrine of suggestion had emerged on the scene at an opportune moment to provide Fascism with a basis for interpretation and investigation. Neither did he disregard the fact that this doctrine opened up an inestimable potential for influence perfectly suited to the ambitions of Fascism. Suggestion permitted the introduction of anything, and in no matter what conditions. 'The heart of the phenomena of suggestion, the property that made them unique, was the ability to produce changes in individuals in the absence of *appropriate objective conditions*' (p. 400; my italics). 'A German shopkeeper in the Sportspalais listening to Hitler or Goebbels revealed a character strikingly different from what he showed in his daily surroundings' (p. 387).

He perceived the scale and the danger of suggestion; it was a formidably potent means of social control.

> It is a matter of considerable import that there should have grown up in psychology a view that decribed social action generally in terms of passivity and equated group influence with arbitrary control. The model was an individual deprived of autonomy, one whose actions stemmed not from an inner direction, but from external influences forcing themselves upon him and taking control away from him (p. 400)

Thus a phenomenon central in both social life and social psychology was characterised by its irrationality and thoughtlessness, and reduced to a matter of pure manipulation. All social behaviour was therefore profoundly irrational from its roots to its overt manifestations. And reason itself was subject to suggestion which assumed the status of a fundamental process. 'The role assigned to thinking was mainly that of an inhibitory process, serving as a brake upon the more primitive and permanent forces of suggestion' (p. 401). Reason was nothing more than a form of resistance to universal suggestion which itself acted in the manner of a powerful and uncontrollable drug.

In contrast to Allport who, as we have seen, based his approach on a purely behavioural social arithmetic, Asch was convinced of the importance of cognitive factors in social life. His focus of interest was, to be sure, the same as that of Allport and all other social psychologists, an understanding of how conditions particular to collective functioning transform individual actions and experiences. But he posed the problem of social influence more precisely, in terms of similarity, commonality, and commitment to erroneous beliefs.

Despite the appalling historical events which he had observed at such close hand, Asch retained an optimistic, positive conception of social life. 'It has been our contention that one fundamental effect of social process is to extend our knowledge to our surroundings, material and social... We know that the help we derive from the observation and instructions of others is of fundamental importance in introducing us to the accomplishment of civilization' (p. 388).

Social life did not seem to him a process of universally orchestrated servitude. Rather it was essential and intrinsic to the establishment and preservation of human dignity. 'It is obvious but necessary to say that we are not victims of one another' (p. 411).

It would therefore be possible to counter the blind or concealed forces of influence, to struggle against them with the aid of personal resources – of character, reason and lucidity – or by drawing upon the resources of the group. And common sense, although conceding the existence of irreducible influences, expects and requires of each that he will exercise his free will, that he will consider the options and maintain his distance from influence pressures, that he will know how to stand out against his fellows. Compliance or sheep-like behaviour is often held up to ridicule.

A rational conception therefore rejects the idea that individuals lack free will. Because it is evidently impossible to elude influence, each individual must choose his sources of influence in deciding about causes, making judgments or weighing things up and finally must accept or reject influence. He will reject any influence which does not provide him with any benefit on the individual or social level. At the extreme this rationality results in a system of exchanges, payments and punishments in which, whatever the circumstances, each seeks to maximise his gains, a system which governs both individual and social life and leads to a clear rejection of the disagreeable and to reasoned preservation of what is agreeable.

In place of the symbiotic relation in suggestion, similar to the archaic merging of hypnotist and hypnotised, we find the gradual substitution of a pedagogic vision of influence. Hypnotic suggestion proceeds on the basis of a series of unquestioned and undiscussed orders. In contrast, researchers from the other side of the Atlantic have sought to emphasise the informative aspect of influence. Even further, in according primary importance to the *object*, influence was to be restricted to the repair of gaps in objective reality.

But Asch was overtaken by events when his rejection of phenomena of suggestion was leading – both in terms of his own experimental research and with respect to the line of research to which it gave rise – to the erection of conformity as the rule because it was subordinate to the properties of the object, to the truth which as soon as it was demonstrated would be accepted by all. Conformity, as the outcome of access to objective realities, was in addition adapted to the functioning of societies, for all was ordered for the best in the best of all possible worlds. It would normally function smoothly, through a consenting commitment to a number of models and rules that would nip in the bud any desire to do or think otherwise.

In order for the system of standardising conformity to attain the optimal degree of perfection, it required only to associate interindividual forms of coercion with the functioning and mechanisms of the group. It was this link that Asch was to make, in his own self-defence.

3   Majority influences

> 'There were five little peas in a pod, they were green, the pod was green, they believed that the entire world was green and for them this was certainly true!'
>
> H. C. Andersen, *Tales*

The individual is delivered bound hand and foot to the judgments of his fellows. This is true in two respects: he fears a negative judgment and seeks to induce positive evaluations; he relies on others in establishing a point of view that agrees with theirs. This proposition and its two corollaries constitute the foundation for research on conformity.

Since Allport, this proposition has been fed, perfected, developed, and theorised about; it rests upon a series of experimental demonstrations the most important of which date from the fifties. Experiments on conformity are legion and it is not our intention to examine them all here. We will only reconsider the most significant and celebrated, those which represent a decisive contribution to the issue of conformity.

Before beginning the presentation of this research, I wish to illustrate my purpose with a well-known allegory. Each of its narrative details corresponds to an aspect of social influence.

The emperor's new clothes

A long time ago there lived an emperor who above all liked beautiful new clothes... Thus begins the story I am about to relate. Doubtless you have already recognised one of the most famous of Hans Christian Andersen's tales, one that is particularly instructive and well suited to our purpose. You can look for resemblances, parallels between these fictitious characters and actually existing people. They are not difficult to find. Furthermore, if this was not truly a nineteenth-century tale, one would swear that it was an experiment in social psychology. We might not be far wrong in supposing it to have been an inspiration for such experiments. But let us not anticipate...

One day two swindlers arrived in the empire. They passed themselves off as weavers and boasted of knowing how to weave the most marvellous cloth it was possible to imagine. But garments made up from this cloth had the strange virtue of being invisible to fools. Thus is identified the pivot of social influence.

Our emperor is delighted to hear this. He will be able to rid his empire of incompetents and eliminate all the fools. He orders the two weavers to set to work.

He is impatient to see if the cloth progresses but nonetheless a little ill at ease. Even emperors can be *uncertain* and have *doubts* about their capacities. He thus decides first of all to dispatch an old and faithful minister, a man of whose intelligence and competence he is certain. Alas! When the two swindlers who pretend to be very busy with their task, request his opinion, the old minister realises that he sees nothing. The *doubt* is implanted; and if he is a fool, if he is incompetent... Even an old and experienced minister can feel uncertain about his capacities. He opens his eyes wide, realising that the most important thing is not to reveal that he sees nothing. He admires the cloth, agrees to the details which the two weavers give him, eager to remember them so that he may repeat them to his sovereign. The same misadventure befalls another wise minister sent by the emperor a few days later. He also pretends to be amazed at the quality of the cloth, which he also reports to the monarch.

The two witnesses *agree*. The two ministers have been able to confirm the quality of the work with their own eyes. The emperor goes in his turn to see the famous cloth. When his two ministers extol to him the quality of the work in this false handicraft, the emperor realises with helpless amazement that he sees nothing of what his two advisers themselves apparently see. Certainly, he is the emperor but divine right is unable to take the place of intelligence. In his turn, he is careful not to admit that he does not see the marvellous cloth. And in his wake, the entire court marvels at the cloth. Then the weavers are requested to sew garments for the emperor, a task to which they devote themselves enthusiastically, mimicking the relevant movements.

The entire population turns out for the ceremony at which the emperor, in his best attire, must lead the cortege through the town. The great day arrives. The swindlers dress the emperor in his marvellous clothes, light as the web of a spider, they say. He admires himself in front of a mirror and the chamberlains bow down to take the non-existent train of the robes. They likewise do not wish it to be known that they see nothing at all.

The cortege crosses the town. And everyone exclaims, everyone express-es admiration for the emperor's beautiful clothes. The concert of praise which salutes the procession is broken by a single voice, a minor voice, the most minority voice of all, the voice of a small child. But even though this voice be ever so weak, it expresses what everyone is thinking in their own inner conscience.

'But he has no clothes at all!' cries the child in the crowd. This cry of innocence is repeated from one to another, first whispered and then amplified into an immense clamour, an enormous burst of laughter as the people jeer at the deceit that has smitten their sovereign.

'The emperor shudders because it seems clear to him that his people are right but at the same time he realises that it will be necessary to hold on to the end of the procession. He draws himself up even more proudly and the chamberlains continue to carry the royal mantle and train that does not exist' (Andersen, 1962, p. 172). Thus ends the tale.

This altogether exemplary story illuminates our argument most effectively. Let us now analyse the facts in their chronological order and in the – possibly less attractive – language of social psychology.

To begin with, the old minister conforms because he thinks that the others – the swindlers – possess greater resources, a greater capacity for access to a true perception of things. He feels *uncertain* of his own judgment, all the more as it concerns himself.

Faced with the need to interpret the social world, the individual is without defences. To achieve an *objective* vision of things he must needs depend on others. In an uncertain or ambiguous situation, the ideal is to converge on a collective definition of the situation, to create a *social reality*, by relying on the false conviction according to which it is impossible to err collectively. Error can only occur at the individual level while truth is social and is imposed by the majority.

The commitment of all to the same conception produces a majority effect. All are required to think the same thing and influence is exercised via a social pressure which *never needs to reveal itself as such*, this also being a sign of its effectiveness. No trace of constraint or explicit pressure exists; each one rallies to the collective vision of his own accord, all participate collectively in the same social reality...up to the point at which one minor, minority voice makes itself heard and finally expresses what everyone had buried in their conscience. But that is another story, and we will come to it in its turn.

Extreme conformity

An epistemological nightmare

Situations certainly exist in which, in order to demonstrate conformity to others, an individual surrenders to declarations contrary to perceptual evidence. The social psychological counterpart to 'The emperor's new clothes' could well be the famed procedure devised by Solomon Asch (1952, ch. 16), and of which Roger Brown has written: 'The situation is an epistemological nightmare' (1965, p. 671).

Asch wished to demonstrate that individuals are capable of escaping

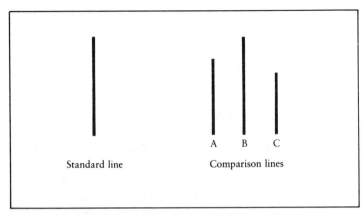

Figure 3.1. Example of the perceptual task in the Asch experiment

from an influence which goes against all the perceptual evidence. To this end, he presented experimental subjects with a task involving comparison of lengths. They had to designate from among three lines of different lengths the one that was equal to a standard line. The task is simple and involves not the slightest ambiguity (see Figure 3.1). The differences between the standard line and the comparison lines that are not equal to it are obvious. These differences averaged one inch and were thus perfectly perceptible to the subjects.

The experimental subjects undertook the experiment in groups of seven to nine. Now, the experimental manipulation consists of placing only one *naive* subject in each group, the others being accomplices of the experimenter who give manifestly false responses on seven out of twelve occasions, responding with perfect unanimity in front of the naive subject. What is this naive subject going to do, embarked without his awareness on a kind of scientific ghost train? How is this individual going to react, plunged into such a baffling situation? Will he continue to give his own response, which is indisputably the correct answer, or is he going to respond 'like the others' and so give false answers? Based on the reactions collected by Asch at the end of the experiment, and imagining what might be passing through the head of a typical subject, Jones and Gerard (1967) performed a light-hearted exercise in social psychology fiction.

This should be a cinch since I know my eyes are real good. I wonder what he is trying to prove. There, he just put up the first pair of cards. That's no sweat, line 2 is the correct one. Let's hear what the first guy says. Sure enough, line 2 it is. Naturally everyone agrees. Now it's my turn, 'line 2'. The last guy agrees too. That makes it unanimous. Okay, here comes the second pair of cards. That's cinchy too, it's line 1. That's right, we're all in agreement. Here comes the third pair. It's line 3. This is the easiest...what did the first guy say? He couldn't have said line 2. It's much too long. I guess I didn't hear him correctly. The second guy just said line 2. What's going on here? Am I seeing things or hearing things? The third guy just said line 2. Maybe my head is tilted. No, whichever way I look at it it still looks like line 3. The fourth guy just said 2. Relax, take it easy, there must be some explanation for this. Maybe it's where I'm sitting. But the guy in front of me is seeing it from the same angle and he just said 2. The fifth and then the sixth guys both said 2. Is this some kind of optical illusion? Maybe they're seeing something I'm not. What am I going to say, it's my turn? I know I'm right but they'll think I'm some kind of a jerk if I disagree with them. They can't all be wrong – or can they? Maybe they're just playing follow the leader. Yes that's it. The first guy made a mistake and now they're all just being sheep. But why would they? What do I do? This is completely mad! Well, it's my turn so I'd better tell him what it looks like to me. 'Line 3.' What a pall just came over the room! They must certainly think I'm some kind of a nut. But what can I do, I have to call them as I see them. This isn't as easy as I thought it would be, although 3 still looks right, or does it? The last guy just went down the line with the others. I sure would have felt better if he had agreed with me. I'd better ask the guy running this what it's all about; maybe I'm doing something wrong... Nope, he says I'm doing what I'm supposed to. Let's see what happens with the next set. There they are. There can be no mistake about it – it's line 1. Let's see what the first guy says. He just said line 2. Well, that's what I thought I heard. But that's too short! One of us is nuts! The second guy just said line 2. Here we go again. My hand is beginning to tremble. I sure wish I could have a drink of water. They must be right but how can they be since I see it differently. It either is or isn't right. There are no two ways about it! They're beginning to look at me kind of funny. I sure wish I had a ruler and could go up there and measure the lines. Then I'd know for sure who was right and who was wrong. Then I could prove my case. I wonder what they would say then. The third guy just said 2. Gee, I'm going to stand out like a sore thumb again! Maybe I ought to go along with the crowd. What's the difference anyway, it's only an experiment. But how can I if I am supposed to tell him which one *I* think is correct. I'm sure they won't speak to me when this thing is over. I can't remember when I've been so uncomfortable about something as I am about what's going on here. I've always relied on other people but how can I here? I've always assumed people see things the way I do. Maybe I don't see things clearly and they are actually right. If I say line 1, I may be wrong and then I'll really be out on a limb. But if they're wrong and I agree with them, then we're all wrong together and maybe that's not so bad. It's my turn. What should I do? 'Line 2.' There I said it. They seem pleased now and I feel a little better about it. Why did I do it though? It still looks like line 1 to me. Next time I think I'll stick by my guns...

Like this archetypal subject whose ruminations lead him to bow to influence, the subjects in Asch's experiment were influenced to an appreciable degree. Over the set of seven incorrect judgments, about one subject in four conformed to the group, and gave an erroneous response; 33.2% of the responses reflected a submission to the majority opinion of the confederates.

Imagine the subjects' difficulty, their psychological distress – such terms are not inappropriate – whether they resisted or whether they went against the perceptual evidence and adopted the point of view of the others. It was a deeply traumatic experience and they said as much. 'This is unlike any experience I have had in my life. I'll never forget it as long I live' (Asch, 1952, p. 467). Likewise, even when they had not submitted, even if they had not given the impression of accepting the unacceptable, they left the experiment very worried. 'The subject insisted vigorously on the correctness of his estimates. Yet, he was deeply disturbed. It seemed that the confidence he felt in his own judgments served to increase further the amount of his disturbance' (p. 466).

Simply describing the Asch experiment is insufficient to convey its many facets. How did subjects give in, how did they resist? Here again, their accounts provide us with valuable information. It is a matter of knowing how they viewed the experiment, if they were involved in it, and finally if they had yielded in order to disentangle themselves from the experiment, the experimenter and his confederates while preserving their own private judgments. If these questions are simple, the answers are less so.

Let us begin by saying that the subjects who remained calmly independent were rare. Everyone would have liked to 'do as everyone else does' and answer like the others.

Asch obtained what is at first sight an astonishing finding but one based on a subtle rationale. Several influenced subjects asserted that they modified their responses because they were certain that the majority had actually given the correct judgments! These subjects, questioned like the others directly after the heat of the action, not only denied the evidence but displayed astonishing assurance: 'I never gave an answer that wasn't right...I didn't give any answer I knew was wrong' (p. 469), one subject claimed. Such an answer can hardly fail to astound us; one subject displayed great surprise when he was told that he had given incorrect responses; he could recall nothing of it, nor could he explain it!

Not all the conforming subjects were equally at ease. Rather than a desire for precision – which they played down – they expressed social motivations. Or else they thought that it was impossible to be wrong collectively, drawing on a deep-rooted representation of group functioning with the result that the more transitory situation they had experienced was never questioned. Or else they revealed a desire not to be different. This rendered them *in*different to the task; they became unconcerned with it, no longer worried about the imprecision of their judgments. Their sole objective was not to stand out, not to deviate. They were entirely conscious of what they were doing. Their clarity on this point allowed them to eliminate any concern or internal conflict: 'I did not want to be apart from the group; I did not want to look like a fool' (p. 472).

The Asch paradigm, one of the most surprising aspects of which is that it actually worked, creates an extreme case of conformity. And indeed the author himself was not a little surprised. At the outset, he had wanted to demonstrate that in the presence of an objective reality, the individual has no need of others in constructing an opinion, and that he is able to draw on the factual evidence in order to resist. Moreover, his own commentary on the experiments makes no secret either of these or the degree to which he was misled.

> A theory of social influences must take into account the pressures upon persons to act contrary to their beliefs and values. They are likely to bring to the fore powerful forces that arise from the social milieu at the same time that they may reveal forces, perhaps no less powerful, that individuals can mobilize to resist coercion and threats to their integrity... Current thinking has stressed the power of social conditions to induce psychological changes arbitrarily. It has taken slavish submission to group forces as the general fact and neglected or implicitly denied the capacities of men for independence, for rising under certain conditions above group passion and prejudice. Our present task is to observe directly the interaction between individuals and groups when the paramount issue is that of remaining independent or submitting to social pressure. (pp. 450-1)

As pertinent as this objective may have been, it remained no more than a pious hope until the first experiments on minority influence. While Asch himself expressed reservations about the effect he had obtained and proposed new approaches and counter-hypotheses, his paradigm was regarded as the basic model for influence processes and radically shaped the research that followed, research in which influence was equated with conformity. '[Asch] has furnished the most striking illustration of conformity, of blindly following the group, evident even if the individual knows that he is following it and turning his back on reality and truth' (Moscovici, 1979, p. 5).

Asch himself sought to determine the limits of conformity. Perhaps the majority error was too slight and so remained within the limits of possibility. It oscillated around a deviation of one inch. But if it became too great, surely subjects would then be able 'to reassert their independence and repudiate the majority more decisively' (Asch, 1952, p. 274). The majority error was thus increased to an average of three inches. Here again, conformity occurred in very significant amounts, influencing 28% of responses! The only difference between this and the first experiment rested in the fact that the subjects were more clearly divided into two categories: the 'independents' who represented about half of the subjects remained so throughout the experiment, while the 'yielders', about a quarter of the subjects, followed the majority in almost all the trials (four out of five). 'The increasing extremity of the conditions seemed to accentuate the reactions of independence and yielding. There was an increase in the proportion of those who were entirely independent. But for the others the conflict was all the more severe' (p. 476).

Likewise, the size of the majority barely affected the emergence of conformity; whether there were three, seven or ten confederates did not substantially change the majority effect. On the other hand, when the subject was not alone in the face of a unanimous error, when another naive subject joined with him, the errors declined very significantly as did the psychological tension.

The moral of this series of experiments is that it is better to be one among many in the wrong than to be the only one who is right. The defence of truth weighs little against the punishment of isolation. But our astonishment is not at an end. Experiments in social psychology have given a good indication of the servile compliance of which individuals are capable when manipulated by the groups to which they belong or under whose authority they are placed.

Submission or abdication

Asch's experiment teaches us the difficulty of discovering the limits of what an individual will do under social pressure. The extreme examples of war or torture are distressingly revealing. And Andersen's tale illustrates in a charming and humorous fashion a fundamental social mechanism.

If the Asch situation contains an 'epistemological nightmare', that devised by Milgram (1964) creates a kind of scientific hell. In this experimental purgatory, there are no little horned devils prodding you with their tridents or tipping you in cauldrons of boiling oil, just a neat, antiseptic, functional laboratory containing consoles for controlling electrical stimulations, electrodes, and one-way mirrors. However, 'observers of the experiment agree that its gripping quality is somewhat obscured in print' (Milgram, 1974, p. 4). The problem, as in the Asch experiment, is to encourage subjects to assert their autonomy and independence in opposition to authority.

Here also the experimenter's expectations were overtaken by events, that is to say by the results. 'What is surprising is just how far ordinary individuals will go in complying with the experimenter's instructions. Indeed, the results of the experiment are both surprising and disturbing' (p. 5).

Milgram distinguished between 'conformity in word', which characterises Asch's experiment, and 'conformity in deed', produced by more powerful and thus more consequential social forces, as much for the subject himself as for others. The basic goal of the experiment is to 'see if a person will perform acts under group pressure that he would not have performed in the absence of social inducement' (Milgram, 1964, p. 137).

Let us briefly review Milgram's experiment. Subjects are apparently participating in a learning task; it involves the learning of words by groups of four persons. In fact, the group includes three confederates. The role each takes is settled by 'drawing lots'; 'by chance' one of the confederates draws the role of 'pupil'. In sight of the *others* he is seated in an electric chair. Another confederate reads the list of word associations to him, first the stimulus word and then four possible responses from among which the 'correct' response must be chosen. The third confederate says whether or not the answer is correct and gives the right response. As for the naive subject, he is placed in front of an electric console, on which are mounted thirty switches running from 15 to 450 volts. Under these switches the following descriptions may be read: 'mild shock', 'moderate shock', 'strong shock', 'very strong shock', 'violent shock' and 'danger, painful shock'. He is supposed to control the 'pupil's' learning by punishing his errors with electric shocks, increasing the intensity of the shock successively each time the pupil repeats an 'error'. The latter reveals himself to be rather a poor learner. The group of instructors must together decide on the strength of the shock to be inflicted; each one indicates in turn what voltage of shock should be given and the lowest of these voltages is then chosen. Thus the naive subject has every opportunity to suggest on each trial a low voltage shock. Now, at each error, the two confederate 'teachers' propose a shock 15 volts stronger than on the preceding trial, so that after the twentieth error for example they concur in asking for a shock of 300 volts!

The behaviour of the pupil confederate who, we should note, actually receives no shock at all and simply pretends, is particularly demonstrative. Milgram describes this as follows:

> The learner indicates no discomfort until the 75-volt shock is administered, at which time there is a slight grunt in response to the punishment. Similar reactions follow the 90- and 105-volt shocks, and at 120 volts the learner shouts to the experimenter that the shocks are becoming painful. Painful groans are heard on administration of the 135-volt shock and at 150 volts the learner cries out that he wants to be released from the experiment, complaining of a heart disturbance. Cries of this type continue with generally rising intensity, so that at 180 volts the learner cries out 'I can't stand the pain' and by 285 volts his response to the shock is clearly an agonized scream. At 300 volts the victim shouts in desperation that he will no longer provide answers to the memory test, and so forth through 450 volts' (p. 139).

In order to determine the strength of the experimental effect a control condition was created in which the confederate teachers were absent. The naive 'teacher' was alone with the 'pupil' confederate. There is one further relevant detail: the experiment included thirty trials in which the confederate pupil made an error.

Would the experimental subjects come to resist the influence of the confederates and refuse to follow their recommendation or would they yield and press switches delivering more and more painful electric shocks? Figure 3.2, which gives the average level of shock at each trial, is very clear, illustrating very well the tendency of subjects to yield to group pressure even if thereby they are induced to commit acts repugnant to them.

In the final trial, naive subjects agreed to administer to the pupil a shock on average of 212 volts, which is hardly a mild tingling! In the control group, the final shock was on average 51 volts, and thus substantially lower. As in the Asch experiment, a study of the distribution of responses revealed two categories of subject, conformists who administered 414 volts on average in the final trial and subjects who resisted, sending no more than 72 volts in the final trial, despite their tension and the social pressure.

In the context of Asch's contribution, Milgram's experiment further extends the limits of individual conformity. Here it is not just a matter of superficial agreement; the subject is obliged to put his money where his mouth is, to press the switches and endure the suffering of his pupil. There is no evasion of the type 'I said it but I did not think it', but instead highly consequential actions which substantially violate humanitarian standards

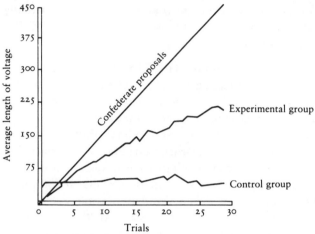

Figure 3.2. Graph of subject response (S. Milgram, 1974)

of respect for another's person. Here conformity proceeds from two norms, the majority norm in a group of peers and the norm of the integrity of the scientific experimenter who has set up the entire situation. Nonetheless, subjects have the option of resisting, they have the power to be more merciful.

Alas, these dramatic experimental situations are still pale reflections, trifles, compared to the evils of torture and other compromises to be found in a harsh reality.

A fictitious prison

The manner in which individuals are incorporated into society structures their perceptions, their behaviour, and their expectations regarding others. It is difficult for us by ourselves to specify the degree to which we are impregnated with our own social context. Here again, there is an experiment (Haney, Banks and Zimbardo, 1973) that can help us to evaluate the significance of this imprint.

The elaborate construction and theatrical character of this particular experiment is not common in social psychology. It all begins with a newspaper advertisement; subjects are being recruited for participation in a well-paid experiment which will last several days. Suitable tests allow selection of subjects who are psychologically well-balanced. They are randomly allocated to 'roles'. And the experiment begins...with the wailing sirens of police cars dispatched to 'arrest' some of the subjects. They are handcuffed and led off to 'prison', located in university buildings disguised to create this effect. Waiting for them there are the remainder of the subjects, 'guards' dressed almost like real policemen, wearing whistles in their belts and very dark sunglasses – no doubt to eliminate any distressing eye contact with the prisoners – and who are given a free hand in organising the incarceration. The 'prisoners' themselves are deindividuated; they are undressed, relieved of all personal effects, and all distinguishing marks are removed from them. They are dressed in a kind of uniform – potato sacks – and their hair is disguised by a stocking slipped over their heads, doubtless to simulate the effect of a shaven head. And then the experimenters stand back to see what will happen.

The consequences were nothing if not dramatic. The situation rapidly became untenable for the 'prisoners', for whom the guards devised numerous forms of persecution, various punishments, 'rituals', untimely awakenings, constant demands, unpleasant fatigue duties. Very rapidly the guards were transformed into veritable tyrants, without experiencing the least need to find any justification or legitimation for their excesses, though they all knew that it was only the drawing of lots which had designated some as 'prisoners' and others as 'guards'. Worn down by the bullying, the prisoners organised a revolt which led to a hardening of the 'regulations'. But the authors found themselves obliged to end the experiment prematurely because several of the 'prisoners' cracked and were no longer able to cope with it. The guards were tremendously disappointed about their loss of earnings; they had fervently hoped that the experiment would be continued to its end.

Let us summarise the experiment. At the start there is virtually nothing beyond the bare essentials: a simple group categorisation in which all possibilities are open. On this slender but significant basis is constructed a process of conformity which proceeds from the accentuation of intergroup differences to the creation of a regime as rigid and closed at the end as it was open and undefined at the outset. The definition of the social environment takes on an increasingly structured form that regulates the behaviour and perception of the individuals.

Superior realities

The language of the body

Thus individuals construe a consensual reality as the basis for their evaluations and behaviours, all the more consensual to the degree that the criteria available to them are limited or weak. A transparent physical reality does not require such an approach; to know whether it is raining it is sufficient to look outside and there is not the slightest problem since all the world agrees on the reality of rain. But in practice evidence which impinges directly on our senses is rare, and very rapidly a degree of interpretation intervenes. Even the simple sensations of hot and cold vary according to individuals and cultures. Walking is, so it seems, the natural mode of human locomotion par excellence and it suffices merely to place one foot in front of the other. Not at all; walking varies according to epoch and culture. To verify this one only has to look at films from the fifties for example; walking and all the gestures are different and indeed seem incongruous. We are influenced by our social environment in everything, up to and including our perception of physical stimuli, especially when an objective foundation is lacking.

Even our physiological state is not objectively given; we must interpret it in terms of socially determined systems of knowledge and in terms of the physical and social context in which it occurs. One of the most elegant experiments in social psychology, that by Schachter and Singer (1962), was carried out to determine the effects of the social context on the interpretation of one's own physiological state and on the occurrence of emotional states consecutive upon these physiological states. We will only describe a part of this experiment here.

The first stage of the experiment was the induction of a specific physiological state. Subjects were injected with a substance activating the sympathetic nervous system, epinephrine. This substance produces an acceleration in the heart rate, palpitations, trembling and muscular contractions, and a reddening of the face. Two groups of subjects were given information about their symptoms. In one case the information was accurate and in the other it was false. The experimenter told the latter that they were going to have swelling of the feet, itching and slight headaches. A third group received no information at all.

The second stage of the experiment was the influence phase. The subjects were required to wait in a room in the company of a confederate who displayed either unrestrained *euphoria* or extreme *irritation*. The experiment revealed that subjects were influenced by the confederate and became either more euphoric or more irritated, the greatest influence occurring when they were given no information or when the information they had been given was incorrect. They were then bound to base themselves on the characteristics of the social situation as defined by the behaviour of the confederate introduced into their presence.

Majority imprecision
In social situations that are even less defined this effect can only occur with greater force. Let us take another example.

Often the so-called 'uninformed' – in effect uninitiated – public judge a painting by the difficulty of its execution and by the faithfulness with which it has been executed, inclinations scorned by the initiated. But how can an objective judgment be made about a work of art which is not supposed to imitate its real model? In this case, it is only possible to rely on the opinion of others or the experts, to take into account the appeal the work has for others.

According to Festinger (1950), when one moves from physical to social reality what changes most fundamentally is the basis of validity. In the first case, one depends only on a tangible reality. It only requires us to test it or experiment upon it, a procedure which suggests that we are able to resist the intrusion of others into our judgments, confident in the validity of the experiment and in our own certainty. Now, the Asch experiment has demonstrated that this is not actually the case; the certainty of our perceptions does not protect us from pressures toward uniformity.

In establishing social reality, uncertainty and dependence are even more predominant. In this case, the solution would be to think in the same manner as others. 'An opinion, a belief, an attitude is "correct", "valid" and "proper" to the extent that it is anchored in a group of people with similar beliefs, opinions and attitudes' (Festinger, 1950, pp. 272-3). The opinion is validated to the degree that everyone thinks in the same manner, something which renders conformity particularly desirable; it constitutes the referent for reality. In its absence the world is abandoned to endless uncertainty and ambiguity. *Normalisation* becomes fundamental not only to better social control but also to the understanding of the world. Every deviation presents a tremendous danger to the individual because he becomes as a result incapable of adequately understanding the world in which he lives. Only unconditional agreement with others sets him back on the right path, namely that of knowledge validated by the consensus of all.

Let us recapitulate Festinger's theoretical contribution. Confronted with an ambiguous social world and deprived of objective criteria, individuals have but one solution, to establish and adhere to a collective truth. This was the very purpose of the celebrated experiment carried out by Sherif in 1936.

> If in due course they come to perceive the uncertain and undefined situation with which they are collectively faced in such a fashion that they give it a certain order, that is to say, if they perceive it as ordered according to a frame of reference elaborated in common during the course of the experiment, and if this frame of reference is shared by the group, we could then say that we have at least the prototype of the psychological process of norm formation in a group. (Sherif, 1936, p. 223)

The experimental procedure uses an illusion well-known to astronomers, the autokinetic effect: if in the absence of any reference marks, an individual fixates on a point of light in absolute darkness, he has the impression that the point of light moves.

The experimental subjects were placed in a totally darkened room, fifteen feet from a small point of light which was illuminated during each trial for five seconds. They had to estimate the degree of 'movement' of this luminous dot in one of two different experimental conditions:

(1) first alone and then in groups of two or three, or
(2) first in groups of two or three and then alone.

Sherif hypothesised that in the individual as in the collective situation, successive estimations would become stabilised around a central value, referred to by Sherif as the displacement 'norm'. The results demonstrated that the subjects who were initially exposed to this situation in groups remained faithful to the norm established by the group when they were subsequently alone. The subjects who had initially established an individual displacement norm converged on an *average* of their previous individual estimations.

Sherif concluded that this experiment illustrates, in a simplified fashion, the fundamental psychological process present in the creation of social norms. The two dimensions of this process are, on the one hand, the ambiguity of the environment in relation to which actors must form an opinion, and on the other hand, the convergence of individual positions in the interaction. As Sherif himself emphasised, this allows of generalisation.

> The psychological basis for the establishment of social norms, such as stereotypes, fashions, conventions, customs, and values, is the formation of common frames of reference, the products of individuals' contacts with each other. Once such frames of reference are established and incorporated in the individual, they operate as important factors in determining or modifying his reactions in the situations with which he is subsequently faced; these include social and even sometimes non-social situations, but particularly those in which the field of stimulation is poorly structured. (p. 233)

In the influence situation as conceived by Sherif, the subject is like a blank page; he has no opinions, no a priori position, no constraints other than those derived from himself. He is uncertain and 'the fact of having doubts about what is correct renders the subject ill at ease' (p. 234). Also, to the degree that the situation involves no crucial interests, he will be dependent on the only social context available to him in order to establish a common code, the estimations of partners. The consensus established between subjects underlines an effect that is very revealing for social psychology: nothing obliges the subjects to agree with others. And yet, as in the Asch experiment and the Milgram experiment, one again encounters this incapacity to diverge, totally incorporated by the subjects to the degree that they are not even aware of it. The fate of social reality is to produce uniformity-enforcing conformity.

Added meaning

The two quasi-contradictory dimensions of reality, physical and social, are reflected in a distinction employed by Deutsch and Gerard (1955) between informational influence and normative influence, and in Thibaut and Strickland's (1956) distinction between task-centred dispositions and group-centred dispositions. For Deutsch and Gerard, informational influence serves to fill gaps in the subject's knowledge and allows him to achieve greater objectivity while normative influence enables him to agree with others within a social reality which is itself ever-changing and requires constant validation:

> ...we come to see objects in the light in which they appear to others. The apple that Adam ate was an object that he approached in the light of the prohibition against eating it and in the light of Eve's experience with it. The relations that others have to things and the control they exercise over them delimit and prescribe my relations to things. (Asch, 1952, p. 179)

This 'addition of social meaning' is fundamental to our understanding of the world. According to Festinger, purely physical meaning comes closest to truth. The addition of social interpretation operates as noise which obscures the true nature of things. Asch is more sceptical about this true nature of things. The same physical or social objects can be decoded in terms of several independent or even contradictory interpretive schemes, each one a self-sufficient system of knowledge. The pertinence of these interpretive schemes is thus totally beside the point. It is their overall character, their internal coherence, and their adequacy to the context which confers on them their validity. 'The physical properties of things are what make them socially relevant; however, we cannot deduce the social from the physical properties alone. However carefully a chemist may examine a bar of gold he will not discover that it is an object of ownership' (Asch, 1952, p. 179).

A functional influence

The research we have described, which assimilated influence to uniformity-producing conformity, is integrated within a coherent, functionalist theoretical framework. In a critical analysis, Serge Moscovici (1976) has offered a systematisation of its propositions. We will now summarise the principal features of this framework as outlined by Moscovici.

Inequality and unilaterality.

This theoretical structure – this model – assumes at the outset a fundamental asymmetry between the source and the target of influence, and the impossibility of reciprocal action between them. In this closed social system, the major pole in the relationship is the source, the positive pole possessing power and resources, and representing legitimacy. The minor pole in the relationship is the target, the individual in a denuded state: '...the majority point of view carries the prestige of truth and norm, and expresses the social system as a whole' (Moscovici, 1976, p. 12). The point of view of the minority is devalued; its variation from the majority point of view can only be expressed as error and deviance. '*Deviate* (noun). An individual who behaves in a manner other than that specified by the *group* or culture in which he is functioning. In research on communication and consensus in discussion groups, it refers to anyone whose views are distinctly different from the mode or majority' (Jones and Gerard, 1967, p. 711).

One thus arrives at a monolithic conception of the group the total power of which excludes any possibility of personal expression. The code of society as a whole is none other than the code of the dominant group.

> Each social order confronts its members with a selected portion of
> physical and social data. The most decisive feature of this selectivity is
> that it presents conditions lacking in perceptual alternatives. There is no
> alternative to the language of one's group, to the kinship relations it
> practices, to the diet that nourishes it, to the art it supports. The field of
> the individual is, especially in a relatively closed society, in large
> measure circumscribed by what is included in the cultural setting. (Asch,
> 1959, p. 380)

The majority point of view represents the absolute standard, whether of truth or legitimacy. All divergent opinion, all differences in judgment constitute deviations from what is real and true. The more prevalent opinions of the majority have a positive value; irrespective of their content, they assume greater weight and more positive value solely because they derive from the majority. The less familiar opinions of the minority, held by individuals devoid of authority, have a negative value and carry little weight. The majority point of view is the only correct or normative choice; the minority point of view is not simply another viewpoint, it is empty, a non-opinion, defined as anomic because non-majority.

In this conceptual framework, the majority is active and open to change while the minority is passive, subjected to and resistant to change. Obviously, within this kind of analysis, the only opposition which creates problems arises from those whom one wishes to change, while opposition to change among the leading circles possesses neither scientific nor political interest. 'In such a context, conformist passivity acquires the positive connotation of being adaptive, whereas activity, innovation, private attitude, acquire the pejorative connotation of being maladaptive' (Moscovici, 1976, p. 13). This chilling conformity, based on submission and represssion, can only be the conformity of passivity and immobility.

Social control

For social control to operate completely, it is necessary that all individuals have the same values, the same norms, the same judgment criteria, and that all accept and refer to them. Just as no one is supposed to be ignorant of the law, each is supposed to know the norm. However, laws are written down; one can refer to them and they have the manifest appearance of external constraints, while norms are not clearly decreed anywhere, they are integrated in each of us. Although conformity to the norm is not particularly rewarded, if there is a disturbance of social tranquillity, if the norm is infringed, it is recalled, and disapproval is expressed because the existence of differences becomes an obstacle to collective functioning.

The process operates in the following fashion: having lost the autonomy which accorded them direct access to their environment, whether on the perceptual or the behavioural level, individuals become dependent on the group for satisfaction of their needs. It becomes obvious that everyone cannot satisfy their desires without hindrance, and thus apparent that normative controls are necessary to the harmony and survival of the group.

Honour to whom honour is due; these norms are not the products of self-directed collective functioning; those attitudes and behaviours most essential to the satisfaction of those persons most powerful in the group are the ones most likely to lead to the formation of norms. Communal norms are at once those of the majority and those of the authorities. In this framework, deviation assumes the appearance of opposition or else deficiency, but in every case it is a sign of inferiority. The ideal functioning of the group – ideal primarily because it allows complete operation of social control – requires uniformity and hence the exercise of pressure to reduce divergencies. And the fundamental goal of influence is to safeguard uniformity by rehabilitating deviants.

> Their specific mechanism consists in making everybody alike, blurring the particularity of persons or sub-groups. The further this process of identification and deindividuation is carried the better each person's adaptation to others and to the environment...it is clear to what extent the stress on non-differentiation, on cohesion, and on normative group pressure is a function of the interpretation of influence as a means of integrating the part into the whole, the individual into the collectivity. (Moscovici, 1976, pp. 17-18)

Dependence

In the functionalist perspective, dependence is one of the fundamental determinants of influence processes. It is a consequence of each individual's need for others. This need is revealed in the search for social approval and leads to affiliation. And acceptance by others leads to a reinforcement of self-esteem. Furthermore, on the cognitive level, the group provides the individual with information which he lacks. It allows him to achieve more objective precision, so as to adjust better to his environment. 'The unavoidable transition from individual adaptation to social adaptation, from direct dependence on the environment to dependence mediated by others opens the way to influence' (Moscovici, 1976, pp. 21-2). The need for social support is imperative if one finds oneself in an ambiguous situation, lacking confidence in one's senses and capacities, doubting one's own intelligence and judgment. We should remember here again the allegory of the 'emperor's new clothes'.

Dependence and malleability are the basic ingredients in the rather unflattering and unexciting 'robot image' of conformists portrayed by authors. Apart from the fact that conformity can be linked to certain kinds of social situation, it also constitutes a set of unvarying personality traits.

> Conformists were said to be characterised by conventionality, conscientiousness, cooperativeness, patience, sincerity and docile socialisation. The self-ratings of such persons emphasised nurturance, affiliativeness, abasement and denial of psychiatric symptoms...the conforming individual is restrained, cautious, submissive, and oriented towards consideration for others. [Conformers were found] to rank low on intelligence, assertiveness, neural reserves, extraversion, realism, and theoretical value. (Steiner, 1966, p. 233)

Conformity is a necessity in social groups but those who yield to it enjoy no great esteem. On the contrary, if anti-conformity is interpreted not as deviance but as elitist action, it becomes preferable to stray from the well-worn path. One has to ask then why so many people cling to conformity. If anti-conformity is not deviance but elitism, it is more gratifying to be anti-conformist, in the same way that it is better to be rich and in good health than poor and sick.

> Those individuals have a high degree of certainty of their own percep-
> tion; they feel themselves more competent or powerful or of a higher
> status than others; they have one or more others in the group agreeing
> with them against the majority judgment; they find the others an
> unattractive source, possibly unlike themselves; and finally they see
> little to be gained by conformity in terms of any important personal
> goals. (Hollander, 1967, p. 558)

In the majority of studies, however, anti-conformity is considered an obstacle to the progress of the group and to personal development. It rhymes with deviance and rejection. Non-conformity is judged unpopular, uninfluential and stands outside the communication network of the group.

Influence is based on the 'needs' of individuals to be liked, and thus to be like others. Let us pass briefly over the tautologous reference to need in this explanation, which brings to mind the 'dormative virtue of opium' as causing sleep, and let us also pass over the naturalistic flavour of the concept. With Moscovici, we cannot see in this explanation any more than a 'symptom of a belief according to which pressure on deviants is always justified, because it answers to certain needs in them and is, to a certain extent provoked by them.' (1976, p. 23).

Rejection of uncertainty

The quest for certainty also corresponds to a 'need'. Lone individuals are helpless in the face of their environment. The ambiguity of the environment leads to influence via the path of uncertainty, in the same way that the instability of the environment provokes interaction as an expedient for constructing norms. The stability of norms mitigates the instability of the physical world. 'Under conditions lacking objective structure in some focal aspect, the individual becomes increasingly uncertain and suggestibility is increased. In other words, he is more prone to be influenced by the words, actions, or other communications of other individuals, groups, and mass media' (Sherif and Sherif, 1969, p. 71).

In an unstructured or overly complex environment, influence leads to uniformity. The more uncertain an individual is of his opinion and judgments, the more vulnerable he is to influence. A fortiori,

> the less certain a person is of his own sensory and intellectual capacities, the more willingly he accepts the influence of someone to whom he attributes greater sensory and intellectual capacities... In a situation where both partners are certain of their judgments and opinions, there is no need for social influence, nor is there any way in which it can come into play, since there is no uncertainty to be reduced. (Moscovici, 1976, p. 27)

The social functioning of individuals is only envisaged as a degraded form of 'ideal' psychological functioning in which they would have direct contact with their environment or nature and would be adequately in accord with it. 'When one is in tune with nature one does not need society; when one is not in tune with nature, then one needs society' (*ibid*, p. 27).

Moscovici expresses his 'bewilderment' at these functionalist claims, raising some pertinent objections. If there is no certainty about physical or objective reality for a given individual, there cannot be any for others; why suppose that others know better than oneself? If the object of judgment is ambiguous, diversity should not be surprising; it should seem normal and permissible. Individuals should have no reason to agree and any actual agreement should provide no reassurance of the validity of their opinions or judgments.

Finally, let us consider a major objection: the experimental facts deny that conformity entails a search for certainty. As Asch himself stressed, in his experimental tasks there is no trace of ambiguity, not the slightest element of uncertainty. It is altogether possible to have a collective agreement which is in error.

The quest for objectivity

In the functionalist model, the search for objectivity is presented as a social norm. Its links with the need for certainty are particularly close. One is all the more confident in a judgment which seems exempt from all partiality. If such objectivity cannot be achieved by means of direct knowledge, then one must try to achieve it by referring to the established consensus concerning the object of judgment.

A basic human requirement appears to be the need for validation of one's opinions. *Although clear information from the physical environ-*

ment contributes to satisfaction of this need, the behaviour of other persons also provides a source of validation. Particularly in situations where he is uncertain or confused – where he does not know how to react – a person can turn to the behaviour of other persons to observe a stable world. This social reality provides him with a reference point for his own behaviour. The more ambiguous *the non-social stimulus situation*, the more likely he is to depend on social reality for orientation. (Secord and Backman, 1964, p. 331, my italics)

This situation nicely illustrates the functionalist conception of influence; it clearly expresses the dichotomy between Society and Environment – Nature, and contrasts relations with objects and relations with people. In the best of all possible worlds, reality as a given and perceived reality corresponds to physical reality, while social reality is reduced to a kind of collective illusion bordering on deceit.

If it is impossible to make an immediate judgment about the environment, the only recourse is to appeal to others and strive to support a point of view which can only be shaky at best. The vision of reality this generates is conventional; it is a product of the group, accepted by each individual only if it is accepted by others, a kind of revised version of the social contract. In consequence, men will live in two types of reality, distinct and mutually opposed: a 'true' or natural reality to which one has access without benefit of intermediaries, and a truncated, refractory reality, a reality by default, which one must accept can only be captured collectively.

In the absence of 'objective' reality, individuals have no alternative but to search for a substitute conventional truth. They are dependent on one another to establish this truth and dependent on this truth for their social identity. Independence, rare and precious, is linked to a correct understanding of reality, based on the possibility of determining its essential features directly, and on the certainty of possessing adequate personal capacity. Only a superman could be capable of such extraordinary independence! For a mere mortal belonging to the group, reaching consensus with it is tantamount to becoming dependent on it and, by the selling of his soul to the group, tantamount to abandoning the independence guaranteed by the physical world. This immediately excludes the case in which the group itself is the carrier of independence and social denial.

Collective functioning itself is subject to the norm of objectivity. If conformity occurs it is because diversity is inconceivable and because it is impossible to have several versions of a single and indivisible objective reality. And in this well-ordered social vision which asserts the accuracy of responses and the objectivity of stimuli, the individual is forced to submit to the group rather than to resist it. To summarise, primacy of the objectivity norm allows the accent to be put on a quasi-biological need for evaluation and on the quasi-physical priority of the environment in judgment, in terms of the contrast between a structured and an ambiguous environment.

A group or individual is more likely to grasp the truth if possessed of sufficient physical or social resources. But frequently this does not occur even in scientific fields, where the truth does not emerge immediately or where it seems an aberration or an error.

The primacy of the objectivity norm implies that relations with others will be subordinated to relations with objects. In the ideal case, the individual has access to information via his senses, and on the basis of this direct access to data draws objective conclusions which in effect he is compelled to accept. The adapted human being can fend for himself all alone and has no need of others. The autonomous individual is more natural than the socialised individual. The group or society only comes into play in cases of deficiency or incapacity; individuals have thus been led to create social rules and relationships to remedy imperfections in their relations with nature.

However, the study of social representations has among other things demonstrated the extent to which it is illusory and erroneous to wish to separate physical and social reality. No reality exists that can be physical without also being social; society does not exist to fill a gap in nature. The means for interpreting all reality rest on a code – language – the rules of which are socially defined.

The primacy of conformity

On the basis of a review of studies on social influence with a functionalist orientation, Moscovici (1976) has attempted to define the range of questions they address:

(a) the nature of the individual and social factors determining an individual's submission to the group;

(b) the role of conformity pressures in the individual or collective psychological equilibrium;

(c) the internal conditions – anxiety, need for affiliation, etc. – which make an individual dependent (rather than those which make him independent);

(d) the external conditions – stimulus ambiguity, hierarchy, etc. – which make an individual more (rather than less) sensitive to influence. (p. 38)

These studies are based on presuppositions which all share an emphasis on the primacy of conformity. Group consensus is necessary in all circumstances and preferable to an isolation based on the certainty of being right against the others. Conformity facilitates social and individual action while deviance hinders it. It is the result of successful socialisation and learning, while deviance is the result of their failure.

The primacy of conformity is so rooted in this mode of theoretical understanding that it is entailed not only in explaining stability and social control, but also, surprising as it may seem, in interpreting phenomena of social change and innovation. For Jones (1965), for example, change in the attitudes of a high-status individual by an individual of inferior status requires a kind of flattery or obsequiousness (which he termed 'ingratiation'): the latter initally voices his agreement with the former, flatters him, and then surreptitiously takes advantage of his entry into the latter's good graces to manipulate his opinions.

The same goes for the study of innovation. It would seem that the imperialism of conformity necessarily leaves no place for innovation. Yet it exists and demands explanation. Thus it is conceived as a particular and valued form of deviance. But who can afford the luxury of this kind of deviance without being driven from the group, and indeed still continue to benefit from all its advantages? Quite simply those who are already in a position of power. How? Hollander (1958) explains it in the following terms: leaders begin first by defending group norms and imposing them on everyone. They thus acquire the respect and confidence of all. They can then accumulate *idiosyncrasy credit*, which once possessed allows them to deviate from the norm and promote changes while avoiding rejection by or dissolution of the group.

In consequence, innovation is only possible if imposed by the high on those lower on the social scale. Thus, social changes are effected smoothly, without the least conflict. Power remains in place and is reinforced. Social relations are maintained.

We saw, in the previous chapter, how the primacy of a uniformity-inducing conformity was the consequence of particular historical changes and a congenial ideological context. We then examined its principal aspects and logic as they are ordered in the functionalist model. This model describes an order of reality present throughout society, but it does not provide access to all processes of social influence and particularly not to change or innovation. This harmonious construction excludes conflicts and eliminates irregularities. In its balance and moderation it ignores aspects of reality which because critical or disturbing cannot be reduced to its terms. It remains for us to underline the partial or biased character of this model which emerged at the critical moment to give comfort to the holders of power, whosoever they were, and to lend a quasi-natural status to submission and respect in relation to the established order.

4 Bases of minority influence

'Audacity, audacity, always audacity.'

Danton

In spite of its coherence, the functionalist model is limited. One major limitation is that it can only accommodate in a partial and pejorative fashion a fundamental phenomenon of social life: conflict. Further, it interprets any expressions of difference, any distinctiveness in relation to the majority group as deviance. In consequence it excludes phenomena of change or innovation that are not initiated by the majority. If the majority point of view represents truth, if it is synonymous with objectivity, if the majority has a monopoly on coercive means for obtaining the commitment of individuals, even when such commitment oversteps the limits of what is desirable or possible, then it is difficult to see what could disturb such a static social order. One is inclined to conclude that a model of conformity as purely uniformity-inducing fails to give adequate representation to phenomena linked to social change.

This being so, we shall take up and extend the critique of the functionalist model that Moscovici has been developing since the late sixties. In his break with the functionalist model and his combination of theoretical analysis and empirical observations, this author has been able to redefine the entire field of social influence as it is studied in social psychology.

Conflict

A history of avoidance
If we were to scrutinise the various studies of conflict in social psychology, we might be surprised at the manner in which they have striven to distort their object. The study of conflict has been principally a study of the avoidance of conflict in all its aspects and forms.

Conflict and discord have been construed as accidents, indeed as pathological states in a social world that is otherwise inherently harmonious and peaceful. Thus the problem consists in retrieving this beneficent state as rapidly and as completely as possible.

107

Social psychology has long taught us that individual needs are the primary explanatory principle in any behaviour with an essentially adaptive goal. Such imperious determinism tends to bring us closer to a physiological or naturalistic explanation of social conduct, because these needs will be the same for all, independent of milieu, epoch or climate. One could, certainly, explain everything in terms of needs and multiply needs infinitely, as formerly was the case with instincts. However, by remaining silent on the origin of these needs, the explanatory system remains tautologous. Social 'needs' in the last resort are hardly more informative than the 'sleep-inducing quality of opium'.

Social psychology assumes nevertheless that individuals tend to maximise the satisfaction of their needs. Reliance on the social environment or membership of the group is necessary to satisfy a need for certainty that cannot be filled by experimenting on the physical universe. There will be reliance on other sources of information to mitigate shortcomings in that provided directly by the environment. The greater the uncertainty, the more important consensus becomes and the more vital it is that it remains stable, solid and univocal; it constitutes the sole foundation for reality.

Sociality is based on the action of individuals circulating in a social world where they are totally devoted to the goal of maximising their own well-being, a well-being identical for all because consequent on satisfaction of the same needs. Correlatively, these same individuals ultimately carry all the responsibility for preserving this fundamentally unifying sociality as well as for disrupting it.

At every level it is the individual and he alone who can and must repair breaches in collective harmony, breaches which are conceived always as threatening occurrences. If we order the various levels of conflict as a function of the threat they constitute for the group, the first level – the least dangerous – is that at which conflict is present and indeed decisive but not externalised.

At the individual level, conflict is introjected. It remains internal to the individual and thus imperceptible to any other than himself. In research on 'cognitive dissonance' (see Poitou, 1974), for example, the absence of agreement between individual and group is resolved by a change in the individual, either on the mental or on the behavioural level. Commitment to the group itself is never in question.

Elimination of intrapersonal conflict proceeds according to a self-regulating mechanism; there is no need here for external intervention. This regulation acts to avoid the occurrence of conflict with the group, the unity of which is thus unaffected. Order is maintained by auto-repression without the group ever being aware of the possibility of a threat. In this self-censure can be seen the true effectiveness of a particular kind of power. Thus is bred the despotism of democratic and egalitarian power, about which Tocqueville expressed concern, with remarkable far-sightedness, in the 1830s.

> After having thus successively taken each member of the community in its powerful grasp, and fashioned them at will, the supreme power then extends its arm over the whole community. It covers the surface of society with a network of small complicated rules, minute and uniform, through which the most original minds and the most energetic characters cannot penetrate, to rise above the crowd. The will of man is not shattered, but softened, bent, and guided: men are seldom forced by it to act, but they are constantly restrained from acting: such a power does not destroy but it prevents existence; it does not tyrannize, but it compresses, enervates, extinguishes, and stupefies a people, till each nation is reduced to nothing better than a flock of timid and industrious animals, of which the government is the shepherd.
>
> I have always believed that servitude of the regular, quiet and gentle kind, which I have just described, might be combined more easily than is commonly believed with some of the outward forms of freedom; and that it might even establish itself under the wing of the sovereignty of the people. (Tocqueville, 1961, vol ii, pp. 381-2)

The study of interpersonal conflict has been diverted into a context which has served as yet another escape from the phenomenon. Cocooned within a form of interaction modelled on the 'prisoner's dilemma', developed in game theory, the individual pursues the goal of maximising his gains and minimising his losses while taking account of his partner's strategy. In this limited context, the only rational long-term strategy is cooperation. Defence of his own interests is clearly recognised as requiring the making of a pact with the other, the trading of his own good will against that of the other. The conflict which each must strive to avoid is a divergence of interests. In such an exchange relation, dependent on multiple concessions, competition could never be the most rational strategy.

The 'prisoner's dilemma' paradigm has served as the framework for all studies of interpersonal conflict and has limited the study of conflict to a single model, at once fictitious and game-like, a model of bargaining gains and losses between partners who are equal at the outset. The possibility that conflict could have other determinants or other objectives has not affected the direction of research to any appreciable degree (Plon, 1972).

At the levels of individual – group and intergroup interactions, there coexist two complementary means for excluding conflicts. The first is described by Festinger in his theory of 'group locomotion': the individual *chooses* to belong to groups which suit him and he is suited to the groups to which he belongs, either because they correspond to what he is looking for or because he adapts himself to them. The second means of excluding conflict involves the issue of deviance which we will develop further on. In brief, if the deviant does not give a lot of trouble, it is necessary and sufficient to reject him; one is thus rid of both the deviant and the conflict. Conformity and normalisation are the means for eliminating conflicts, that plague of (majority) groups.

Return to sources
We are all of us aware that the experience of conflict is never a pleasant affair. It is, for those involved, a critical, disagreeable and distressing time. But can one for all that say that it is invariably a negative thing? Is this not to confound the experience of conflict with its importance or value on the social level? And is it not to renounce any attempt to clarify the fundamental links which unite conflict and negotiation to influence and social change?

At the beginning of this century, it seemed obvious to Georg Simmel that conflict is involved in the regeneration of social systems. Adopting a position which only appears paradoxical, this author saw in conflict one of the most deep-rooted forms of interaction, a means for achieving a certain degree of social unity and an entirely legitimate form of sociability. Such conceptions require that one avoids thinking of change in terms of a disorder that disrupts a society which is dependent on the reassurance of stability. On the contrary, for Simmel, stability is the result of a more or less temporary balance between forces in interaction. Thus the apparent disorder of social forces in perpetual motion can result in a transitory order.

Simmel did not set himself up as a moralist. He did not seek to distinguish between pure gold and base metal in social life. Are not rain and fine weather two complementary aspects of climate, whether or not we prefer one to the other? 'Just as the universe needs "love and hate", that is, attractive and repulsive forces, in order to have any form at all, so society too, in order to attain a determinate shape, needs some quantitative ratio of harmony and disharmony, of association and competition, of favourable and unfavourable tendencies' (Simmel, 1955, p. 15).

Moreover, he thought, quite rightly we believe, that an accurate description of social life would make no reference to individuals' affects, not because he was indifferent to these affects but simply because they are not relevant to the description of social life. Clearly, this does not mean that individuals do not suffer considerably in conflict situations. But the true social significance of conflict does not reside in the well-being of each person, or indeed in the 'satisfaction of their needs'. 'Since discord unfolds its negative, destructive character between particular individuals, we naively conclude that it must have the same effect on the total group' (p. 19). The attempt to elucidate explanatory mechanisms of conflict and influence should not be envisaged as a task of conciliation.

Conflict may often be difficult to live through for the individuals concerned but it does generate structure. 'Our opposition makes us feel that we are not completely victims of the circumstances' (p. 19). For the actors or individuals involved, conflicts represent a key occurrence in the anchoring of judgments, feelings and actions. For their targets they constitute challenges which provoke them either to revitalise enfeebled ideas and routine activities or to abandon them. Actor-groups just as target-groups must work out some position in relation to the conflict and, if possible, rebuild their unity around it, equipping themselves with a new and more adequate language.

Restlessness and stability

It is possible to envisage other models of functioning for the world than those which stress the primacy of stability. The models of biology and modern thermodynamics open up for us a fertile avenue of thought. They raise questions which force us to move beyond the sterile and totalitarian analogies between physical and social worlds if we are to analyse the terms in which it is possible to envisage the problem of change.

In thermodynamics, one starts with an original state of disorder in which stabilities are local and transitory solutions. 'Stability', wrote Prigogine and Stengers (1979) 'is no longer the attribute of a state as such but the outcome of an examination which leads to the regression of all possible fluctuations' (p. 154). 'Irreversible fluxes can, in a predictable and reproducible fashion, create the possibility of local self-organising processes' (p. 156). Thus thermodynamics allows us to conceive the possibility of an original state of disorder and mobility in which order and equilibrium are secondary phenomena. '[Living things] function far from equilibrium in an area where the processes producing entropy, the processes which dissipate energy, play as constructive a role as sources of order' (p. 190).

These new conceptions are in stark contrast to the classical conceptions in which permanence is primary. Contrary to these latter, the former demonstrate that disorder is a source of renovation.

Here, where classical science has emphasised permanence, we now see change and evolution, we see elementary particles which transform into one another, which collide, disintegrate and are born. (p. 285)

The classical science of flux, from Archimedes to Claudius, stands in contrast to the science of turbulence and bifurcating evolution, a science which reveals that...disorder can give birth to things, both to nature and to man. (p. 285)

What is fundamentally challenged by these new scientific theories is precisely what seems to rule in the social world, the primacy of stability and order. 'Here, where science had revealed an immutable and pacified stability, we believe that no organisation, no stability as such is guaranteed or legitimate, none is imposed by right, all are products of circumstance or at the mercy of circumstances' (p. 295).

This assertion, if pertinent to the universe of the exact sciences, is, a fortiori, perfectly transposable into that of the social sciences where disturbance, divergence, ambivalence, and uncertainty coexist with stability; and stability itself should not blind us to this. Blindness with respect to social entropy arises from an unequal struggle with history. By posing circumstances as the basic determining factor, one helps to rid social psychological approaches of unwarranted naturalism; it is then no longer 'needs' that energise social life, largely by default, but contexts favouring either stability or change in group activities.

Constructive conflict

Conflict may also be a source of structure in social psychology. Conflict is an occasion for renewal of communications, one significant aspect of which is the establishment of a process of negotiation. This acceleration of expressions and exchanges of views has a motivating effect, acting as a catalyst to development and change. In the group dynamics methods developed by Lewin (1947), the object was to change fundamental attitudes concerning eating habits. If these attitudes are governed by 'objective norms', provision of new information of a culinary, dietary or economic nature, for example, should be sufficient to change them. Now, eating habits and tastes are deeply rooted in a culture and difficult to modify. The French eat neither roast python nor grilled locusts, but they greatly enjoy snails and offal. Americans have no taste for any of these foods. Nonetheless, under the conditions of economic hardship caused by the Second World War, it was necessary to promote the consumption of offal. With this goal, Lewin placed individuals either in a lecture situation or in discussion groups. The information made available was the same in each case. The objective was to influence these individuals and lead them to change their eating behaviour, by demonstrating that not only does offal have a high nutritional value but it can also taste good. In the lecture situation, the individuals were in a passive role; they assimilated a certain amount of new information but they changed little. In the group situation, they were able to express their tastes, ask questions, and show their disagreement. They were active participants in the situation and this gave a vigorous stimulus to the life of the group, provoking intense emotional or 'cathartic' reactions. Thus, according to Lewin, it was possible for change to occur by overcoming the forces of stability, allowing a decrystallisation, a shift, and then a re-crystallisation of attitudes. Influence here is mediated by the dynamic forces expressed in the conflict.

Approach-avoidance

In the functionalist model, influence occurs with the object of preventing conflict. But active regulation and negotiation of conflict also provoke influence. This is one of the fundamental differences between majority and minority influence. We have previously considered the various aspects of majority influence. But this form does not encompass all types of influence. In particular, influence aimed at innovation or change and which plays on the management of conflict, is exercised by minorities asserting their differences and refusing to have these treated as deviance.

In majority influence, the result of conformity is elimination of conflict, while normalisation creates a compromise position out of initial differences.

If cohesion, the principal foundation of the group, is based in similarities and in agreement on the part of all members of the group, all dissimilarity is threatening. As such, it must be dealt with in the framework of those interpersonal relations which constitute the cement of the group, by an arsenal of pressures brought to bear on the culprit.

In contrast, for a minority, conflict has a totally different significance. It allows the minority to challenge the majority group through a general questioning of the reality it supports. Interest centres no longer on the actors in the conflict, but on the object of conflict itself, for which the minority proposes a new definition. Concurrently, this new definition of reality is for the minority a source of resolve and unity. Simmel (1955) gives an excellent illustration here: he proposes that a political party could benefit from a reduction in the number of its members, and hence an increase in its minority character, if this resulted in elimination from its midst of any timorous elements or those inclined to compromise. And this benefit is all the more vital to a minority group embroiled in an acute conflict.

> When, for instance, in 1793, the Whig party was already melted down greatly, it was strengthened by the defection of all elements which were still somehow mediating and lukewarm. The few remaining, very resolute personalities were only then enabled to engage in a wholly

united and radical political action... For this reason, groups, and especially minorities, which live in conflict and persecution, often reject approaches or tolerance from the other side. The closed nature of their opposition, without which they cannot fight on would be blurred... Every concession of the other side, which is only partial anyway, threatens the uniformity in the opposition of all members and hence the unity of their coherence on which the fighting minority must insist without compromise. (Simmel, 1955, p. 97)

By insisting on its difference and hence its opposition, and thus accentuating the conflict with the majority, the minority magnifies the contrast, distinguishing itself yet more radically from the majority. Thus, from the outset it holds a trump card in the negotiation which as a result pivots on its own positions.

For minorities, conflict represents a weapon; it allows them to create the conditions necessary for change or innovation; it generates the circumstances capable of giving rise to change. Through conflict, the minority establishes the conditions for attracting attention and getting a hearing, while in the absence of conflict there is every likelihood that its activities will remain insignificant. Here again, the relevance of a propitious context reveals the inadequacy of the functionalist model.

Order by fluctuation leads to the study of the play between chance and necessity, between provocative innovation and the system's response, it leads to a distinction between the states of the system in which all individual initiative is condemned to insignificance, and the areas of bifurcation where an individual, an idea or a new behaviour can overturn the median state... Therefore, no more than it accepts the opposition between chance and necessity, does the concept of order by fluctuation assume the distinction between functional and dysfunctional (traditional, in certain schools of sociology). What is at one given moment an insignificant variation in relation to normal behaviour, can in other circumstances be a source of crisis and renovation. (Prigogine and Stengers, 1979, p. 190)

Deviance and minority

The rejection of the deviant

In the majority model, all deviation from the norms is synonymous with deviance. Now, if it is to exercise influence, the minority must indeed resist being identified with deviance. The theme of deviance has caused more ink to flow than almost any other in the social sciences. Nevertheless, deviance remains an unclear and profoundly subjective concept. In order to manage the distinction between minority and deviant more adequately, we must analyse the way in which deviance has been approached. This should allow us not only to understand it rather better, despite the over-abundance of interpretations, but to appreciate more fully the spirit in which it has been studied, namely as the negative and recalcitrant object of social control.

How can deviance be precisely defined or characterised? We should be clear that this is one of the most imprecise concepts in the social sciences, indeed the most extraordinary intellectual ragbag it is possible to imagine. Let us begin, as if we were complete innocents, by consulting the entry on *deviance* in *The international encyclopedia of the social sciences* (Sills, 1968). Deviance is represented here as simultaneously a behaviour which violates norms – crime, for example; as a statistical abnormality – a different state or behaviour; and finally as a psychopathological anomaly. 'This definition includes mental retardation, illness of all sorts, blindness, ugliness, other physical defects and handicaps, beggary, membership of ritually unclean castes and occupations, mental illness, criminality and a shameful past, homosexuality...' Replete with irony, this whimsical enumeration did not prevent its author from emphasising the relative character of deviant behaviour. Albert Cohen (1966) teaches us that this generic term includes behaviours as diverse as cheating, malingering, trickery, disloyalty, crime, haggling, feigning, embezzlement, immorality, dishonesty, treason, corruption and bribery, perversity, and offences against decency. Only the absence of a racoon[1] from this sociological bric-à-brac prevents it being truly comic, except that these nebulous, impressionistic definitions have had the most calamitous consequences, both on the theoretical level and at the level of practice.

The first conclusion which we can draw from such contradictory definitions is that deviance, which others have discussed with such assurance, is a far from clear concept. One has to doubt the value of assertions founded on definitions which at the outset sink in the sands of imprecision.

State of default
Deviance can only be understood in relation to a uniform order. At first sight this seems to involve a hierarchical, unidirectional relationship. Ugliness, for example, can only be deviance if one views it from the perspective of the canons of beauty. If wealth or financial power is the reference point, poverty is deviance, rejection, and despair. Deviance is a

---

[1] This is an allusion to a poem by Jacques Prévert, 'L'inventaire', the comic effect of which is due to the accumulation of whimsical objects.

concept forged by the superior group to stigmatise the absence in others of whatever it possesses. It also expresses guilt, hatred and fear on the part of the privileged with respect to the dispossessed. It confounds the phenomena of anomie, which include criminality and alcoholism, with those of exclusion in which entire social categories (women, homosexuals, immigrants, blacks, artists...) are identified as lacking economic, cultural and intellectual qualities. More generally, on an ideological level it allows concealment and distortion of the reality of the hierarchical order.

This inexhaustible concept embodies a three-fold paradox. In practice, everyone wishes his uniqueness acknowledged, while despising the 'other', the stranger. One gives priority to one's own individuality, one's own self-actualisation, but one detests the other's difference. One stigmatises deviants, one accords them a separate, lower position, but simultaneously one holds them responsible for their deviance and their exclusion. Finally, deviance seems simultaneously to threaten the group and to forge it into a sacred union. 'The deviant has always been described as an individual who is in need of others; deprived of independent psychological resources, he is willing to subscribe to the opinions and judgments of the majority and of authority. The state of deviance, the state of being different is thought of as an uncomfortable position, one with purely negative connotations' (Moscovici, 1976, pp. 43-4).

The distinction between minority and deviance is a recent one. For a long time researchers in the social sciences had regarded all minority phenomena as manifestations of deviance. The minority was in a situation of alienation in relation to the majority. The latter remained the universal referent and signifier, playing on the need to dislodge the minority from its threatening, insubordinate position. In practice, the definition of the majority as the universal referent opens the door to ostracism and racism. The many studies of intergroup relations have taught us the fundamental consequences of categorising others as 'in-group' or 'out-group' (Tajfel *et al.*, 1971). But in the case of majority – minority relations, this categorisation operates instead asymmetrically; one is either in or outside the majority group. It operates as a form of normative hierarchy which simultaneously combines notions of status and legitimacy, of number and of deviation from the norms. To be part of the majority is to be placed automatically within the group considered, to be part of a minority is to be placed outside, and in most cases below.

Lewin (1947) emphasised the importance of minority versus majority membership in relations between groups. He clearly demonstrated the projective character of discrimination; in no case was a minority group proved to be responsible for the discrimination to which it was subjected.

In recent years, we have started to realise that so called minority problems are in fact majority problems, that the Negro problem is the problem of the white, that the Jewish problem is the problem of the non-Jew, and so on... One of the most severe obstacles in the way of improvement seems to be the notorious lack of confidence and self-esteem of most minority groups. Minority groups tend to accept the implicit judgment of those who have status even when the judgment is directed against themselves. (Lewin, 1947, p. 214)

In his brilliant analysis of racist ideology, Guillaumin (1972) defines the racist group as the majority group and the racialised group as a minority group. The first is the referent, the measure of everything, and the 'natural' fault of the second resides quite simply in not being the first, an irreparable flaw, and so one invests the minority with a wrong which it cannot undo.

They are presented as a *particular* in relation to a *general*. They are marked with the seal of idiosyncrasy no matter what concrete form they assume. In this they are different from the majority, itself devoid of idiosyncrasy, which preserves for itself all social and psychological generality. The relation between minorities and the majority has assumed the mark of difference. The majority is different from nothing, being itself the referent; whosoever is enclosed within it escapes all idiosyncrasy. Idiosyncrasy, on the contrary, constitutes the minority in as much as it differentiates minority from majority (p. 87).

This deviatiation from the majority referent justifies oppression.

Rather than designating them as 'minorities', one might refer to those at the margins or in some form of custody, either for transgressing the norms or through incapacity to conform to them, those whose difference condemns them to an inferior status, as 'minors'. In this case, to comply is to accept the dominant frame of reference and one's own position within it. But this in nowise means being integrated into the dominant group itself; that would be impossible. 'The more shrewd the monkey', writes Memmi (1966), 'the better he imitates, and the more irritated the coloniser becomes' (p. 160). To become integrated into the dominant frame of reference is to turn against oneself the devaluation it asserts. It is to direct against one's own group the violence it exudes, or to direct against oneself the potential for destruction which it engenders and so descend into madness. The cultural heritage of the minority, from which it derives its place in the world and its explanation of that position, its uniqueness and its dignity, is transformed by the majority into deviant, laughable activities. Examples abound; we might refer here to all the manifestations of colonialism, to cultural destruction and ethnocide. All the things which form the rhythm of life from birth to death, from cooking to magic, from

117

the everyday to the sacred, become shameful, ridiculous and contemptible; but without them there is no other alternative but self-destruction.

Rational consensus

Examination of various considerations regarding deviance leads us to three questions. First, how is the point reached at which groups in a subservient position are convinced that they themselves are the source of their situation? Second, by what subtle social mechanism are they induced to accept responsibility for their difference and their submission? Finally, a subsidiary question: why do difference and submission become sources of guilt? The answer to these enigmas is not to be found in a Manichean vision of the social universe, nor in a manipulative conception in which various powerful groups or individuals orchestrate the subjugation of the masses. The reality is at once less easily grasped and more mundane; everyone is enmeshed in a web of minor daily obligations and in a network of tenuous but ubiquitous meanings.

The dominance of the majority group is founded on the myth of a society of equals united by consensus. 'The first prerequisite to organised human activity is that there be *some* understandings, however arbitrary they may be' (Cohen, 1966, p. 3). Consensus is thus a basic necessity and in these terms deviance is dysfunctional. In the context of the postulated equality of individuals, the necessity of consensus turns on two complementary notions: the normality and conformity in relation to which deviance is defined.

All disagreement challenges the consensus, the definition of reality itself. Disagreement is not equivalent to a simple divergence, it resurrects a cosmic battle between universal truth and error. 'As soon as disagreement makes itself felt, it is experienced as a threatening, anxiety-inducing state. It gives notice that the fragile contract of relations, beliefs, and consensus is about to be challenged' (Moscovici, 1976, p. 98). The appearance of a disagreement represents a leap into the unknown, accompanied by anxiety and doubt. All social dissent is, in the last resort, interpreted as a difference between the normal and the deviant, between opinions on our side and opinions on the other side. Deviance represents failure and maladaptation. Conformity on the other hand, conceived as a requirement of the social system, leads to adaptation, equilibrium and consensus.

In the same way that a living organism rejects any element which it does not recognise as its own, so also the phobia about deviance comes to be expressed on the collective level in some form of rejection. This wholesome, immunising logic has been the subject of an extensive literature, both theoretical and experimental, concerning the only rational outcome with respect to the deviant, namely his ejection from the group. Festinger

(1950) states that in a coherent group, 'any dissent entails efforts at persuasion on the part of the majority to reconvert the deviant. If he cannot be brought around, he is rejected, and the group redefines its boundaries.'

The democratic denominator

Conformity and normalisation are functional and rational. Numerous studies have illustrated the fact that the influence of the group results in normalisation, that is to say, the movement of extreme responses towards a central value. The normalisation of attitudes, a process that has the flavour of moderation and renunciation, ensures that group cohesion is safeguarded. But it leads to attitudes which exclude anything that smacks of originality or idiosyncrasy. Compromise ensures a levelling of differences in a group, preserving its integrity while avoiding exclusion of its members; it allows an understanding of the environment that stays as close as possible to a 'true', collectively defined median. Through a set of reciprocal concessions, the group reduces the differences between individuals and out of this achieves the conditions for its own survival.

> Individuals forgo any attack on the group consensus, they forgo presenting or defending their own personal opinions. Such behaviour seems in this case the most rational. Now, in a group, one is confronted with divergent judgments and positions. It follows that no one is altogether wrong and no one altogether right. Nonetheless, by adopting a solution which takes the middle road between the various opinions and judgments, one achieves a result both satisfying to all and optimal as regards the possible gap between truth and error. (Doise and Moscovici, 1973, p. 118)

In addition, the rationality of individuals and groups coincides with a democratic ideal. In groups, the combination of individual attitudes is rational because statistical; it corresponds to an average of the individual positions. Each member of the group is treated as equal with respect to the possible combination of his attitudes with those of others. It is thus clearly an egalitarian vision, giving an equal weight to everyone.

Derived in this fashion, the democratic ideal coincides with a social order based on uniformity. To attribute an equal weight to each individual entails a levelling of the most extreme or divergent among them, and hence of those most threatening to the tranquillity of the group; it means creating an environment of moderate individuals. Everything overhanging the Procrustean bed is cut off. This normalisation ensures a limitation of the group's boundaries, limits which no one may transgress. Beyond the group is barbarism, the unforeseeable, the unconstrained, the abnormal, everything one must distance oneself from if one wishes to remain within the reassuring bosom of one's fellows.

One of the best experimental illustrations of this collective moderation is that devised by Schachter (1951). He organised groups to discuss the fictitious case of a young delinquent, Johnny Rocco. The arguments concerned the penal sanction to be imposed. While the subjects were rather lenient – they inclined towards rehabilitation rather than punishment – a confederate present in the groups advocated the greatest severity and consistently urged the harshest punishment.

Apart from this extreme confederate, two others were present; one was a conformist; he consistently adopted the modal position of the group. The other was 'influenceable'; he began by adopting an attitude of extreme severity and then progressively moved towards the general position defended in the groups by the five to seven naive subjects.

Schachter anticipated that the extreme confederate would be rejected.

> It is assumed that there is a parallel between the process of induction and communication; that is, communication is the mechanism by means of which power is exercised. Therefore one method by which deviation from a group standard may be maintained is cutting off the deviate from communication with the group. Lack of communication may result from little initial contact between the individual and the group or rejection from the group. In the latter case, if the magnitude of the change that the group attempts to induce is greater than the force on the individual to stay in the group, the deviate will want to leave the group and/or the group will push the deviate out of the group. (Schachter, 1951, p. 19)

Does Schachter's experiment prove that the confederate is indeed rejected? Contrary to the author's claim, this does not actually seem to be the case. He was, it is true, rated negatively on the post-experimental sociometric questionnaire. But in the group discussions, the confederate was indisputably the centre of attention. The other participants addressed themselves to him extensively and increasingly so as the discussion wore on. It was only towards the end of the sessions that a decrease in communications to this deviant confederate began to appear. Nonetheless, it appeared that he drew attention to himself, probably as a result of the surprise created by his extreme attitude. His position did not make him attractive, certainly, but he was intriguing; he was provocative and interesting. This was not true of the conforming confederate; he seemed no more interesting than the other members of the group, and they only occasionally addressed themselves to him. As for the influenceable confederate, the more closely he conformed to the median attitude of the

Table 4.1. *Amount of communication addressed to the three confederates during successive phases of the group discussion*

| | Time spans (in minutes) | | | |
	5–15	15–25	25–35	35–45
Deviant	0.71	1.33	1.70	0.98
Conformist	0.13	0.06·	0.06	0.10
Influenceable	0.53	0.55	0.21	0.17

group, the less interested they became in him. The communications addressed to him, frequent to begin with, rapidly underwent a sharp decline (see Table 4.1).

Thus in the end Schachter did not succeed in showing that difference is a reprehensible behaviour, interpreted as deviance and so justifying rejection. Now, the entire social psychological tradition has ignored this failure, perceiving instead a wicked deviant justly punished by exclusion, a colourless conformist distinguished by his social invisibility, and an influenceable individual attracting less and less interest the more he was influenced.

Are deviance or independence truly asocial or antisocial responses to social pressure? Sherif and Sherif (1968) have hypothesised the existence of a normative bias in the social perception of radicalism. 'Perhaps our view of persons who take extreme stands has been coloured excessively by a norm of "liberal moderation". In other settings, extreme stands may be viewed as strong convictions rather than as symptoms of personal disturbance' (p. 119). The egalitarian view of group functioning distorts our interpretation of collective processes. It also induces in us the inclination to erase any inconsistencies or rough edges from our behaviour and disposes us to avoid conflict with others and search instead for empathy.

The functionality of deviation

Can one still assert that opponents or contenders are outside the social system even when in every quarter they are increasingly making themselves heard, taking action, introducing innovations? They are the people through which the forces of renovation in societies are expressed. Immobility and stability give rise to little but boredom or gloom. Changes and prospects of change are revitalising.

Instead of rejecting idiosyncrasies, they may be taken as standards or rallying points. Today there are several categories of deviant that are seen as active minorities, groups that have altered their position in society by asserting their peculiarities and the claims which these imply.

Social change has its source in opposition to the existing order. Power in itself may modify or reform but it cannot transform. It always seeks to maintain the same equilibrium, consolidating the solidity of the structure it represents, shoring it up as necessary.

In his analysis of deviant behaviour, Merton treats it as a product of the same social structure as conformist behaviour. Some deviations must be regarded as new forms of behaviour. They appear in sub-groups opposed to the institutional norms supported by more powerful groups or by legislation. According to Merton such non-conformity is both useful and adaptive to the social system, filling the necessary function of system regeneration. 'Under certain conditions public non-conformity can have the manifest and latent functions of changing standards of conduct and values which have become dysfunctional to the group' (Merton, 1961, p. 365). Undue rigidity in a social system can often lead to its collapse.

Non-conformity does not necessarily arouse universal opprobrium. At the beginning of this century, it was depicted in enthusiastic and lyrical terms by Cooley. But it no longer attracts unmixed admiration. In the mythical and idealised vision of an equilibrated society, it is something reprehensible, a thing to be expelled. But non-conformity expresses more than rejection, it also expresses an affirmation of the self, autonomy, a desire to break away from an oppressive destiny.

If such wishes are expressed, does one respond with indifference, non-communication, does one ignore them? Or does one immediately react repressively or reproachfully? In practice, attempts at rejection run into irreducible disagreements. What is surprising, and deplored by Merton, is how often this disharmony has been obscured by otherwise clear-sighted theorists in the social sciences.

Unless the distinction between types of non-conformist and deviant behaviour is maintained, conceptually and terminologically, sociology will by inadvertence continue on the path it has sometimes begun to tread and become the science of society which implicitly sees virtue only in social conformity... It is not infrequently the case that the non-conforming minority in a society represents the interests and ultimate values of the group more effectively than the conforming majority. (1961, p. 365)

Merton's clairvoyance here, his own thoughtful reflections, have not fundamentally shifted him beyond a functionalist tradition which makes a virtue of conformity and deviance of non-conformity.

Deviance assumes a variety of forms. Conceived as a form of transgression, it can only be anomic, devalued and devaluing. In contrast, if it offers solutions to change it is constructive. It derives its strength from the protests and contradictions which it discerns in the society it fights.

Many categories of deviants and minorities represent groups which have been placed in an inferior position, excluded from the society's idea of normality by various forms of discrimination – economic, social, racial. They are blatantly, in a direct or hypocritical manner, deprived of rights that the social system and political or religious values grant to everyone else. Such a conflict between principles and reality not only creates internal conflicts, but also a sense of guilt. For the Christian to have slaves, the democrat to prevent blacks from voting by insidious manoeuvres, the egalitarian to live with striking inequalities all around him, all represent contradictions. (Moscovici, 1976, pp. 73-4)

Certainly, it is still possible to devalue a category of 'sub-humans' in order to legitimise domination. But when these 'pigs', these 'dogs', these 'rats' refuse to hide or be silent, the situation becomes deeply embarrassing and conspicuous for the majority. With no further means of evasion, it is necessary to confront them, to get involved and make compromises.

The minority pole

By asserting its opposition, the minority produces a polarisation in the social arena and out of this a degree of coherence emerges. The minority relies on the power to split the group by opposing the inertial force of consensus. It demonstrates that it is willing to take risks. Non-conformity exposes individuals and groups to the risk of insult, ostracism and even persecution. At the same time, those who dare risk such abuses are envied; the attraction of the deviant is confounded with the attraction of the cause he symbolises. 'We should take note of the extreme non-conformist who enters on his public course of non-conformity with full knowledge that he runs the risk, so high a risk as to be almost a certainty – of severe punishment for his behaviour by the group... He is prepared to accept, if not to welcome, the almost certain and painful consequences of dissent' (Merton, 1961, p. 364). The deviant is the object of an ambiguous attitude of approach-avoidance, even on the part of those he challenges. 'Acting openly rather than secretly, and evidently aware that he invites severe sanctions by the group, the non-conformist tends to elicit some measure of respect, although this may be buried in thick layers of overt hostility and hatred among those who have a sense that their sentiments, their interests and their status are threatened by the words and actions of the non-conformist' (p. 365).

By their claims, minorities oblige others to look for reasons for their behaviour and hence to consider an alternative reality, even if only to refute it. The majority can, as in the past, continue to devalue the minority. But by this stage this mechanical defence is no longer credible; a defence which reveals the majority's bad faith more than anything else is bound to become suspect. Having achieved visibility, the minority can then force the majority into its sphere of influence.

Social recognition

The emergence of minority claims breaches the unity of the social system. The majority meanwhile strives to preserve universal commitment to a shared symbolic system in which on one side are the cherished children while on the other are the outcasts. This entails a single system of reference for defining both majorities and minorities, the former in a constructive fashion, the latter destructively; it incorporates a single dimension of identity, in which the former define the positive pole and the latter the negative pole.

To constitute an identity of its own, the minority must reject the option of negative identification in relation to the majority; in the process it must overcome doubt, confusion, distress and denial. Identification with the minority takes on connotations of self-affirmation. Moscovici was the first to emphasise how the stress placed on difference becomes a strategy of assertion.

> Groups which were defined and which generally defined themselves in a negative and pathological manner in relation to the dominant social code have become groups possessing their own code and moreover presenting it to others as a model or solution to change. They illustrate the concrete fashion in which the psychology – and why not the sociology? – of deviants is metamorphosised into the psychology of minorities; one sees men marked by anomie create their own *nomos*, while passive members of the social body are transformed into active participants (Moscovici, 1979, p. 11).

Minorities on all sides clamour for their 'right to be different'. Such attempts at differentiation face not just disapproval but also violent opposition. Sometimes it is necessary to resign oneself to a 'programme of absolute disorder', following the formula of Franz Fanon (1967). It is no longer a matter of begging or imploring, it is necessary to win over, to uproot, to indulge in excesses, in order to get a hearing.

The quest for social recognition is an integral part of the process of minority affirmation. A highly celebrated field study, *When prophecy fails* (Festinger, Riecken and Schachter, 1956) can be reinterpreted in these terms. Following reception of extra-terrestrial warnings in the form of automatic writing, a little sect was formed. The direct recipient of these warnings was one Mrs Keech, a person whom nothing seemed to have predestined for her astonishing prophetic fate. The sect waited calmly for the end of the world, predicted for 21 December one year in the fifties. Its members had nothing to fear; they were the elect; they would be saved by the flying saucers sent by their extra-terrestrial protectors just before the catastrophe. The fateful night of 20 December was marked by a redoubling of their fervour. But, happily for them and for the rest of the world, the apocalypse failed to materialise. Having overcome an initial period of tension, the members of the sect were not at all discouraged. The world was indebted to them for its avoidance of the cataclysm; it had been saved by the grace of their prayers. Thus they were able to reinforce their faith and legitimacy. They went further still; they sprung into action, seeking a confrontation with the external world in order to bring it the good news and to influence it. As surprising as it may seem, they threw themselves into an active campaign of proselytising. They at last had decisive proof of their rightful place; their belief had averted the end of the world. They had now to put their hands to the plough and bring the good word to all.

Emergence of minority influence

Minority action requires management of conflict. But as we have seen, it is not an easy task to take on conflict. From whence can be drawn the strength necessary to confront such a distressing situation? How can doubt be overcome, the greater number defied, rejection suffered? How can attention be roused, negotiation compelled?

Such questions lead us to a closer scrutiny of the minority style of behaviour – that sequence of actions whose goal is self-assertion and the production of change in others – and to an examination of its characteristics and its degree of generality.

Minority influence arises from the emergence of a conflict which actualises differences and increases their salience. The emergence of this conflict itself entails the expression of a specific behavioural style. This latter expresses simultaneously the desire for influence upon others and the wish to resist others. At the same time it also expresses the importance that the subjects' positions have for them and the clear alternatives it offers.

Now, the first condition for appearance of such behaviour resides in the extremity of the positions advocated. As Sherif and Sherif (1968) emphasise, 'Extreme positions are frequently stated in an unambiguous form ...the greatest variability in categorising usually occurs in the intermediate range' (p. 131).

Extremism possesses a clear meaning for everyone and the more significant the attitude object becomes, the stronger the tendency to extremism, the more unacceptable becomes the demand to modify positions, and the more stubborn becomes the defence of attitudes. The behavioural style of the minority at the same time symbolises confidence in their enterprise and clearly delimits the alternatives with which everyone is confronted. One of the major obstacles for the minority group, which it has to overcome if it wishes to exert any influence, is surely indifference and lack of attention.

Consistent repetition

Originally, refusal to change or steadfastness was operationalised as *repetition* which seemed to represent and indeed symbolised the complex behavioural style defined as 'consistency'. It was necessary at the beginning to show that a minority subject expressing a constant preference in a judgment situation would induce other majority subjects to adopt his response, even when this involved overturning an implicit norm of the group.

Two experiments by Faucheux and Moscovici (1967) provided the first demonstration of the effectiveness of consistent repetition.

The first of these was presented as concerned with the transmission of information in aerial navigation. It involved determining whether there exist 'preferences' for certain parameters when decoding information 'intended to increase the legibility and discrimination of information transmitted to air traffic controllers'. This represented the 'cover story' of the experiment; it was intended to provide the experimental situation with some credibility and to distract the attention of the subjects from the true purpose of the experiment or at least to reduce any strong assumptions in this regard. This purpose was to demonstrate the link between minority influence and consistent behavioural style.

The experimenters explained to the subjects that they were going to participate in an experiment which would recreate in a simplified form a situation of perceptual choice analagous to those of aerial navigation.

They were presented with a series of pictures varying according to four dimensions: size – large or small; colour – red or green; form – rounded or angular; contour – continuous or dotted line. The subjects were asked to give only one response from among the four possible, the one which seemed to them the most appropriate at a given moment for a particular drawing.

Two experimental conditions were created, a control condition involving only naive subjects and an experimental condition in which the groups included a confederate who invariably chose 'colour' from the first to the last trial. The main results confirmed the hypothesis: choice of the response 'colour' increased significantly in the experimental groups. The experimental groups gave on average 21 colour responses while the control groups gave 15.

The second experiment was more sophisticated and allowed manipulation of two types of deviation in relation to the norms, one conservative and the other innovative. The authors used lists of word associations as the experimental materials. To each stimulus word, for example 'orange' there corresponded two response words, one being a qualifier, for example 'round', and the other a superordinate, for example 'fruit'. In the experimental groups, the confederate always chose the superordinate response. Two lists were constructed. In the first (list A), the probability of association of the stimulus with the superordinate response was greater at the beginning. Thus at the start, the association chosen by the confederate corresponded to the norm. Then this probability declined to some degree so that the stable response of the confederate became 'conservative'; it symbolised a refusal to change. In contrast, with respect to list B, at the beginning the confederate gave a form of response which was infrequent but which became less and less deviant as the probability of this form of response increased; thus his mode of response symbolised originality and innovation.

What can we learn from the results? Generally, they again confirm the initial hypothesis: an increase in the number of superordinate responses is apparent in the experimental groups (Table 4.2).

Furthermore, there is no great difference in the frequency with which superordinate responses appear when the confederate is conservative at the beginning compared to when he is initially deviant. It appears that initial conformity is insufficient to explain minority influence. The effect of the minority requires a specific explanation; it is quite inconsistent with Hollander's hypotheses regarding innovation.

But let us go back a little and ask ourselves, as did Faucheux and Moscovici, the following question: is the Asch effect, that massive conformity effect, that effect which apparently so clearly exemplifies

Table 4.2. *Means of superordinate responses*

	List A	List B
Experimental groups	74.01	63.67
Control groups	57.61	53.89

majority influence, perhaps just an example of the effect of repetitive consistency?

The authors offered this rather paradoxical proposal to emphasise the radical break they envisaged with the traditional view of conformity. Even today this break has not been totally accepted, the functionalist enterprise and faith in conformity remaining the major sources of resistance.

Let us see first of all what there is in Asch's experiment to justify the authors' proposal, however far-fetched it might seem at first sight. In fact, three of the conditions that underlie minority influence are combined in this experiment. First of all, one may argue that the confederates introduced into the presence of the naive subjects, whatever their number, constitute a clear *minority*. From the point of view of the naive subject, they are the only persons that he has ever met who have asserted with such certainty and unanimity that two manifestly unequal lines are well and truly equal. The subject who takes part in the experiment comes with his past experience, an entire system of reference, commitment to self-evident truths and truisms which the experimental manipulation cannot remove by use of instructions or the creation of a situation circumscribed in time and space. Nevertheless, the subject finds himself alone against a 'minority' that is *deviant* in its use of perceptual codes which everyone is known to adhere to, except that in the situation here and now the minority position is supported unanimously. Coherence and *consistency* are expressed by the agreement which is revealed to exist among all the confederates when they simultaneously give the same false responses.

In contrast, as soon as this consistency weakens, influence substantially diminishes. This occurs when a single additional confederate is introduced into the group and, in the face of the false responses given by the other confederates, gives the correct response like the naive subject. On the other hand, when the subject confronts all the others alone, then this 'minority' appears to stick to its point of view and to do so systematically. A conflict is thus born in the opposition of two frames of reference, that promulgated by the group to which the subject momentarily belongs and that of the group to which the subject habitually belongs. From this conflict results the influence achieved over a significant proportion – a quarter – of the subjects involved.

Unwittingly, Asch's experiment provides, according to these authors, additional proof of the fact that a coherent minority can, in certain circumstances and sometimes against all expectations and all credibility, transform a majority norm.

We have examined this demonstration here because, quite apart from the paradox, it stresses the effectiveness of consistent repetition, whether it be minority or majority. However, there is no doubt that so far as the reactions of Asch's subjects were concerned, they had perceived the situation in terms of majority pressure, even if the source of this pressure may have operated in terms of a minority frame of reference. We have to concede that processes of influence are not univocal, they assume meanings which differ as a function of the contexts in which they occur.

The blue and the green

Let us stay with the perceptual domain, with this surrealist universe, constructed by social psychologists, in which lines are elastic and where 'the earth is blue like an orange'.[2] Indeed, it is blueness we will consider next, specifically the perception of colours, and the key experiment by Moscovici, Lage and Naffrechoux (1969) in which for the first time the celebrated blue – green procedure was developed, an experiment in which the existence of minority influence was made the object of extensive study.

Imagine that you have agreed to take part in an experiment on the perception of colours. Apart from yourself, five others are present. You begin by collectively taking part in a test of colour perception. You are able to ascertain that no one has any visual anomalies and that everyone in the group of which you are part identifies colours in the same fashion. In fact, none of this seems particularly difficult or very distressing.

But at this point things get more complicated. The experimenter tells you that he is going to show you a series of slides and you must call out the colour – you must only use simple colour names, not composites – and the luminous intensity. The experimenters introduced this second variable to break the monotony of the task a little; thirty-six projections of the same slide can be tedious.

Then the second phase begins. The experimenter projects a blue slide on the screen and the subjects respond. Strangely, two subjects answer

---

[2] Translated quotation from the French surrealist poet Paul Eluard.

'green'. They must have been mistaken, you think. But your astonishment is only beginning; the same two subjects persist in their error, invariably answering 'green' right to the end of the experiment. What do the other subjects do? And what would you do in this case? You cannot presume defective vision, given the test of colour perception undertaken before the start of the experiment. On the other hand, you are under no constraint whatsoever to adopt their mode of response; from the beginning you were not the only one to answer 'blue' and there is no explicit obligation upon the group to try and reach a consensus. As far as you are concerned there is nothing to stop you ignoring these answers and continuing to answer 'blue' each time. Nevertheless, these two strange confederates, lost in a group of six people and clearly diverging from the answers of the group, *exercised influence* on the responses of other members of the group.

Some figures will indicate the scope of this influence. First, consider the fact that this influence caused each subject to give *at least four 'green' responses*; this was true of 32% of the experimental subjects, divided between 43.74% of the groups. Taking all the responses given by all the subjects, then 8.42% of responses were 'green', attributable to the presence of a consistent minority. In contrast, in a further experimental condition in which the consistency of the minority was markedly weaker, the influence exercised was quite negligible. These results, which clearly confirm the existence of minority influence, are further reinforced by the demonstration of a secondary effect, in which influence occurred not at the verbal level but at the level of the perceptual code itself.

After the experimental phase, the subjects took part in a test of colour discrimination to determine the threshold at which they would give a 'green' response when they were presented with colours changing gradually from blue to green. Compared to the control group, the experimental subjects perceived green earlier. But this was not all; they perceived green even earlier if they had not succumbed to influence during the experimental phase.

Despite the final debriefing phase, people who took part in the 'blue – green' experiment were deeply disturbed by the experience. One of the confederates in the experiment told us how she would come across subjects in the corridors of the university and they would stop her to express their irritation or resentment or wry amusement long after the experiment!

Behavioural style
This demonstration made two things clear: on the one hand the effectiveness of minority influence and on the other the decisive role of behavioural style, in this case consistency, manipulated experimentally as a repetitive

behaviour simultaneously expressing certainty and refusal to change, and translating aspirations into action.

The experimental operationalisation we have described, repetitive behaviour in the context of perceptual tasks, cannot hope to encompass minority influence in all its complex facets. The aim was simply to recreate consistent behaviour in a precise and workable fashion. But it would be unduly restrictive to conceive minority behavioural style purely in this fashion. The 'blue – green' experiment was a first step; it was the first deliberate and convincing demonstration of minority influence and it opened up a fertile area for research.

But first let us go back and examine the minority behavioural style. It involves *a structured set of answers, of actions*, integrated within *a structured set of representations*. It would be inappropriate and simplistic to interpret minority behavioural style as no more than repetitive consistency. It remains true, though, that consistency has been studied experimentally more than any other style, both in its positive sense of certainty and in its negative sense of rigidity.

The concept of behavioural style refers to an organisation of actions characterised by the timing and intensity of their expression. These styles are codified in some way so that they carry a meaning which is accessible to everyone and so that in consequence they elicit an appropriate reaction. Thus most people will be able to decode a behavioural style in a particular context and make a prediction regarding future interactions. Behavioural styles incorporate at the same time both information and meaning. In terms of their content, they concern the object of the interaction and in terms of their structure the disposition of the actor.

Minority behavioural style includes several interrelated elements. Consistency, if not confined to repetition, involves notions such as steadfastness, firmness, and stability. It is expressed in the strength of assertions or convictions. Both consistency and involvement are linked by a principle of coherence or non-contradiction which gives the minority behavioural style credibility and sincerity.

In social exchanges, the styles of behaviour which exert influence are those which demonstrate that the group or individual involved is strongly committed to a choice freely made, that the goal pursued is highly regarded, to the point where personal sacrifice is voluntarily accepted. Determination makes any risks possible.

Involvement is linked to the extremity of positions, as many studies have shown (Sherif and Sherif, 1968; Paicheler, 1974); it seems absurd to declare oneself 'firmly without opinion'. Involvement is a preliminary to the expression of certainty. The necessary minority visibility is achieved by these three elements, involvement, extremism, certainty, and by the subsequent indication of refusal to change. Involvement carries a sense of courage in the face of risks, obstinacy whatever the goals pursued, and intransigence whatever the consequences for the self or others. Even though the minority has no power, these are certain trump cards in any negotiation!

Independence

Minority behavioural style will have neither the same meaning nor the same impact if it appears to have been produced by remote control, imposed on the group or individual by circumstances over which they had not the slightest control, or if it seems to result from some form of dependence.

Minority behavioural style must reveal autonomy, autonomy being regarded as a commendable attitude that invites emulation. It has several aspects, including an independence of judgment and attitude which reflects determination to act in accord with one's own principles, and a certain objectivity, that is to say, the capacity to take all the relevant factors into consideration and to draw appropriate conclusions, without letting oneself be deflected by subjective considerations. 'When an individual seems to have autonomous opinions and judgment, and is neither domineering nor particularly inclined to compromise, he will be perceived, characterised and probably responded to as an advocate of a particular model or set of values' (Moscovici, 1976, p. 115). This minority will give the impression of being in control of its own conduct. This individual or group will be heard and will, furthermore, have power in relation to other individuals. This ascendancy will be all the more potent if it is difficult to attribute manipulative intentions to the individual or group. It is their independence, their distance from authority and their refusal to temporise which inspire respect and admiration and lend value to their example.

Autonomy is inseparable from the freedom the group or individual reveals in relation either to others or to institutions. This was demonstrated in an ingenious experiment by Nemeth and Wachtler (1973). It was based on the representations contained in the connotation of an individual being placed at the head of a table. Whether it be in the Cabinet, in administrative meetings or at the family table – and in an infinity of other situations – the position at the head of the table is a mark of power and prestige. Consequently, in a group, without which the situation does not arise, one expects the person who occupies this position to have a role of authority. Moreover, even if he or she does not clearly exercise this role, one still tends to make the attribution.

After the usual fashion, the experimental design contrasted an experimental group, containing a confederate, with a control group in which no confederate was present. Variations were introduced in the experimental conditions: the confederate either occupied the place *at the head of the table*, or a *side* position, and he either seemed to *choose* his position, or else the experimenter *assigned* one to him. The experimental phase involved group discussions among five persons who simulated juries deliberating on a case involving awards of costs and damages for an injury sustained during an accident at work. The legal maximum compensation was $25,000. The average of the proposals by subjects prior to the experimental phase was $14,500. The confederate himself always suggested awarding $3,000 to the victim, using a predetermined list of arguments, which remained the same across all the experimental conditions. The confederate's position was at the same time clearly both deviant and consistent.

Autonomy was operationalised in terms of whether or not the confederate had apparently chosen his place at the table. The importance of autonomy was confirmed by the results; only when the confederate had chosen the place at the head of the table did he exert any influence. In contrast, when this place had been assigned to him or when he chose to occupy a side position, the confederate had no influence. When he chose the place at the head of the table, the confederate simultaneously expressed autonomy and self-confidence. Thus the representations and expectations which correspond to this position could operate without hindrance, which is clearly not the case when this highly significant position is imposed.

Thus independence works. But we should be careful not to confound it with egocentrism or selfishness. The individual or group which seems to be seeking satisfaction only of its own desires or its own particular interests arouses hostility and/or greed and is likely to encounter various obstacles to the pursuit of its aims. Thus independence must be accompanied by a certain degree of disinterest or even altruism, in order to attract admiration. It is only credible if it is accompanied by a disregard for the consequences to the self of the actions undertaken. Political figures are well aware of this. They never miss an opportunity to declare that they are not fighting to safeguard their own personal interests or privileges but rather that they are struggling on behalf of the general interest, for the collective good – including in this the interests of the ungrateful or ignorant who did not vote for them – and that they are above partisan struggles.

Scarcely had the minority influence model been demonstrated when it was already being questioned. A simple repetitive conception of the power of persuasion had to be quickly abandoned. Nonetheless there is little dispute that repetition can play a not insignificant role. Le Bon (1896) had already proposed this without the benefit of any systematic methodology:

'Repetition of a few evidential truths gives the strength of tyrants.' However, the minority influence model is not a model of legitimate power, if indeed clearly delimited and fixed power exists, but of a particular kind of power, and with a definite form, in the sense that it refers to the existence and strength of a certain kind of elite.

Whether we are talking of majority or minority influence, what is primary is the existence of a pressure from which individuals cannot escape. The difference is that the pressure has its source either in those who are already established or in those who wish to capture this position. All things considered, in minority influence, power is only a question of time, assuming that time works in its favour. This influence carries a risk; it can be lost, but even when it fails the fact remains that its objective was to win. In this sense, Nemeth and Wachtler's experiment is very revealing; the minority gained in influence when it succeeded in attributing to itself, and having attributed to it by others, signs of power.

Let us now conclude this part of our argument. We have emphasised the importance of two conditions essential to the appearance of minority influence: conflict and difference. Now, we have endeavoured to identify within these different aspects one of the fundamental means by which this influence is exercised: behavioural style. We have relied on research in which this minority influence has appeared to be clear and explicit. But these studies also demonstrate in various ways that this influence is complex, in particular that it is not only at the explicit level that it occurs. Once agreed on the existence of this type of influence, researchers took on the task of refining their investigations, of identifying both positive and negative effects, and of establishing the degree to which these effects are conscious. This takes us on to evidence of latent forms of influence, forms which cannot be located only on a rational level. Their mechanisms are not accessible to subjects, whose actions are affected nonetheless, sometimes with irresistible force; in effect they appear to represent a kind of unconscious influence. This muted influence lacks the power of hypnosis, certainly, but sometimes finds a concealed path through the subject's defences. In this sense, it constitutes an intriguing matter, and one which we will now attempt to elucidate.

5 The hidden face of influence

Limits

Interiorisation and Exteriorisation

The possibilities for conformity seem infinite. It may not be easy to procure all the ingredients of the recipe for conformity proposed by Walker and Heyns (1967), but this recipe is certainly effective. Furthermore, it has the merit of summarising all the elements of the functionalist model.

> If one wishes to produce conformity for good or evil, the formula is clear. Manage to arouse a need or needs that are important to the individual or to the group. Offer a goal which is appropriate to the need or needs. Make sure that conformity is instrumental to the achievement of the goal and that the goal is as large and as certain as possible. Apply the goal or reward at every opportunity. Try to prevent the object of your efforts from obtaining an uncontrolled education. Choose a setting that is ambiguous. Do everything possible to see that the individual has little or no confidence in his own position. Do everything possible to make the norm which you set appear highly valued and attractive. Set it at a level not too far initially from the starting point of the individual or the group and move it gradually toward the behavior you wish to produce. Be absolutely certain you know what you want and that you are willing to pay an enormous price in human quality, for whether the individual or the group is aware of it or not, the result will be CONFORMITY. (p. 98)

This recipe presents the 'gentle touch' in which the assent of individuals seems to be the consequence of their own characteristics and those of their environment. Conformity is the result of a combination of enduring and situational factors. It is also much more than this; it is the result of a manipulation that is more or less conscious, so far as both actor and target of influence are concerned. It does not just *change* the individual or the group, it is also constitutive of them.

However, for the moment let us confine ourselves to the hypothesis that conformity introduces a change in the behaviour of a person, having the effect of a real or imagined pressure emanating from one or more people. This definition contains no surprises; it is a distillation of the definitions to be found in most American textbooks. Even accepting this minimal definition, it must be modified. Conformity is not monolithic; it varies according to the conviction which underlies it, assuming a variety of forms.

Kelman (1958) introduces a distinction between different types of conformity, distinguishing between internalisation, identification, and compliance.

Internalisation is the most permanent of the three, the most solidly based effect of influence. It is at once both a tenacious and subtle form of conformity. The subject adopts actions or systems of values to such a degree that he is no longer able to see that he has been the object of influence. Internalisation renders these actions or systems of belief highly resistant to change.

Internalisation in this sense can be compared to the process which Blake and Mouton (1961) called 'conversion', defined as effects following pressures to conform which persist when these pressures are removed. If influence is still exercised when the constraint is absent, then a genuine conversion effect has been obtained.

Identification is a more fragile form of behaviour. The individual wishes above all to be like the source of influence, whatever the object of influence may be. Identification involves adopting the behaviour, attitudes or opinions of those one likes and wishes to resemble. It is not that the acts or thoughts resulting from influence are satisfying in themselves, but that these acts or thoughts allow a definition of the self which creates the possibility of a satisfying relationship with the persons with whom one identifies, and consequently with oneself. With every tournament at Roland Garros or Wimbledon great and small flock to the courts, under the spell of a MacEnroe or Noah practising a magic sport which renders them – or seems to render them – like gods of the stadium, with very little effort or willpower on their part.

Identification is a fundamental psychological device and one of the major means of pedagogic action. Freud (1955) accorded it considerable importance in social and emotional life, and indeed in power relations.

The comic effect of a Woody Allen film, *Zelig*, depends in large part on identification. Zelig, the chameleon man, becomes exactly like those in whose presence he is placed; by turns he becomes an Indian, a fat man, a

Nazi, a society writer, a boxer, etc... And of course it is difficult to treat him; among psychiatrists he transforms himself into a psychiatrist. He cannot bear to be different, not, as he reveals under hypnosis, to avoid rejection, but in order 'to be liked' and to like his own self.

Compliance is a more servile behaviour. It is public acceptance of a behaviour or system of values without any private commitment to them. In appearance, individuals accept influence, they yield. They thus manage to avoid disagreements, but internally, they resist, they preserve their own beliefs and are prepared to change back as soon as circumstances allow. They swallow their revolt but it seethes within them, ready to gush out.

Compliance is conformity, but it is also a sly means of resisting influence. We should, however, beware of exaggerating its significance; this private, buried resistance seldom results in any explicit display. It remains a derisory power of the weak. If weakness exists, it is the result of compliance in the face of power, whether real or symbolic. Two conditions are necessary for the emergence of this response: the impossibility of escaping the situation and the threat of sanctions in the case of explicit resistance (see Festinger, 1953).

Leporello, for example, at the beginning of *Don Giovanni* rails against his master. He 'no longer wishes to serve and wishes to be the gentleman'. He no longer wishes to lead an unceasingly disturbed life, satisfying the most extravagant buffoonery of his master. But the master only has to appear and he cannot but obey, carrying out the basest tasks, showing disconsolate lovers the door while making a fool of others, being drubbed in his turn. He remains powerless in the face of his master's impious provocations. He can only obey and assume a contented air, his thorough complicity reinforcing his master while sticking in his own throat. He is and will remain nothing but the servant. Don Giovanni risks his life in splendid fashion, while he follows on in a fashion rather more cowardly.

Like many other taxonomies, Kelman's classification is not perfect; his categories are neither exhaustive nor exclusive. But they do have one virtue: they allow emphasis on two aspects of influence, depth and ambiguity. They remind us, if it were necessary, that influence is neither univocal nor stable. They demonstrate at the same time the limits of conformity and the complexity of the process, by distinguishing internal and external aspects of influence. Following Kelman, we also must attempt a more fine-grained analysis of this dichotomy.

Majority constraint

Let us return to the celebrated Asch experiment and consider the implications of his results. To induce a quarter of the individuals, under conditions of majority pressure, to give a response contrary to the most obvious evidence is no trivial achievement. We have only partially clarified why subjects yielded or resisted and we have ignored the extent to which this influence was superficial or profound, transitory or lasting.

These same questions were raised by the author himself. To try and understand what went on in the heads of the subjects, he questioned them after the experiment. The method is not without weaknesses; it is difficult to get beneath their rationalisations. But even an examination of the brain based on something as sophisticated as nuclear magnetic resonance would still not enable us to detect what people *really* think. Truth drugs are placebos both for those who ask the questions and for those who answer. Lie detectors are more likely to be anxiety detectors...and so on. Given our prehistoric methodology, we must be content with what people say or do.

We know that the traumatic quality of the Asch experiment was evident in most of the interviews. Recall the subjects' reactions. Even though they had been subject to no explicit pressure, they had felt themselves constrained by the opinions the others expressed, even though the evidence available in the task left not the slightest doubt about the correct response. All the subjects voiced their distress, whether they had ceded to or resisted the majority pressure.

Not a single subject remained calm and untouched. 'It is more pleasant if one is really in agreement with the group' (Asch, 1952, p. 468) one of them affirmed. Said another, 'Frankly, I considered momentarily the policy of agreeing with them and reserving my judgment, but I decided against it' (p. 468).

This experiment is rich in surprising findings. Among the influenced subjects, a very small number found nothing 'remarkable' in it. They claimed to have followed the majority because the latter were giving the correct answers. Certainly, they had the most economic attitude psychologically. 'I never gave an answer that wasn't right' this subject said and then corrected himself '*I didn't give an answer that I knew was wrong*' (p. 496; my italics). Asch commented 'His lack of awareness apparently permitted the subject to speak and act in a straightforward, calm way without any trace of evasiveness or embarrassment' (p. 469).

Not all the conformists were as much at ease as this subject. They knew very well that they had given incorrect responses, but they retreated behind social motives. Finding themselves confronted with such unanimity gave rise to disconcerting doubts, sapping their confidence and energy to resist. Convinced of the fact that collective error is not possible, they then convinced themselves of their incapacity to judge correctly. 'They were so positive, and so of the two [alternatives] I'd give the one they gave. On a couple I felt they were probably wrong, but I wasn't ever absolutely sure' (p. 471).

Other conformists clearly and simply expressed not doubt but the desire not to be different. They became completely uninterested in the task and seemed no longer concerned with whether or not their judgments were correct. For them the single imperative need was not to deviate, to remain at one with the group, not to risk exclusion. These subjects were clearly conscious of what they were doing. They did not doubt their own judgment but in the situation they refused to distinguish themselves, at least by their courage. They protected themselves by a split which was for them the best means of escape in the situation without loosing too much face. 'Scientifically speaking, I was acting improperly, but my feeling of not wanting to contradict the group overcame me' (p. 472).

How ill at ease he is finding himself confronted with his own weakness! 'I condemned myself for lacking the force of my convictions. I had a sense of guilt and anger against myself for not having been entirely conscientious' (p. 472).

The pressure of the group provokes a tendency to avoid acting differently. The constraint of the majority induces conformity in the form of compliance. This set of recollections provides us with the entire gamut of reactions possible in such a situation. It indicates that there was no profound integration of any new way of thinking, but a transitory and circumstantial adoption of a particular behaviour.

The term 'behaviour' is crucial here for it was a matter of what could be seen or objectively observed in the subject's actions. Compliance implies behaving or seeming but not changing inner convictions.

We need assurance finally that Asch's results do indeed indicate compliant behaviour. The post-experimental interviews considered above are useful but only a further experiment in the appropriate form could provide definitive proof.

It would be desirable for any replication of Asch's experiment to include certain modifications. Instead of requiring subjects to give their answers publicly, in the presence of others, they could be asked to give them privately, in writing, after being made aware of the 'judgments' of other members of the group. These would be the same as the evaluations of the confederates in Asch's experiments. If the confederates' unanimous but false answers really convince subjects, their private and public evaluations should be identical. On the other hand, if subjects are displaying compliant behaviour in public, adopting the others' responses merely to avoid disagreement with the group and remain in its good graces, the private estimations should be quite different from the public ones.

Using Asch's material, Deutsch and Gerard (1955) set about comparing

139

private and public situations. After presenting the lines for comparison, the 'answers' of other 'members' of the group were illuminated on a console; these were similar to those given publicly by the confederates in the Asch experiment. The subject responded knowing that his own responses would not be transmitted to the others. In this case, conformity totally disappeared; knowledge of majority judgments was practically without effect on private judgments.

Reactions to influence

Explicit or public commitment to the positions of an influence agent can signify a transitory resolution of a dispute. Subjects yield to pressure in public and then return to their own positions in private. They respond explicitly as they think the situation and social norms demand but they reserve their position. To study this experimentally, one requires a situation where the answer can be expressed first publicly, with more or less constraint, and then privately. An experiment by Paicheler and Bouchet (1973) was constructed according to such a plan.

It was concerned not with perceptual evaluations but with the expression of attitudes in which the subjects were deeply involved. It was carried out in a junior high school a little after May 1968. The atmosphere was charged; extreme left wing students were getting a wide hearing for their convictions and meeting little opposition. It seemed evident that they occupied a position of authority. Events had seemed to confirm the validity and relevance of their case. Their opponents had little or nothing to say and had retreated to low-profile, moderate positions.

The subjects, final-year students, had to discuss various aspects of their educational conditions and, over the course of the discussion, to reach some agreement on a certain number of points.

The experimental design was of a simple classical form. The initial attitudes of subjects were assessed (*pre-consensus*), using an attitude scale consisting of items referring to various issues related to educational conditions. They then discussed these same issues with the aim of adopting a position common to the group (*consensus*). Finally, they responded to the attitude scale once more but this time in private (*post-consensus*).

The authors observed the anticipated effect; attitudes became more extreme during the course of the discussion. But there was a boomerang effect; the subjects tended to revert to their initial positions after the discussion.

This reversal was more accentuated when the group included one or more extreme individuals, while the change in attitude was more stable in groups of individuals who were more uniformly moderate. The extreme individuals had thus exerted a very strong pressure to which subjects had yielded during an interaction that proceeded in a tense and constrained atmosphere. Under the subsequent conditions of anonymity, they had then returned to their initial positions, hence rejecting the agreements forced from them in the group.

Conversion or secrecy

Forced submission signifies public acquiescence to an opinion promoted by a powerful group or individual. However, this public submission does not necessarily remain a purely superficial response. The theory of cognitive dissonance (Festinger, 1957) teaches us that forced compliance can result in a genuine change of attitude. Individuals will endeavour to reduce the psychological gap between their actions and their thoughts, their public opinions and their private beliefs.

This tendency is demonstrated in an experiment by Joseph Nuttin (1972) which may be illustrated here with the case of 'Jean-Marie'. Jean-Marie is a second-year chemistry student at Louvain. He is a left-winger who supports university reform. We are at the beginning of the seventies, in the middle of the period of university upheaval. He meets 'by chance' a young woman who asks him to take part in a television broadcast dealing with reform of the examination system, and organised as a debate between professors and students. Jean-Marie accepts and is invited to present himself at the recording studio. In fact this studio is a fake; moreover nothing is due to chance in this experiment. At the studio it is explained to Jean-Marie that there are too many supporters of reform available for the broadcast and it would be good if he would speak against the motion to enliven the debate. To this end, he needs to prepare an argument lasting five minutes *against* university reform. Of course, he is at liberty to refuse, but again he accepts. He then finds himself being offered the sum of 20 Belgian francs (about 20 pence) for his participation or 'collaboration'. Thus he doesn't have the solace of being manipulated for a reasonable fee. He prepares his argument, is broadcast and is then able to watch the broadcast at his leisure on videotape. Before Jean-Marie finally takes his leave, the experimenter asks him to indicate his position on a line – a continuum – running from *altogether opposed* to *altogether in favour* of university reform.

The results compared the subjects who had been induced to agree and a control group of subjects drawn from the same population but who were asked only to indicate their position on the continuum. These results clearly demonstrated that subjects induced to draw up an argument against their own opinions had become less favourably disposed to university reform. Five weeks later this difference in opinion still remained highly significant.

Yielding to an influence contrary to one's own opinions can occur to differing degrees. It depends among other things on the strength of the pressure and the strength of the opinion. The history of the Inquisition is rich in examples of forced conversions which split individuals internally and resulted in covert pursuit of proscribed practices. This was true of the Marranites in the strongly Catholic Spain of Ferdinand and Isabella in the fifteenth century (Poliakov, 1961). The Inquisition pitilessly hunted down Jews and Moriscos. Either they renounced their faith and embraced the Holy Church, or they were put to the sword or the fire. The margin of choice was narrow... Some converted and became convinced Catholics. But these 'new Christians' were still mistrusted and barred from any official positions; they were unable to vouch for the 'purity of their blood'. The line was a fine one between these new Christians and the 'conversos', recently converted Jews, of whom it was impossible to be certain that they had erased all trace of Judaism from their practices; they were people to be avoided, potential traitors under constant surveillance.

As for the Marranites, they chose to be covert. Forced to yield, they put on a pretence. They annulled their Christian prayers with blasphemies uttered under their breath and continued to practise their religion in secret. But the Inquisition lasted a long time, until the beginning of the nineteenth century, and time had right on its side. Most Marranites were assimilated in the end, if they had not been driven out or burned. Little by little, they had lost the substance and significance of their rites, preserving only the necessity for secrecy. If the pressure is too strong and the resistance excessively secret, the former will often triumph over the latter.

A certain solace

The constraint of influence has graduated effects, according to its force and duration. It arouses some degree of resistance because it is disagreeable to let oneself be influenced against one's will. One has a feeling of having been pushed or compelled. One draws from this conclusions about one's own personality – I am weak, I have let myself be made a fool of, I have neither character nor independence – and other rather disagreeable conclusions.

To be influenced is to lose face, to admit that one possesses an unworkable system of beliefs or practices. This is why one may, as a means of self-defence, refuse to adopt judgments that are too discrepant with one's own in the presence of others, particularly if it is they who support them. Let us suppose that despite this rejection, the others' judgments remain very stable and that this stability is surprising given that the situation is ambiguous and thus that points of reference for verifying any particular judgment are weak. One might then attribute the discrepancy and the stability of the others' responses to a deliberate intention to influence. One would then resist. But once the others are absent, the psychological obstacles to influence collapse. It becomes possible to consider their point of view, to put oneself in their place without feeling harassed by their advice. They are no longer there to observe or enjoy their victory. This type of situation may be observed in daily life when we are violently opposed to another on a particular point and refuse to concede, and then, as soon as his back is turned, we think that perhaps after all he was not so wrong...

Moscovici and Neve (1972) created a situation of this type experimentally. Following Sherif (1936), their procedure relied upon the auto-kinetic effect. It may be recalled that this key experiment by Sherif demonstrated a convergence in individual estimations and stabilisation around an average response. In Moscovici and Neve's experiment, confederates gave estimations very different from the average estimates of the naive subjects; they consistently overestimated the illusion of movement in the point of light. The experiment was conducted with pairs of individuals; a confederate and naive subject responded in one another's presence.

The manipulation was as follows. The confederate claimed he was late for an appointment and left the room 'before' the end of the experiment. The naive subject remained alone and continued to give estimates of movement of the luminous point. In the control group, the confederate remained present to the end.

The manipulation worked; 83% of experimental subjects shifted their estimates towards those of the confederate after he absented himself, while 92% of the control subjects shifted their estimates further away during this final phase of the experiment. The confederate's absence lifted the constraint aroused by the lack of agreement.

Underground action
In the framework of majority influence, constraint bringing about behavioural compliance can lead little by little to a genuine change. Often, external behaviour precedes any internal change. This dissociation of the public and private levels is either maintained or attenuated. The examples we have given make it clear that the delay between levels can take a variety of forms.

The same delay can be observed in the exercise of minority influence except that here the effects are less clear-cut. In the key experiment by Moscovici, Lage and Naffrechoux (1969), the existence of just such a dissociation between public and private effects was observed.

The authors wanted to go beyond the explicit effects observed in the experimental phase, that is during the interaction. They were also curious about the depth and stability of the effects. If modification of the social response is accompanied by a change in the underlying perceptual code, then the effectiveness of minority influence would be indisputable.

We wondered whether the subjects experienced an influence which, even if it did not result in a change in verbal response during the experiment, did have a lasting effect on their perception. We expected a shift in the blue-green designation threshold which would reveal a reaction that was repressed during the social interaction. Certain subjects did refuse to adopt openly the minority response, feeling compelled to remain loyal to the general norm, even when they themselves began to doubt its validity. Here one might expect a latent attraction manifesting itself by an extension of the designation 'green' to stimuli in a zone which a control group would call blue. (p. 370)

In a variation of the 'blue-green' experiment, the authors ran a blue-green discrimination test following the experimental phase, with the aim of detecting any subsequent deeper change in the perceptual threshold. Subjects took this test alone and gave their responses in writing. The material they were given to evaluate consisted of sixteen discs the colours of which lay in the blue-green area of the colour spectrum. Three discs were clearly blue, three were clearly green and the other ten formed a continuous gradual change from blue to green. These discs were presented ten times, in random order. The control group subjects also took this test so as to provide a basis for comparison.

Three values were used to estimate discrimination thresholds. The 50% threshold was the point in the sequence of discs at which a subject gave as many blue as green responses. The lower threshold was the disc to which a subject gave 75% green responses and 25% blue, and the upper threshold was that to which a subject gave 25% green responses and 75% blue.

The threshold for discrimination between blue and green was clearly modified in the experimental subjects (see Table 5.1). As an example of how this table should be read, and to indicate the extent of perceptual change, let us take the values 484.1 for the control groups and 480.3 for the experimental groups. Chromatically these values are very close to one another. Now, at the point where only 25% of the control group responses are green, 50% of those given by the experimental group are now green. This shift is consistent across all the threshold values in Table 5.1. And it should be emphasised that this alteration in perceptual thresholds involves subjects rather than changes in verbal responses.

The authors also found that in the groups where there had been no change in verbal response, where the green response had been 'repressed', there were more green responses in the discrimination test. The minority

144

Table 5.1. *Displacement of threshold for the perception of the colour green (mean wave lengths in centimetres)*

percentage of green responses	control groups	Experimental groups
75	461.6	468.5
50	473.9	480.3
25	484.1	491.9

had exerted a greater influence on the subjects' perceptual code than on their explicit evaluations.

These results reveal the existence of a latent influence, one of which individuals are all the more unaware to the degree that they reject overt influence. The absence of explicit effects should not be allowed to obscure the fact that changes are produced at other levels. The discovery of these latent effects has had an impact on subsequent research on minority influence. Experiments have since been designed to allow more explicit attention to be given to these effects.

Two cycles of influence

Majority and minority influence

We have now identified the existence of complex forms of influence. To bring some order to the tangled web of possible influences, it was necessary to simplify at the start. Thus, in the most basic terms, two contrasting types of influence can be specified, conformity and innovation, or majority and minority influence, respectively.

But we must then ask whether they are different and in what way they are different. For Latane and Wolf (1981) these two processes are governed by the same quasi-arithmetic principle: social impact. This is a function of the strength, the proximity and the number of individuals able to exercise influence. The more numerous, close and resolute they are, the stronger is their influence; the difference between majority and minority influence is a matter of degree, not kind.

Serge Moscovici, the first to demonstrate the influence of active minorities experimentally, vehemently rejects this position which he regards as reductionist and retrograde.

> Most seek to renovate and safeguard the old, preserving the familiar hypotheses intact simply by introducing ad hoc modifications which allow them to incorporate new data. (1980, p. 16)
>
> I know nobody who has been able successfully to accomplish the intellectual feat of demonstrating that making an innovation is an attempt to get back to the same structure which enforces respect for order and sustains the uniformity of behaviour and opinions. (p. 37)

Moscovici and Lage (1976) took on the task of demonstrating the aspects that distinguish minority and majority influence.

Again using the blue-green paradigm, the authors showed that minority influence involves levels of evaluation which are both manifest and latent, while majority influence creates superficial agreement and results in surface conformity. The authors compared two experimental conditions. The confederates were either in the majority or in the minority relative to the number of naive subjects in the groups.

As in the original experiment, the results showed that a consistent minority could exercise significant influence. However, it was less influential than a unanimous majority on the explicit level. The latter affected 40% of the answers while the minority modified only 10% of them.

At the latent level, this difference was totally reversed. The subsequent colour discrimination test clearly revealed that subjects confronted with consistent minority influence modified their blue-green discrimination threshold, perceiving green in the composite colours more often than the control groups.

Here again, this modification was not limited to subjects who had been influenced during the interaction phase. It was apparent whether a subject had yielded to influence or not. In contrast, no such deep change in perceptual thresholds could be found in the majority influence situation.

The authors concluded from this that there clearly was a difference in kind between majority and minority influence.

> A minority, without obtaining substantial acceptance of its point of view at the manifest level, can nonetheless influence subjects to revise the very basis of their judgments, while a majority can make them almost all accept its point of view if it is unanimous, without affecting the underlying perceptual-cognitive system. In other words, majority

influence works on the the surface, while minority influence has deep-lying effects. (p. 163)

We should beware, however, of confounding the depth of change with the effectiveness of influence. Often surface conformity is socially more effective than a response which is so deeply buried that it never sees the light of day, or has to undergo profound change before it can ever be expressed.

Copy conformity or non-conformity

Influence induced by the majority is an influence towards complete identity, towards adopting the opinions or actions of the majority in every detail; it is imitative conformity, rigid and subservient. In contrast, the minority offers an example of originality, it invites not simply direct imitation of its opinions or actions, but the adoption of difference in general. Minority influence is not direct but one step removed; it encourages, by example, a search for new solutions.

Nemeth and Wachtler (1983) were able to demonstrate this with an experimental task involving comparisons of more or less complex figures. While the majority provoked compliance, the minority stimulated a search for new answers which were different from their own. Moreover, subjects confessed to feeling more inadequate, embarrassed, alarmed and frustrated, and less happy in the majority situation. Minority influence seemed more stimulating, less constricting. The majority restricted the possible alternatives to two, their own – the good ones – and other or bad ones.

It is not in the least surprising that majority and minority pressures differed in their effects. A majority tends to isolate subjects if they fail to share in the position of the greater number. They are constrained to accept majority influence if they are to escape the conflict. As soon as they are out of the situation, subjects are able to revert to their initial position without any remorse. The minority, in contrast, offers no such threat. Here conflict is born instead out of resemblance with the minority. However, the impact of the minority is such as to suggest that it should not be analysed in terms of manifest reactions alone. Minority influence initiates long term effects and these only emerge when the link with the initiating conditions has become sufficiently tenuous.

Latent minority influence

To explore and understand these covert phenomena requires an appropriate methodology. A decisive step in this direction was achieved by incorporating into the experimental procedures a well-known effect from the field of perception, an optical illusion, namely the 'after-image' effect.

Briefly, if you fix your gaze on a colour for several seconds and then look at a white screen, you will see the colour complementary to the previous one. For example, if you have fixated on red, the after-image you see will be green.

The preceding experiments have shown that the effects of minority influence go beyond overt signs. There is influence on the latent structure of responses. But how can we be sure of the robustness of these results? Do they really allow us to conclude that a modification has occurred in the perceptual code? It is possible to advance a counter-hypothesis. The effect of influence could be explained simply as the effect of verbal contamination. Having frequently heard the response 'green' during the course of the experiment, the subject could unknowingly have become so impregnated with this response that he uses it more often. To this counter-hypothesis one could object that if there was truly verbal contamination, it is not clear why subjects in the majority condition were not nearly as affected by it as subjects in the minority condition. They would have heard the response 'green' even more often and yet no modification in the perceptual threshold was observed in this group.

The after-image effect allows a test of the possible parasitic effect of verbal contamination. If influence can be shown at the level of the after-image, then we can be sure that the effect is both deep and well-anchored. If subjects are consenting to a superficial modification of their answers in saying 'green', the colour perceived following a blue slide should be located in the yellow-orange zone of the spectrum. On the other hand, if the subjects' perceptual code has truly changed, they should, whether or not they have answered 'green' and thus yielded to the influence of the confederates, perceive the colour complementary to green, and thus shift towards the purple zone of the spectrum. We should stress that this is a very strong hypothesis and its experimental verification would provide a decisive confirmation of the latent effects of minority influence. The hypothesis was put to the test in an experiment by Moscovici and Personnaz (1980).

In order to evaluate the effectiveness of majority and minority influence both at the level of manifest verbal response and at the latent level of the perceptual code, some variations were introduced into the blue-green paradigm. A naive subject took part in the experiment in the company of one confederate. The experimenter projected a series of blue slides which the confederate consistently judged as green. Minority and majority were defined not in strictly numerical terms but in terms of their symbolic value; the confederate was not in himself the majority or a minority but 'representative' of the majority or of a minority.

We will describe the sequence of events in this experiment, as the experimental variables were introduced successively through the course of the experiment.

The first phase, the *pre-test*, involved five trials. The subject and the confederate gave their responses concerning the colour of the slide and then that of the after-image privately in writing.

The response sheets were collected up. Then the experimenter informed the subjects that he was going to give them some information about the answers given by previous subjects. It should be understood here that this information was fabricated. It allowed introduction of the first experimental variable, categorisation of the subject and confederate respectively as minority or majority. Subjects were given a sheet on which were indicated the percentages of individuals perceiving the slide as blue or as green. These percentages clearly differentiated a majority (81.8%) and a minority (18.2%) response. Thus in one experimental condition (majority source of influence) the confederate appears to belong to the majority and the subject to the minority, while in the other (minority source of influence) the reverse is the case.

The second phase was the influence phase. For fifteen trials, responses were spoken out loud, and the confederate consistently answered 'green'. During the third phase, the slide was projected fifteen more times. Here subjects again gave their responses in writing, both for the colour of the slide and for the after-image.

Before the fourth phase, the *post-test*, has begun, the confederate, under the pretext that he is likely to miss an appointment, hurriedly leaves the room. The subject is now alone and continues judging the colour of the slides and after-images.

Moscovici and Personnaz anticipated that on the one hand the influence exercised by a consistent minority source would modify the subjects' perceptual code while influence exercised by a majority would not have the same effect. On the other hand, they expected that modification of the perceptual code would be greater when the source of influence was absent than when he was present, that is, when the constraint of his presence was removed.

The objective of this experiment was to establish some rather delicate effects. It is difficult enough to manipulate overt behaviour experimentally, while taking all the necessary precautions to ensure that the experiment adequately addresses the questions posed. Investigation of latent phenomena, which are often more tenuous and difficult to pin down, requires of necessity particular experimental rigour.

The results obtained by Moscovici and Personnaz confirmed the existence of latent influence operating on the after-image. In the minority influence condition, estimations of the after-image by subjects were shifted towards the colour complementary to green. This shift was accentuated after the departure of the confederate.

In a replication of this experiment, Doms and Van Avermaet (1980) obtained comparable results for the after-image effect in the minority situation. But they obtained a similar and indeed more marked effect in the majority situation. A further replication was required.

Subsequent replications have supported the hypothesis of a specifically minority conversion effect. Personnaz (1981) repeated the Moscovici and Personnaz experiment, perfecting assessment of the after-image effect by adding an intermediate measure, more reliable than the verbal response. The use of a spectrometer, an apparatus for measuring the spectrum of light and therefore colour, avoided the need for verbalisation of the after-image colour. Instead of using a verbal scale from yellow-orange, the complement of blue, to red-purple, the complement of green, the author asked subjects to set the spectrometer to the precise colour corresponding to their perception. Using this apparatus, the subject could scan across the entire visible spectrum and stop as soon as he found the colour he had just perceived, whether of the slide or of the after-image. This allowed the use of a very precise metric scale, namely wavelength.

The experimental design was the same as that employed by Moscovici and Personnaz. During the second or influence phase, when confronted with the confederate's 'green' response, the subject first responded orally, and then adjusted his response on the spectrometer, both for the colour perceived on the slide and for that of the after-image.

The results obtained were in the same direction as those in the Moscovici and Personnaz experiment. Again it appeared that individuals exposed to minority influence modified their perception of the slide itself, something which did not happen under conditions of majority influence. This effect was greater when the source of influence was absent. The minority influence on overall perceptual activity, perception and after-image, was thus confirmed.

A supplementary finding provided some interesting clarification of the subjects' psychological functioning. It opened up the beginnings of an interpretation that went beyond the mere presentation of numerical results. In a post-experimental questionnaire, the author asked subjects to reconstruct from memory the percentage of individuals perceiving the slide as blue versus green, the fictitious information with which they had been provided at the end of the first phase. It was found that 'minority' subjects had a tendency to magnify the majority percentage and minimise that of the 'minority' to which they apparently belonged. In other words, minority identification seemed particularly marked. Overevaluation, by minorities of the majority to which they did not belong accentuated their status as exiles. The beginnings here of an explanation require some examination of the meaning of minority identification.

Possible or impossible identification

Majority and minority identities

The study of intergroup relations provides us with some valuable indications about the mode of functioning of majority and minority groups. The tendency to overevaluate the membership group is well established (Tajfel *et al.*, 1971), but it is not universal. Exceptions exist, and these indicate in particular that disfavoured and devalued groups lack the option of construing themselves in such a way as to allow them a positive image of themselves or devaluation of other groups, especially those which are reference groups.

At issue here is the meaning of majority and minority identification (Moscovici and Paicheler, 1978). These vary according to whether group membership is valued or devalued by the members of the group itself and by members of other groups. If a majority group is able to achieve a positive identity, because it is stable, legitimate, valued, or secure, then it will display a courteous, equitable attitude towards other groups. There is no threat to its identity and it can play the enlightened party. In a similar situation, minority groups, weaker by virtue of their small numbers, are inclined to be closed, to value themselves and devalue others, and assertively to exaggerate distinctiveness. Majority groups with less stable, legitimate or valued identities also tend to emphasise distinctiveness. This seems to be a defensive attitude; they close ranks and try to increase the difference between themselves and others, the only obvious mark of their threatened superiority. Minority groups devalued by others have a tendency to devalue themselves as well. They are genuinely in a deviant position, a burden with which they must come to terms.

Fear of difference

Rejection of minority influence arises from a fear of being different. Individuals or groups seek to avoid the threat of being categorised as deviant. What is perceived to be most salient about a minority is its difference and not the content of its arguments. Its arguments are accorded meaning first in terms of the minority position they occupy, not in terms of what they express. If individuals or groups openly adopted the perspective advocated by this minority, they would at the same time risk being identified with, and identifying themselves with, the minority. They possess neither the conviction nor the determination that would allow them to claim this difference. Rejection of the minority point of view is, initially, the only way of remaining within normative limits, though this does not mean that subjects remain totally impermeable to less direct minority influence, as research on delayed influence shows.

Individuals generally expect that interactions with others will confront them with opinions little different from their own. When this is likely not to be the case, they either avoid the situation or psychologically prepare themselves for it. If, unexpectedly, they find themselves confronted by individuals who express different points of view, they are all the more prey to uncertainty if the discrepancy is acknowledged. This uncertainty sows seeds of doubt about their own capacity to make judgments.

Divergence from the majority produces efforts at social comparison in which the emphasis is placed on difference versus similarity. It implies an attempt to attend to others rather than attending to the object, as the majority response is a priori taken to be true. Its validation is based on the concordance of responses. It is impossible, initially, to challenge the majority judgment. Thus an interpretation for the occurrence of divergence must be sought in judgment criteria external to the majority. One may begin by asking oneself about one's own difference. The alternative is challenging a deep-rooted representation which postulates an equivalence between majority, right and reason.

To prove the majority judgment false or unworkable, one must have access to criteria other than the criterion of consensus. Given that consensus symbolises truth and thus requires no further verification, this criterion is particularly potent. Hence, escaping from its pull is both socially and psychologically costly. Individuals, as we well know, are often happier agreeing with one another, making judgments which are uniform rather than true, and preferring to be wrong with others than right against them and alone.

In contrast, the minority response immediately seems ambiguous. The difference in response and the persistence of the minority will be attributed to an intention to influence, not to a superior capacity for judgment. Thus to adopt the opinion of the other would be a public acknowledgment of weakness, of an inclination to yield. It is obvious that individuals are going to be reluctant to do this.

The minority's consistency helps to overcome this doubt and encourages reconsideration of the validity of their alternative. The coherence and certainty of their view sets a process of validation in motion, an intense intellectual and perceptual effort to test out the relation between the minority judgment and reality and to try and see or know things as the minority sees or knows them. The minority's assurance arouses curiosity.

One is inclined to try and put oneself in the other's place and understand how it is possible to be this way, not to 'be like everyone else'.

Although this empathic effort makes the other appear less different, it also initiates a process of rejection. One feels more threatened by the possibility of identification with the other if he becomes more accessible. To think like the other is to become like the other, to be included in a general representation of the other, a symbolism of otherness which entails discrimination, guilt, projection and rejection.

We can now better appreciate why minority influence is so difficult to exercise during the course of interaction and becomes so much easier once the danger of being categorised as deviant declines. The other's response, no longer threatening, carries information useful to the construction of one's own judgment. Transformation of one's own response in the direction of the minority response no longer has the appearance of incompetence or submission. In the absence of the influencer, the attribution of an intention to influence is reduced and so loses its constraining implications.

Removal of resistance

The latent dimension of minority influence is now well established. The next step is to test out the mechanisms. These are likely to be organised around the defence mechanisms of individuals or groups exposed to this influence. Subjects' resistance to minority influence is greater if they reject identification with the source of influence. This resistance is translated into a modification of latent responses, without the subject being aware of it. If it were possible to reduce the intensity of the conflict aroused by the discrepancy in responses and by the deviant quality of one set of responses, for example by reducing resistance to the minority response, a resolution might then be achieved on the manifest or public level. Subjects might then yield to influence publicly and make immediate concessions.

With this in mind, Moscovici and Doms (1982) introduced, in a variant of the experiment using the after-image effect, a sensory deprivation condition. Let us clarify first what sensory deprivation is. It involves conditions of isolation; the individual is immobilised and his visual and tactile sensations are reduced. His auditory perception is altered through acoustic isolation, in practice by white noise. Sensory deprivation lasting several days induces perceptual disturbances, modification of perceptual and cognitive thresholds, learning difficulties and emotional problems, rendering the individual more vulnerable. In extreme cases, there may be anxiety, distress, irritability and a dissociation of the personality to the point of psychosis, reduced only with difficulty after cessation of the sensory deprivation. Sensory isolation can enable a more effective manipulation of individuals and has often been used as a subtle form of torture.

Research on sensory deprivation suggests that subjects deprived of auditory or visual input react to influence attempts in a manner analogous to hypnotised subjects. Like hypnotic suggestion, sensory isolation effects a lowering of resistance.

The experiment by Moscovici and Doms was similar to the Moscovici and Personnaz experiment except for one small detail: it included a sensory deprivation phase. After the first phase of private responding and following distribution of the fictitious response percentages, which differentiated subjects and confederates as majority or minority, they were placed two at a time for forty-five minutes in complete darkness, as the experimenter informed them, 'in order to eliminate any possible effects of the initial colour perceptions'. Then followed the influence phase and the two post-test phases.

Very marked effects were immediately apparent at the level of overt influence during the interaction, particularly in the condition in which the subject was paired with a 'majority' confederate. Following the interaction, the percentage increase in influenced responses was comparable in the majority and minority conditions (see Figure 5.1). Overall, more influence was apparent if subjects' resistance had been reduced by sensory deprivation.

Influence at the latent level was weaker than in the experiment by Moscovici and Personnaz. The conversion was effectively cancelled out by the occurrence of explicit influence. In a more refined analysis of the data, the authors were able to demonstrate interesting differences between subjects publicly influenced by the minority source and those who resisted.

Those who were so influenced showed no modification in perception of the after-image, continuing to perceive the colour complementary to blue. In contrast, subjects who were not influenced were more inclined to perceive the colour of the after-image as closer to that complementary to green.

When the influence source was majority, the after-image effects were less marked. However, subjects who rejected overt influence and stuck with the blue judgment perceived the after-image as closer to the complementary to pure blue as the projected slide was closer to a turquoise blue. It seemed to be a case of counter-influence in subjects who had rejected any expression of submission.

This experiment creates conditions in which overt influence in response to a consistent minority is accentuated while latent influence is inhibited. Sensory deprivation achieves the desired effect; it lifts the barriers against

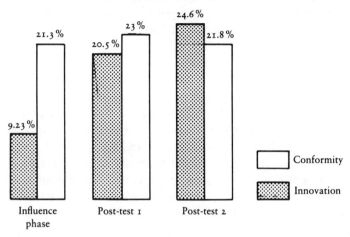

Frequency of green responses

Figure 5.1: Measures of overt influence

exercise of overt minority influence by attenuating the conflict that leads to rejection of identification with the minority.

Minority proximity
Individuals or groups will resist direct minority influence more strongly if they perceive themselves as close to the minority. They are more conscious of the possibility of influence and all the more resistant to any explicit association with the minority. The closer the minority, the more vital it becomes to invest energy in differentiating oneself from it, and the more imperative it becomes to treat it with disdain, against the risk of being confused with it. Such censure on direct influence could result instead in the occurrence of indirect influence.

An experiment by Aebischer, Hewstone and Henderson (1984) clearly illustrates this mechanism. It concerned changes in the musical tastes of adolescents. Among the forms of musical expression in vogue, the authors selected three: 'hard rock', 'new wave' and 'contemporary'. The great majority of young people preferred 'hard rock'. But despite this almost universal preference, several among them were susceptible to 'new wave' and 'contemporary' music, which are similar in their sound and harmonic qualities.

The aim of the experiment was to subject adolescents to influence so as to modify their musical choice, rendering them less favourable to 'hard rock' and more so to 'new wave'. According to whether they resisted explicit influence, the manipulation could produce either an overt change or latent effects. The demonstration of an indirect influence could be managed by testing preferences for 'contemporary' music, similar to 'new wave' music but not the object of explicit influence.

Throughout the experiment, the subjects hear pieces of music two at a time, indicating their preference for one or the other. One is always a fragment of 'hard rock', the other, depending on the phase of the experiment, either a piece of 'new wave' or of 'contemporary' music.

The experiment was conducted in three phases. The first was the pre-test phase. Subjects listened to musical extracts and made comparisons of twelve pairs: six of 'hard rock-new wave' and six of 'hard rock-contemporary'. If in the first series of comparisons they expressed a preference only once for 'new wave', they were defined as 'pervious'. If they expressed more than one such preference they were eliminated from the experiment. If they expressed no preferences at all for this music they were defined as 'impervious'.

The second phase was the influence phase. Subjects made comparisons of six pairs of extracts or 'hard rock' and 'new wave'. The subjects were junior high school pupils. During this phase for each comparison of musical extracts and before they responded, they were given fictitious information about the preferences of other subjects. They were told that an inquiry had been carried out on the musical preferences of junior high school pupils like themselves (a majority source), or on technical college pupils (a minority source). The technical college pupils have a lower status that the junior high school pupils. To be attending a technical college is a mark of failure and they constitute a kind of social minority. The information given the subjects was as follows: they were told that the fragment of 'new wave' music was preferred by 80% either of junior high school or technical college pupils. The information was contrary to their own preference. Finally, influence was 'strong' if all six 'new wave' exstracts appeared to have been preferred by other pupils and 'weak' if the 'new wave' extracts had been preferred in three cases out of six.

The third phase was the phase of indirect influence. Subjects made comparisons of six 'hard rock-contemporary' pairs.

The 'pervious' subjects were in general less sensitive to direct influence than the 'impervious' subjects. It is likely that the first were more protected against what they perceived as an attempt at influence, while the latter were more likely to feel the attraction of a new opinion. Consistency, in the 'strong' influence condition, appeared overall more effective in producing direct influence. And it was particularly effective if the influence source was minority. The resistance of the 'pervious' subjects was confirmed by the results for indirect influence which was greatest for this type of subject. Finally, the minority exercised more influence overall than the majority.

These results point to open resistance by subjects close to the minority, who refuse to be compared with it. Conflict is never greater than when individuals or groups from which one wishes to remain distinct get too close. This is when efforts at differentiation are at their strongest, and at the slightest hint of danger barriers are erected against access by the minority, or indeed access to the minority. If, for example, the racism of poor whites is so virulent, it is because the disadvantaged whites are so close, socially, economically, and ecologically, to the blacks.

Delayed influence

Minority influence does not always produce an obviously overt effect. Nor is any effect necessarily immediate. Each of us can probably think of examples in our own daily lives of the following psychological mechanism: it sometimes happens that we consciously and indeed forcefully reject an opinion, form of behaviour, or fact which nonetheless surreptitiously insinuates itself until we accept it so completely that we are no longer able to recognise its external origins. Jacquard (1982) gives a nice example of this reaction.

> One morning, having, without any apparent cause, developed an idea, in truth a very fine and to my mind particularly original idea, I was feeling 'very clever'. In the afternoon I couldn't resist the pleasure, at the end of a meeting at work, of announcing this fundamental new truth to various colleagues; instead of the expected compliments, one responded with a mocking smile. 'Do you not find this idea interesting?' 'Yes, certainly, but it figures centrally in my thesis.' I had eighteen months earlier been part of the examining panel; I removed my copy of his thesis from my library at the earliest opportunity; rapidly, we found the passage expressing 'my' idea almost word for word; in the margin I had noted 'no, wrong'. (p. 88)

We frequently forget the origin of an idea completely while remembering its content. We may regard an idea or opinion first suggested by others as the product of our own thought. This again is a latent influence mechanism. It has been demonstrated in numerous studies of attitude change, and American researchers have shown a great deal of interest in an analogous effect which they have labelled in vivid fashion the 'sleeper effect'. Initially there is a rejection of the source (individual, group, medium...) from which the message (opinion, behaviour, information...) derives. The emitter seems to lack credibility, or for some reason or other one is disinclined to believe it. Then when sufficient time has elapsed the message and its source become dissociated; the message has registered but its origins are forgotten. In accepting it now, one no longer experiences any risk of being identified with its source. Time has got the better of the defence mechanism and it ceases to be a barrier to influence.

It is possible to link this effect to diffusion of minority innovations. Such innovations meet obstacles and resistances, some of which are associated with unwillingness to be identified with the minority. Moscovici, Mugny and Papastamou (1981) have attempted to track down delayed minority influence experimentally.

In an initial phase, subjects completed an attitude scale concerned with problems of pollution. Items on this scale were of the following type:

Households are deeply implicated; they make inconsiderate use of the most polluting products such as cleaning products or other detergents or *Supermarkets and manufacturers of chemical fertilisers have combined to adulterate natural products.*

Hence, these items attribute responsibility for pollution either to individual acts committed by *determinate social categories* (women, motorists, peasants) or to *industrial groups or companies.* Subjects evaluated each item on a seven-point scale from 'valid' to 'invalid'.

The distinction between social categories and industrial groups was based on the fact that dominant conservationist arguments treat selfishness and individual unawareness as causes of pollution while an innovative minority argument claims that it is industrial groups which cause the most pollution and which pose the greater threat to natural balances, sacrificing everyone's well-being and health in the pursuit of profit. As for the subjects in the experiment, they had no well-entrenched opinions at the start; they attributed responsibility for pollution as much to individual selfishness as to the pursuit of commercial profit.

The influence phase took place a week later. The experimenters informed the subjects, with the aim of influencing them, about the 'answers' given by other groups. The source of influence was of course fictitious; it was either a government commission (majority source) or a marginal ecology group (minority source). These appeared to have responded to the same attitude scale as the subjects to whom 'their responses' were transmitted. In each case, their responses were extreme and uncompromising; the majority source attributed responsibility for pollution to social categories, the minority source to industrial concerns. The transmission of these responses must clearly have appeared to the subjects as a constraint, an explicit attempt to exert influence, and in consequence should have brought about a reaction by the subjects against this pressure. Let us recall that in the 'sleeper effect', influence is initally rejected. To test this the experimenters had the attitude scale completed a second time with respect to those questions to which the responses of either the government commission or the marginal ecology group had been provided.

Subjects were also given the text of an argument 'drawn up' by the majority or minority source of influence. This text proposed a certain number of measures to check pollution. These measures would be taken against either the social categories or the industrial concerns. They were either *rigid*, recommending severe repression, or *flexible*, recommending the use of inducement, information and persuasion.

The experiment consisted of two similar post-test phases. The subjects filled out an attitude scale on the subject of pollution, just after the influence phase and then three weeks later. It should be added that this attitude scale consisted either of items *directly* linked to the argument of the influence source or *indirect* items, that is, items dealing with the same problems touched on in the first questionnaire and in the text but in different terms.

An examination of Figure 5.2, indicates that there were strong influence effects in the second phase. Providing subjects with the responses of the influence source clearly operated as a constraint which was translated into compliant behaviour both in the majority and the minority influence conditions. This pressure was much more apparent here than in the first post-test where influence was weaker in all the conditions and even weaker on the indirect items than the direct items. For the indirect items, there is even a modest counter-influence when the source is a majority. The subjects appeared to have reacted negatively to an influence that was too obvious and thus one they felt too constrained by.

The delayed influence effect, in the second post-test, is particularly clear on the indirect items. There is a marked contrast here between the results reflecting latent minority effects and those reflecting majority compliance effects. The majority source produces a substantial counter-influence while the rigid minority produces a positive influence. This latter effect is attributable to the explicit conflict and opposition aroused by confrontation with a source of influence which is both minority and rigid.

Subjects confronted with a minority influence remember well enough three weeks later that it was a minority. By contrast, when the source of influence had been majority, they recall its characteristics less clearly. Thus their recall of the surprising information is better. On the other hand, what time erases is the conflict aroused by a blunt and coercive confrontation with a rigid minority. It seems clear that consciously, the subjects reject identification with the rigid minority source and, according to the authors, do so for two reasons.

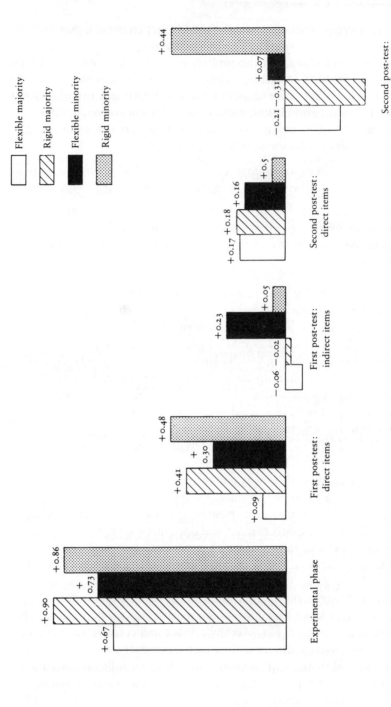

Figure 5.2: Mean changes in opinion (on a seven-point scale; a positive sign indicates positive influence)

Flexible majority

Rigid majority

Flexible minority

Rigid minority

Experimental phase

+0.67

+0.90

+0.73

+0.86

First post-test: direct items

+0.09

+0.41

+0.30

+0.48

First post-test: indirect items

−0.06

−0.02

+0.23

+0.05

Second post-test: direct items

+0.17

+0.18

+0.16

+0.5

Second post-test: indirect items

−0.21 −0.31

+0.07

+0.44

160

First there is a lack of ideological agreement between subjects and source; it was seen in this experiment how subjects had incorporated the dominant ideology regarding pollution which holds individual selfishness responsible, something to which the minority was radically opposed. On the other hand, recognition of the minority nature of the source induces in subjects mechanisms of stigmatisation, which in particular entail negative connotations of the minority. (Moscovici, Mugny and Papastamou, 1981, p. 217)

Once the danger of too blatant an identification had passed, subjects were all the more influenced by a minority message that was clear and intransigent.

Conclusion

In the attitude domain, in the domain of prejudices, and in the domain of social influence we are confronted with the same contradiction. If we attribute a strictly rational approach to individuals, it is difficult to reconcile ourselves with the fact that there is a discontinuity between what is said and what is done, between what a person thinks and how he acts. This hiatus is not perceived by individuals so that in extreme cases, though still in all good faith and conscience, they will assert such enormities as: 'I am not a racist, but I don't like the...' The road to hell is paved with good intentions that we fail to act upon.

Such disjunctions occur with constant regularity in every area of social life. It is clear that our systems for the explanation of action must incorporate ambiguities and contradictions, for if they do not they are nothing more than the stiffened veneer of a mask on the face of a ceaselessly mobile reality.

The findings from research on influence represent an increasingly coherent and complete pattern. The importance of majority influence we have always known about. It was necessary to look beyond its too familiar presence and identify its limits. Now, the extremes of majority influence are to be found in the phenomena of compliance, in circumstances where, whatever is felt, heads must be bowed, mortifications endured, and revolt postponed sometimes until the impulse is so changed that it never happens. In our submission we come to forget both our revolt and our reason for revolt, while the gestures we make in taking on the behaviour forced upon us come to convince us of its sure foundations. And we create for ourselves a comfortable, undisturbed world, but it is a world of resignation, of stifled aspirations and crushed revolts, all meekly executed by ourselves.

But minority influence can arrive unexpectedly and in the nick of time to generate turmoil and change. The emphasis given to the determinants,

161

effects and manifestations of latent influence has allowed enlargement of the investigation and establishment of effects.

Throughout this sometimes complex account, through the multiple interrelations that we have tried to clarify, we have made various references to the inferences that subjects make about their relationships with others, with themselves and with the situation. Expressed in more mundane terms, we have followed numerous other authors in advancing hypotheses about what is going on in the subjects' heads, and about the way in which what goes on in their heads is linked to the influence situation, and the manner in which their immediate conditions of life are incorporated within a more general social context.

We must now go further in this direction, and try to move beyond propositions which, even if coherent, do not constitute irrefutable proofs. To this end we shall now describe some research whose object has been to manipulate the meaning of different aspects of the influence situation directly.

6   Two-way influence

Thirty years on

During the last decade there has been much debate about the issue of experimentation in social psychology. The artificiality of the situations and their distance from reality have been criticised. Henri Tajfel (1972) questioned the validity of results from experiments conducted in a 'social vacuum'. This vacuum is perhaps two-fold: the emptiness of the experimental situation as compared to a concrete social context, and the vacuum attributed to subjects regarding their repertoire of representations, cognitions and interpretations. The essence of this vacuum consists in regarding the subject as a 'black box', a container of impressions only of those elements introduced by the experimenter in his paradigm. Sherif and Sherif (1968) unwittingly underlined the irony and discontinuity entailed in speaking of attitudes and attitude change when asking subjects to estimate the number of beans contained in a jar. It is obvious that some processes can only be brought to light or adequately understood by operating within a context of rigorous experimentation which requires that the situation be considerably simplified, literally purged. But this effort at rigour should not also substitute for reflection upon the social phenomenon one proposes to study.

Replication of a major experiment can give some perspective on the possibilities and limits of investigations in social psychology. We are of the opinion that this discipline cannot aim to demonstrate universal and immutable laws of collective human behaviour, but only to show the manner in which human sentiments, thoughts and behaviours are shaped by membership in a particular community at a specific moment. What becomes fundamental in this perspective is the ubiquity not of particular modes of functioning but of the way in which immersion in a given society moulds human activities, giving them a meaning which renders them possible, desirable or necessary. Such behaviour does not carry within it a single, universal meaning; it will be interpreted as a function of the contexts and situations in which it appears.

In the same way, influence is located in a context which gives it a particular meaning, rendering it possible or even inevitable, or else forming a barrier against it. We will now attempt to demonstrate the various meanings inherent in majority and minority influence.

Oppression and conformity

What has become of Asch's celebrated effect, some thirty years after his first investigation? Is the extreme tendency to conformity which he demonstrated truly universal? Research on minority influence has already shown us that this is not the case. But there is only a single study which, after all this time, has been devoted to the apparently quite straightforward goal of replicating this key experiment. This is the study by Perrin and Spencer (1981).

These authors did not repeat the experiment simply to see what would happen. They worked with very precise hypotheses which they hoped to use the experiment to test. And they made these hypotheses clear at the outset. 'It is argued that the classic Asch studies of conformity may not be universal but rather reflect the historical and cultural state of the USA in the 1950s' (p. 205). The authors were doing nothing less than returning to sources, and specifically to Asch's initial questions regarding the role of cultural factors in influence. Rather than cultural factors, which in social psychology are so often turned into sterile and meaningless contrasts between individuals of different origins, Perrin and Spencer referred to both the historical and the social context in order to clarify different forms of influence. 'It is our contention that the social and cultural conditions which obtained in the USA and to a lesser extent in Europe, in the 1950s and 1960s, were contributory rather than incidental to the demonstration of the Asch effect' (p. 205).

Since then times have changed. Conformity is more difficult to demonstrate today than it was in the fifties in the United States, in the heart of the period of McCarthyism's ascendance. At least, it is likely to be less apparent among contemporary English students than among their American counterparts of thirty years earlier. On the other hand, it should still be apparent among subjects in a disadvantaged or devalued position, for example, among young delinquents on probation if the group of confederates and the experimenter are deputies of the probation service, or else among young blacks when the experimenter is white.

To test their hypothesis, the authors used a simple experimental design, replicating the renowned Asch experiment (1952) with three contrasting populations, British students, delinquents, and young, unemployed West Indians. The students and the West Indians were confronted with a majority of confederates appparently similar to themselves, the delin-

Table 6.1. *The Asch effect: results for difference experimental groups*

	Asch	Larsen (1974)	Perrin and Spencer (1981)		
			Students	Delinquents	Unemployed West Indians
Mean number of errors	4.41	2.17	0	3.25	3.25

quents with a majority of confederates presented as deputies of the probation service. Thus for the last group the 'social costs' of non-conformity were stressed.

Here again, the results exceeded the authors' predictions. The difference between their student sample and that of Asch was so 'striking' that they wondered if the lack of effect among the former was not the result of some kind of bias (see Table 6.1), a possibility contradicted by the post-experimental interviews.

Only the subjects whose circumstances of objective oppression were reinforced by the experimental situation showed any tendency to conform. Perrin and Spencer obtained not the slightest degree of conforming behaviour amongst the students, who nonetheless reported that they had been upset, plagued by doubt, inclined to accept the majority point of view, but had resisted. It seems clear that the style of response to pressures to conform has changed with time. To conform would be to show evidence of 'weakness', 'foolishness', 'stupidity'. We have witnessed an extinction of the tendency to conform, a sign of a very general change in mentality. To conform is no longer to be on the right path, the right side, the side of truth. To be a conformist is to be dull, sheep-like, uncreative. The aspirations that surfaced at the end of the sixties have dealt a decisive blow to the old representation of conformity. Originality and creativity, the pursuit of individual goals, increasingly these are valued more. Desires give much better returns than duty.

Absence of meaning
The article by Perrin and Spencer was followed by a response from Asch (1981) who viewed their results as something of an enigma. To attribute the difference in their results to historical or socio-cultural conditions

seemed plausible but too general. According to Asch, psychology lacks the conceptual or methodological tools for attacking such vast problems.

> Thus, the McCarthy period produced effects vastly more serious and radical than what psychologists could study with their diabolical (but fortunately feeble) procedures. Perhaps it should be acknowledged that phenomena such as personified by McCarthy – not to mention Hitler and Stalin – can be best approached with the powers of the human mind and imagination, assisted by historical understanding, and that the discipline of psychology in its present form lacks the means to confront them. (p. 233)

Undeniably, however, Perrin and Spencer raised an important question, an issue which in one way or another runs throughout social psychology: is it possible to practise anything called 'social' psychology if one does not refer to socio-cultural, historical or ideological contexts? Can we seriously believe, as social psychologists, that the only contexts which permeate our subjects are those we create and manipulate in our laboratories? Even if this were the case, do we have any control over the manner in which subjects are going to decode or interpret these contexts? The heritage of behaviourist individualism is too burdensome: the 'black box' subject, the stimulus-response situation, and directly observable psychological functioning on the level of individual behaviours, a trilogy in which the substantive core of true scientific psychology is concentrated.

Happily this model has become a little dated. It is beginning to spring leaks all over. Even the great figures of social psychology, who could by no stretch of the imagination be accused of unbridled impressionism, now refute it and stress not behaviour but meanings.

> To the degree that the social sciences, particularly political psychology, have applied a methodology conceived within a technical cognitive perspective without discrimination, they have in general neglected the fact that the action of man must be understood by reference to the 'meanings' it possesses for the actors and their audience; the action of man is rooted in the intersubjective contexts of communication, in the intersubjective practices and forms of life which have defined historical meanings. Blind imitation of the technical orientation of the exact and natural sciences has also led a number of specialists in the social sciences to refuse to see the degree to which their theoretical and empirical work, that is to say, their scientific activity, is influenced by the implicit hypotheses, the axiomatic positions, the ideological tendencies and the political and economic perspectives of the circles to which they belong. (Deutsch, 1983, p. 248)

Social anaesthesia

A stress on social meanings, themselves located in their proper historical and cultural contexts, allows an appreciation of the primacy of conformity in the American studies of influence not as the revelation of an absolute scientific truth, but as the operation, in the heart of social psychology, of a general ideological conception. The culminating point in this primacy of conformity was in the 1950s. At that time, conformity was an integral part of the 'American character', governing a general vision of the world.

> In the face of a conspiratorial theory of politics fueled by McCarthy, it became necessary to demonstrate loyalty as an American... In this sense, concern with conformity was part of the *Zeitgeist*... But conformity became interwoven with matters of style of life in a more general sense... And so social scientists joined journalists and other 'opinion leaders'...in creating worries about conformity. (Meyerson, 1979, p. 98)

The tree should not be allowed to conceal the forests. It was only possible for conformity to become so preeminent in this way under McCarthyism because it was overdetermined in the American context ever since the freely consented creation of communities of equal individuals with sole responsibility for themselves.

Bounded thinking

In the nineteenth century, Tocqueville analysed the dialectic tension between equality and freedom and stressed the alienating character of majority rule, ubiquitous and diffuse, and so difficult to evade because it is not embodied in any material reality but infuses minds themselves. 'In America, the majority raises very formidable barriers to the liberty of opinion' (1961, vol. i, p. 310). 'It seems at first sight, as if all the minds of Americans were formed upon one model, so accurately do they correspond in their manner of judging' (*ibid.* p. 314).

Similarity is created at the level of the production of ideas, and this production is in turn shaped by and derived from a particular social logic. There is nothing violent in this subtle form of servitude; it is a necessary product of the forms of thought themselves. 'The excesses of monarchical power had devised a variety of physical means of oppression; the democratic republics of the present day have rendered it entirely an affair of the mind, as that will which it is intended to coerce' (*ibid.*, p. 311). Under the reign of democracy, difference gives rise not to brutal chastisement but to permanent psychological ostracism.

> The sovereign can no longer say, 'You shall think as I do on pain of death', but he says, 'You are free to think differently from me and retain

your life, your property and all you possess; but if such be your determination, you are henceforth an alien among your people... You will remain among men but you will be deprived of the rights of mankind. Your fellow creatures will shun you like an impure being; and those who are most persuaded of your innocence will abandon you too, lest they should be shunned in their turn. Go in peace! I have given you your life but it is an existence incomparably worse than death.' (*Ibid.*, p. 311)

Such rejection, however, remains the exception, for the ascendancy of psychological control closes the door on every expression of idiosyncrasy. 'The Inquisition has never been able to prevent a vast number of anti-religious books from circulating in Spain. The empire of the majority succeeds much better in the United States, since it actually removes the wish of publishing them' (*ibid.*, p. 312), a far more effective result and one achieved with greater economy of means.

Majority rule is based on a universe of meanings shared by all and limiting each to a single interpretation of reality and of his own behaviour. The majority defines the relationship with the real but it does much better than simply expressing its will; it universalises its point of view. Any deviation threatens not only the self-confidence of members of the majority, but reality itself.

Moreover, the explicit meanings of behaviours based on equality and similarity often come to conceal the true direction of majority influence and power. In the service of a substitute reality, the majority forms a screen against all other reality. But it is always necessary to refer to this idea of a screen with the greatest care. It signifies that there exists a reality 'other' than that upheld by the majority.

Now this is relative; it is located elsewhere than in the majority point of view, in other times or other places. But for those who are a part of the majority system of thinking, it is impossible to conceive of this somewhere else. Similarities of viewpoints attest to their validity.

> The moral authority of the majority is partly based upon the notion, that there is more intelligence and more wisdom in a great number of men collected together than in a single individual, and that the quantity of legislators is more important than their quality. Thus theory of equality is in fact applied to the intellect of man. (*Ibid.*, p. 299)

Mild violence
Having noted the 'moral' or ideological ascendancy the majority has over individuals, Tocqueville goes on to consider further consequences of equality. Not only does it result in a closure within the majority group but it also provokes constant anxiety and unending frustration at the indi-

vidual level. Again one of the axioms of the functionalist model of social influence is encountered here, that of uncertainty and the desperate quest for an assurance based in similarity with the greatest number. Tocqueville is more enlightening however because he analyses the origins and the reasons for this uncertainty, locating them at the heart of the relation between the individual and the social.

> It cannot be denied that democratic institutions have a very strong tendency to promote the feeling of envy in the human heart; not so much because they afford to everyone the means of rising to the level of his fellow citizens as because those means perpetually disappoint the persons who employ them. Democratic institutions awaken and foster a passion for equality which they can never entirely satisfy. This complete equality eludes the grasp of the people at the very moment at which it thinks to hold it fast, and 'flies', as Pascal said, 'with eternal flight'; the people is excited in the pursuit of an advantage which is more precious because it is not sufficiently remote to be unknown, or sufficiently near to be enjoyed. The lower orders are agitated by the chance of success, they are irritated by its uncertainty; and they pass from the enthusiasm of pursuit to the exhaustion of ill-success, and lastly to the acrimony of disappointment. (*Ibid.*, p. 230)

The pursuit of this impossible equality creates an anxious society in which one is unceasingly reminded of what must not be done, while remaining unclear as to what is desirable. The consequence of this is a turning in on oneself, a search for refuge in individualism, a disengagement or flight from, and indifference to, the public sphere. 'It must be acknowledged that inequality, which brings great benefits into the world nevertheless suggests to men ... some very dangerous propensities. It tends to isolate them from each other, to concentrate every man's attention upon himself' (Tocqueville, 1961, vol.ii, p.25).

An egalitarian society produces temperance, a moderation enhanced by the fact that it is sustained through a set of minute and diffuse powers against which resistance is virtually impossible. The well-being it procures is in proportion to the undefinable anxieties it arouses. The uniformity it generates is hardly attractive; no stirring grand designs but minor objectives to be completed each day.

> I do not assert that men living in democratic communities are naturally stationary; I think, on the contrary that a perpetual stir prevails in the bosom of those societies and that rest is unknown there; but I think that men bestir themselves within certain limits beyond which they hardly ever go. They are for ever varying, altering, and restoring secondary

matters; but they carefully refrain from touching what is fundamental. (*Ibid.*, p. 306)

There is no longer here any harsh power or authority against which one struggles or is broken, but a softer form which deadens all revolt, enmeshing it in a multitude of insignificant habits and unconscious consents, a power which is 'minute, regular, provident, and mild' (*ibid.*, p. 381), 'not fierce or cruel, but minute and meddling' (*ibid.*, p. 166).

Similarity and moderation facilitate the coincidence of general and particular interests, the convergence of one's own well-being with the general well-being. Here again, the little compromises, the little controls create the greater social stability.

The principle of interest rightly understood produces no great acts of self-sacrifice, but it suggests daily small acts of self-denial. By itself it cannot suffice to make a man virtuous, but it disciplines a number of citizens in habits of regularity, temperance, moderation, foresight, self-command; and if it does not lead men straight to virtue by the will, it gradually draws them in that direction by their habits. (*Ibid.*, p. 147)

Equality, the anxiety it creates, the isolation it implies, the multiple and miniscule moral manipulations it effects, result in social uniformity by means which individuals do not even suspect.

Men who are equal in rights, in education, in fortune, or, to comprise all in one word, in their social condition, have necessary wants, habits and tastes which are hardly dissimilar. As they look at objects under the same aspect, their minds naturally tend to analogous conclusions; and though each of them may deviate from his contemporaries and form opinions of his own, they will *involuntarily and unconsciously* concur in a certain number of received opinions. (*Ibid.*, pp. 309-10; my italics)

Tocqueville's analysis stresses the psychological forces associated with a social system. These provide him with the basis for his explanation of the interindividual similarities he observed in the United States in the nineteenth century. They are of two types: psychological forces internal to individuals which incline them quite 'naturally' to seek after conformity so as to assure and reassure themselves that they are indeed similar and thus equal to others; and psychological forces emanating from a group of equals and tending to nip all dissidence in the bud.

Now the causal chains described by Tocqueville are treated not as natural facts – such as, for example, the need to reduce uncertainty – but as sociological observations in which the psychological appears dialectically as a consequence and reinforcer of the social order.

We often speak today of 'pressures for conforming', without thinking much about what creates them; Tocqueville's analyses of ambition and egalitarian passions were a dissection of the origin of these pressures, and his conclusion was that they arise not out of the smugness of those seeking to make others conform, but out of their very need to validate the meaning of their individual frustration and their sense that nothing is ever enough. (Sennett, 1979, p. 121)

Now, this frustration flows precisely from their membership of an egalitarian system of rights.

The myth of fusion

Tocqueville considered democracy and equality as acquired facts in the society he observed. Nonetheless, questions can be raised about the reality of this equality and one may ask whether it has actually been achieved. One consequence of the individualised and individualising control on which conformity rests is that it diverts people's attention from the reality of social relations, providing them with a limited interpretation, and stifling all public and political claims through an emphasis on private life.

Sennett (1979) stresses that there is not the slightest necessity that equality exist in practice for the effects described by Tocqueville to come about. He adds a supplementary level to the analysis of the meanings found in an egalitarian society. Even if equality does not exist in practice, the determining factor is that individuals believe it exists and act as if it does indeed exist. 'People behave as if they were equal in condition. If, in fact, they do not move roughly within the same band of action or at least form part of the same action in order to feel that they belong to a common social order, they change their tastes, habits and outlook to appear as if they did' (p. 123).

One now understands better why appearances, the surface of things and actions, occupy such a place in conformity. The important thing is to regard oneself as similar and to appear similar to others. This objective takes precedence over everything else: finding a basis for similarity and identifying those characteristics of objects about which one agrees. The result is that social relations, conflicts and interests are obscured, and emphasis is shifted to individual effort and responsibility.

For Tocqueville, the consequence of dissatisfaction, envy and anxiety, aroused by the conditions of egalitarian life – or life perceived as such – is that individuals no longer wish to involve themselves in social affairs but desire instead to be disengaged from them. But if they turn away from social affairs, the latter nonetheless permanently impinge upon them, structuring their understanding of reality, substantially by masking and distancing them from its objective characteristics. Egalitarian, conformist ideology works effectively even when the material conditions generate inequality. Sennett (1979) argues that egalitarian ideology produces a two-fold process.

> Challenges to the structures of inequality are deflected in a gross manner by the illusion that 'fundamentally' everyone is the same. They are deflected in a more subtle way by the induction of an individualist mentality in the members of society so that they conceive of the responsibility for gratification and personal development as an individual matter, one that plunges them into an unending, restless search. (p. 132)

The causal links developed by Sennett are certainly not so direct, from egalitarian illusion to individualism. We have already considered how the development of individualism in Protestant sects, promoting solitary dialogue with God and responsibility for personal salvation, was integrated with the foundation myths of America, generating egalitarianism and conformity.

By emphasising the mythical character of conceptions of equality and community, Sennett wished to demonstrate that the social sciences must move beyond the level of appearances, or the way actors discuss their condition, if they are to shed light on the discontinuity between beliefs and facts. But there is an additional point that we must not lose sight of: in the final analysis, collective beliefs themselves constitute the facts. 'What modern researchers have uncovered, particularly in affluent cities and suburban areas, is that men frame for themselves a belief in emotional cohesion and shared values with each other that has little to do with their actual experiences together' (Sennett, 1970, p. 32).

For Sennett, the social relationship experienced is in terms of belief and this belief is based on error. But the fact that everyone makes the same error at the same time converts collective error into social reality. This mythical social reality suffers no contradiction, precisely because of its relative fragility.

> The feeling of common identity is a counterfeit of experience. People speak of their mutual understanding and of the common ties that bind them, but the images are not true to their actual relations. But the lie they have formed as their common image is a usable falsehood – a myth – for the group. Its use is that it makes a coherent image of the community as a whole; people draw a picture of who they are that binds them all together as one being with a definite set of desires, dislikes and goals. The image of the community is purified of all that might convey a

feeling of difference, let alone conflict, in who 'we' are. In that way, the myth of community solidarity is a purification ritual. (*Ibid.*, p. 36)

Such a communal ideological construction is only stable if all individuals are perceived as alike with respect to their most mundane, anodyne activities, even if there is no real equality among them. The resulting conformity is not a process of passive manipulation, in which individuals are the victims, nor a process of blind obedience from which they derive no pleasure. This description would be far too flattering. Individual consent to conformity is on the contrary an active psychological process in which the compensation for submission is the petty power that similarity permits one to exercise over others, to keep them on the straight and narrow as defined by the social group. 'When the desire for communal sameness is understood as the exercise of powers developed in everyday life rather than as the fruit of some abstract culture called "the system" or "mass culture", it is inescapable that the people involved in this desire for coherence actively seek their own slavery and self-repression' (*ibid.*, p. 40).

The myth of a community of similar individuals is an act of censure against the self, rendered acceptable because it is accompanied by a similar censure of everyone else. What this vision of society effectively produces is unity against differentiation and rejection; it simultaneously represents both a totality and a referent. The reassuring feeling of unity in practice ensures non-differentiation in two ways, first by a subjective equalisation and second by a simplification both of the object and of the social group. It is as if the mechanism which produces and results in this feeling of unity was a necessary and sufficient social objective in a group of 'similar individuals'.

The stress on unity tends to mask social relationships, exclude conflicts and obscure differences. Ultimately, it imposes a binary division on the social world, a simple and simplifying partition that takes several parallel and equivalent forms: legitimate-illegitimate; positive-negative; similarity-difference; sense-nonsense; etc.

This division may be symbolised by the majority's opposition to the minority such that the majority is presented as the group and the minority the out-group. The latter is identified with rejection and the threatening spectre of differentiation. It represents a dangerous idiosyncrasy, not only to the majority but to the entire social system.

All forms of rationalism postulate *good sense*, a *sensu communis*, a reason identical in every human. But this 'every' does not strictly include every specific case. In the best scenario it holds only for the *majority* and always leaves a *minority* to one side. It offers not a genuinely transcendental position... but only a conformist, average, popular position...

Two-way influence

Humanity divides itself in two, on the one side the mass of those content
to be no more than replicas of a model, examples of the rule, and on the
other side, inevitably excluded in any claim to unanimity, the minority
of eccentric, or as one also says, 'singular' (in the sense of *uncommon*),
cases. (Descombes, 1979, pp. 184-5)

Community of thought

The effectiveness of any influence – whether it involves suggestion,
conformity or innovation – works through a fusion of influencer and
influenced. This unity involves shared representations more or less dis-
placed from the reality to which they refer.

All explicit influence implies a community of thought between influencer and influenced, knowing and sharing in the same social codes. We
have analysed extensively the mechanisms relating to normalising conformity. The sharing of myths located within a well-established world
view – such as the myth of equality – underlies any given influence just as
much as does being part of any more transitory and specific contexts.
Taking these basics into account enables a more rigorous analysis and a
better understanding of the influence processes at work.

In our discussion of suggestion we referred to the work of Mandrou
(1968), who quite explicitly subtitled his book 'an analysis of historical
psychology'. He was able to highlight the extent to which the study of
possession and the reactions to which it gave rise depended on studies of
the representations current in the historical periods in which they occurred. These representations may themselves have been related to the
religious beliefs and social practices with which they were concurrent.
Suggestion emerged in the context of essentially asymmetrical power
relations, and unshakeable beliefs in the existence of irrational or inexplicable phenomena, phenomena which everyday experience could only
confirm, and finally in the context of an archaic dependence of the subjects
of suggestion on the manipulators of suggestion. This type of influence
functions on and relies upon consent; the subjects offer no resistance and
no criticism, in effect no rational objection.

Consistency with variable meanings

Contrasting representations

Compared to suggestion and conformity, two highly effective forms of
influence though contrasting in meaning, minority influence proceeds by
rather contradictory routes. Here again, social meanings and the possibility of sharing them are the conditions that determine the possibility of

influence. However, matters are complicated by the fact that influence can operate at the latent level, even when it is consciously rejected. An experimental procedure will help us analyse and understand the processes at work on the semantic levels of minority influence.

Let us begin by positing as a fundamental proposition that majority and minority influence are based on quite different processes of representation, or forms of understanding, of reality. We have already seen how these two types of influence differ in their development, in the conflicts they arouse, and in the depth of their effects.

It has been demonstrated that a disagreement with the majority leads individuals to focus their attention on those with respect to whom they differ, while a disagreement with a minority leads them to give more attention to the object of judgment. One study provides some additional clarification by demonstrating experimentally that the fact of being majority or minority and simultaneously of being opposed to a minority or a majority activates different sets of representations. Guillon and Personnaz (1983) used a quasi-natural group discussion and conflict situation. Subjects discussed abortion in groups of four. These groups included either a majority (three) or a minority (one) of confederates who consistently maintained a position critical of abortion. The discussion was recorded on videotape. Immediately after the discussion, subjects viewed the videotape in ten-and-a-half minute segments and indicated what they had thought or felt during each period. The way their accounts developed was analysed using mathematical classification and representation of form theory. The authors were able to establish that,

> faced with a majority, the minority subjects seemed to be so preoccupied with social relationships that they talked only about the links between themselves and the others, seeing the latter in a negative light; when confronted with a minority, the majority subjects, who have no problems of identity in relation to the others, focussed on the content of the minority's argument, on the object that was the source of contention. (p. 76)

In Guillon and Personnaz's experiment, the minority or majority of confederates took up minority positions by opposing abortion, but their stand was also deviant and reactionary. It is hardly surprising that they aroused strong conflict among students generally quite favourable towards abortion, and that they were not in the end very convincing.

Impossible innovation

But innovation itself proceeds by very tortuous routes. The need to provoke a conflict in order to acquire visibility and present issues in new terms has its limits; these include obstruction and expulsion, determined by the capacities for understanding of those to whom innovation is addressed. Consistency, in so far as it constitutes the minority's behavioural style, will itself be interpreted in terms that vary according to the location and content of what is defended. There is a positive feedback between rejection of influence and the categorisation of minority action as rigid, obstinate and even mad.

Thirty years before Pasteur, in 1847, Semmelweis, a Hungarian doctor working in Vienna, discovered the mechanism by which infections are transmitted. More precisely, he described the process without ever identifying the fundamental causal agent, microbes. Instead he talked of 'miasmas', or 'particles in decomposition'. Perhaps only thirty years before Pasteur but in other respects light-years earlier, this passionate doctor struggled valiantly to reduce the mortality of women in childbirth, a scourge which seemed to cause little concern to the obstetricians of his epoch; they were more concerned with anatomy than therapeutic improvements.

Semmelweis learned his craft from an obstetrician practising in the homes of a rich and private clientele who were accustomed to giving birth in clean, perfumed sheets. This exemplary practitioner claimed that childbirth is a normal process in which, as far as practical, nature should be allowed to take its course without constant internal medical examinations; he achieved excellent results, eliminating considerable suffering.

Upon becoming an obstetrician, Semmelweis worked in the First Maternity at the Vienna hospital where medical students learned childbirth techniques, the Second Maternity being reserved for students of midwifery. Maternity departments generally were not in the least bit inviting at the time. Antiquated, dirty, poorly ventilated and badly maintained, they mainly gave shelter to destitute women who were unable to give birth at home but also served as a sanctuary for all manner of needy people. But the First Maternity at Vienna was particularly terrifying; mortality through infection or puerperal fever was as high as 33% of all pregnancies while it was 'only' 9% in the Second Maternity.

Semmelweis was deeply distressed by this appalling slaughter, by the terror of the women in childbirth who even during labour would try to flee this deadly maternity ward. Having observed the excellent results of his first master, he thought it was his duty to understand and try to reduce this mortality. Supposing that the sickness could be detected in the bodies of the deceased, he threw himself into a frantic inquiry, undertaking numerous autopsies of women dead from puerperal fever. In vain. Not only did he find nothing but the mortality increased during the course of his duties. Then one of his medical friends, following an autopsy examination, also died of puerperal fever. Semmelweis had the first element of his explanation: contact with the 'miasmas' of cadavers with open wounds produced the infection because these 'miasmas' remained on the hands of doctors and students who then passed without changing from the autopsy rooms to the confinement rooms. He then discovered that puerperal fever could be caused by 'the putrid miasmas of suppurations and infections in general' (Thuillier, 1982, p. 149). As a consequence of this discovery doctors and midwives were required to wash their hands carefully between each examination or birth and after autopsies, and disinfect them with a suitable solution.

This discovery was to be Semmelweis's downfall. It had practically no influence on his colleagues, who saw in it nothing but the whim of a disturbed man; they ridiculed him. He tried to gather more evidence, examined hundreds of cases and records, drew attention to the excellent results he obtained...to no avail. At best he was heeded politely by people who nonetheless took care not to change their habits. He even had trouble in getting the sheets properly washed. His career was compromised.

Convinced that he had found the truth, he tried desperately to communicate the fact. He wrote a long treatise on puerperal fever, the preface to which began as follows:

> It could be considered evidence of my aversion to polemics that I have never answered the numerous attacks of my adversaries. It is because I believed that truth speaks for itself. I believed that what I had found was so evident that my discovery would come to the attention of the entire world and that there would be no further need to say or write more about it. For thirteen years I have seen no progress among my adversaries, who have sacrificed so much human life through ignorance, and now I feel myself responsible for all these useless deaths. I must reveal the truth. (Thuillier, 1982, p. 239)

He distributed this book all over Europe. Again in vain. Instead, cabals were formed against him; his efforts were dismissed in a peremptory phrase; he was mocked. His clients did certainly have confidence in him and he even practised in the Hungarian royal court. But the lives he saved were as nothing beside all those which could have been saved simply by the washing of hands.

His irritation grew. He became angry, insulted his colleagues, describing them in open letters as assassins. He even had placards posted in Budapest declaring: 'Father of the family! Do you know what you are doing by calling a doctor or midwife to the bedside of your wife in childbirth? You are inviting death into your house and you run a readily avoidable risk for your companion' (Thuillier, p. 274). His rages became excessive, he lost

177

consciousness, he became incoherent and degenerated into madness. He was interned and rapidly died in 1865 of gangrene from a poorly tended wound. Ten years later, the existence of microbes was demonstrated...

Semmelweis's role as precursor had been tragic and almost useless. A hygienic precaution which seems elementary to us, a matter of simple common sense, was not available to doctors of the period; they lacked a theoretical framework which allowed them to assimilate it. His discovery was beyond their understanding and his insistence only hastened his rejection. In his case at least, behavioural consistency had not made innovation possible because it was interpreted negatively as dogmatism, deviance and finally madness. Semmelweis remained trapped within the madness attributed to him, for he was too premature a visionary. 'Semmelweis's madness was the reason of a single man which clashed with the injustice of a reason that was the blind madness of all his colleagues', wrote Thuillier (1982, p. 11).

Relative consistency

Consistency is not sufficient in itself to compel influence. At least as important is the meaning attributed to it. In his initial research, Gabriel Mugny (1982) directed his attention to representations of the behavioural negotiation styles of minorities, manipulating their variability in order to generate 'rigid' or 'flexible' styles. His first experiment led him to suggest that it is not rigidity or flexibility as such which is decisive in the exercise of influence, but the way in which these behaviours are interpreted in different situations. The respective effects of flexible and rigid negotiation are not comparable in quantitative terms; they must be related to a complex organisation of representations producing a stable and uniform social discourse.

Nemeth, Swedlund and Kanki (1974) had already raised the question as to whether consistency is a matter of simple persistent repetition or if it derives its persuasive force from an internal logic. Adopting the blue-green paradigm, they demonstrated that a rigid repetition of responses produces less influence than a consistent response which obeys some principle of systematic variation, even if without foundation. In their experiment, confederates who answered either green or green-blue according to the luminosity of the slide exerted more influence than confederates who systematically answered green.

However, it would clearly be impossible to carry out any systematic investigation of the connotations or representations of behavioural style using a perceptual paradigm of the blue-green type, since one cannot in this situation take into account any particularly significant aspect of ideological functioning. An understanding of the mechanisms of minority influence very rapidly necessitated the use of experimental paradigms involving concrete and contentious social issues, and almost simultaneously several studies appeared which moved in this direction.

From intransigence to intolerance

Mugny's (1982) experimental studies have clarified some of the complex mechanisms involved in accepting or rejecting minority influence. The content of consistent behavioural style, and its social meaning are factors which either facilitate or hinder the progress of minority influence. Mugny has revealed the limits of consistent behaviour as a function of its multiple and sometimes contradictory connotations and representations. He has also demonstrated the effectiveness of some of the ideological barriers against the exercise of minority influence.

Mugny (1982) went on to extend the theory of consistency by locating it within a cluster of factors interrelated by several levels of analysis, intra-individual, interindividual, intergroup, social, and ideological. His objective was to set his studies in a social and historical context. He proceeded on the assumption that the diffusion by a minority of an innovation occurs within a complex social context of change and resistance to change. To understand this process better, he enlarged the model of minority influence to include three elements: established power, the population – which might also be called the masses or the silent majority – and finally, minorities. Between each of these entities are sustained specific and fundamentally different relationships (see Figure 6.1).

These distinctions allow us to conceive the influence relation between minority and population in terms of its deeper connections with the antagonistic relation between minority and power. The minority-population relationship by itself gives rise to study of negotiations between these two entities, essentially in terms of greater or lesser rigidity of style on the part of the minority, but also studies of forms of understanding, or representations, of the minority in the population. We then begin to find that these behaviours and representations take their meaning from the links between these influence relations and the power relations in which the population is embedded. Finally, Mugny demonstrates how differing interpretations may be made of the antagonistic relation between minority and power and how these can lead to widely divergent influence effects.

It has become evident that consistency of behavioural style is necessary but not sufficient for interpretation of minority phenomena. Consistency itself can be differentiated or graduated and so result in more or less acute conflict and hence different styles of conflict negotiation. But the population participates in the ideology disseminated by the institutions of power. It is thus going to be opposed to the alternative minority position. Conflict

Two-way influence

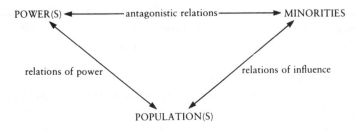

Figure 6.1. Relations between power, population and minority.

is therefore located at the ideological level and influence operates within the framework in which this conflict is negotiated, a negotiation in which the minority will display more or less rigidity or flexibility.

Perceiving the minority behavioural style as rigid will limit and modify influence, forcing it to take more circuitous routes or even eliminating it. A certain flexibility on the other hand can enhance the impact of minority influence. In fact, the effectiveness of each of these types of behaviour, rigidity and flexibility, is a function of minority objectives and of the situation. Flexibility may be less effective than rigidity in as much as very resolute behaviour can bring about delayed influence.

Minority influence is mediated and determined by representations or forms of understanding of the minority by the population. Rigidity clearly enhances an impression of obstructiveness. Obstruction becomes an anchoring point around which other dimensions are organised, and this produces a paradoxical effect: the more acute the effects of rigidity the less consistency is perceived. It induces a categorisation in terms of dogmatism and difference, provoking both rejection and resistance to identification.

Inducing a particular representation of the minority is thus going to determine the nature of the influence it can exercise. Now, fundamentally there exists a strong psychological defence mechanism against minority influence. This mechanism works by obscuring the social relationships between minority, power, and population, isolating minority behaviour as a repellent idiosyncrasy. One already demonstrated example of this is *naturalisation* which consists in undermining the ultimate credibility of a minority source by attributing its actions to natural or naturalised categories. This frequently employed mechanism consists for example in claiming that the inferior educational performance of blacks or women or the Portuguese is attributable to genetically based flaws in brain functioning.

Dogmatism and rigidity

Minority behavioural style is not an immutable given. It is reconstructed

180

by the target population on the basis of certain fundamental criteria, with the result that it either accepts or rejects this influence. For this reason there is no rigidity or flexibility as such. These are the consequences of conflicts which, depending on the situation, cause the population to interpret minority actions either as flexible or as rigid. Rigidity is thus related to the minority's dogmatism and closed-mindedness. Perception in terms of rigidity implies rejection and rejection implies perception in terms of rigidity.

Mugny set out to demonstrate this experimentally. His experiments took the classical form of three phases: pre-test – an initial measurement of attitudes; experimental phase – the influence phase; post-test – second measurement of attitudes. The attitudes at issue in these experiments concerned ecology and minority influence processes at the level of society in general. The attitude questionnaire concerned assignment of responsibilities for pollution. It consisted of twenty propositions which were equally divided between holding industry responsible for pollution and blaming various categories of individuals (housewives, peasants, etc.). Table 6.2 gives four examples of the items, to which subjects responded on seven-point scales from 'valid' to 'invalid'.

The objective of the influence attempt was to convince subjects, who in general thought that social categories and industries were equally to blame, that only industries were culpable and that accusations made against social categories served only to conceal the truly guilty party, namely the politico-economic system. This influence attempt was introduced via a written text, which took up some of the themes in the questionnaire and thus also allowed a distinction between 'direct' items in the questionnaire, those linked directly to the minority case and 'indirect' items which were not so closely related to this case.

In a period in which sensitivity to the pollution issue has grown, it remains true that a position that blames only the politico-economic system and rejects any individual responsibility is very much in the minority, as compared to the powers that be or to the majority, but also compared to movements for the conservation of nature, which themselves tend to emphasise the importance of individual actions.

The text which the subjects read was punctuated with slogans, in heavy type. These slogans varied according to whether the minority was presented as rigid or flexible. The flexible slogans corresponded to a conciliatory position; for example, they suggested imposing damages and fines on polluting industries. The rigid slogans defined an extreme position that would not readily recruit subjects' commitment; for example, they advocated the close-down of polluting factories, or an immediate halt in production.

181

Table 6.2. *Examples of items from the pollution questionnaire*

– The manufacturers of detergents are all the more responsible for continuing to make and promote the sale of products whose harmful effects they are perfectly well aware of.

– By judicious distribution across the country and avoidance of unduly high concentrations, the factories built in the countryside demonstrate an enduring concern to preserve nature.

– How can peasant farmers be blamed when one well knows that they are obliged against their will to employ chemical fertilisers, or else go under.

– The indiscipline of Sunday walkers contributes substantially to the gradual but irreversible deterioration of nature.

The experiment ended with a questionnaire designed to evaluate the image of the minority source on two central dimensions: degree of consistency and degree of flexibility or rigidity. This questionnaire consisted of a list of forty adjectives; ten adjectives involved a positive evaluation in terms of consistency: assured, effective, vigorous, logical, etc.; ten adjectives involved a negative evaluation in terms of inconsistency: confused, irresponsible, inconsistent, superficial, etc.; ten involved a positive evaluation in terms of flexibility: cooperative, open, realistic, sociable, etc.; finally ten involved a negative evaluation in terms of rigidity: authoritarian, stubborn, intolerant, harsh, etc.

In the first experiment to be described here, Mugny expanded a little on the basic experimental design described above. He sought to give a different image (rigid or flexible) to the same text. The text was presented with only the flexible slogans included, and then instead of presenting subjects with the adjective list, they were given fictitious judgments by persons who were supposed to have read the text before them, judgments concerning the authors of the text. In the case of *induced rigidity*, the authors were judged unfriendly, obstinate, harsh, rigid, intolerant, hostile, stubborn, dominating, authoritarian and arrogant. In the case of *induced flexibility*, they were judged sociable, coherent, tolerant, sympathetic, realistic, balanced, agreeable, open, cooperative, and adaptable.

The results were conclusive; experimental induction of different images of the *same text*, either as flexible or rigid, modified the influence effect; it was less if rigidity was stressed. The content as such did not constitute the means for exerting influence in favour of the minority position; it is not so much the nature of the alternative position itself which matters as the perception one is led to have of it as a function of various characteristics of the situation or context.

The importance of the cognitive processes at work, processes of understanding with respect to the situation, had earlier been demonstrated in an experiment by Ricateau (1970). This experiment showed that rigidity runs counter to perception of consistency. In particular it demonstrated the feedback between actual behavioural rigidity and the rigidity revealed on the cognitive level in the forms of understanding of this type of behaviour by subjects. Use of a small number of judgment scales to evaluate another induced the belief that this other himself used few judgment scales and thus few subtleties in his own evaluations.

The originality of Ricateau's experiment lies in the fact that he actually manipulated the rigidity of the forms of understanding of a rigid be-haviour. First, subjects were presented with the case of a young man guilty of a delinquency; a sanction had to be chosen in terms of a scale of punishments from extreme severity to maximum tolerance. The subjects, psychology students, were inclined to favour the more tolerant options. Then began the second phase involving group discussion of the same case; a unanimous recommendation was required. A confederate was present who rigidly defended the most severe position and refused to negotiate; this was also the most unpopular position. He thus obstructed any possibility of negotiation or agreement. The discussion itself was inter-rupted every ten minutes for the subjects to evaluate each of the other group members either on *two*, or *five*, or *eight judgment scales*, each consisting of contrasting adjective pairs of the type: active-passive, realis-tic-romantic, etc. The aim of this manipulation was to induce a form of interpretation of others which was more or less simple or multidimension-al, and thus greater or lesser rigidity in the perception of others. In the same way that pictorial caricatures select and accentuate certain character-istic and salient features, producing an image that derides and ridicules, so also consideration of a reduced number of characteristics in the perception of another produces a deformed representation in which the subject will be particularly inclined to differentiate himself from the other. It was assumed that the less multidimensional the judgment, the more salient obstruction of the negotiation would become and the more resistance to influence would increase. This is exactly what the results of the experiment indicated. As the number of judgment scales increased, so did the influence of the extreme confederate.

Rigidity accentuates conflict and structures perception of minority behaviour. So, by manipulating categorisation, the author succeeded in modifying the influence effect, by accentuating or attenuating rigidity, by attracting or diverting attention from the conflict and the obstruction of negotiation.

Resistant categorisations

Categorisation reduced to simple, clear cut elements, allows emphasis of the idiosyncrasy and peculiarity of the minority position. As a defence mechanism against influence it can take various forms: naturalisation, individualisation, psychologisation... If this is indeed the case, then logically it should suffice to inhibit these mechanisms in order to lower resistance and facilitate minority influence. Such was Mugny and Papastamou's (1980) objective in the experiment we will describe next. The paradigm used is again that of pollution.

The influence-inducing text was presented either with rigid slogans or with flexible slogans. In addition, it was attributed either to one or to two minority sources; in the latter case the text was divided between two parties. The first half was attributed to minority 'A', the second to minority 'B'. The results indicate that a single rigid minority induces less influence than a single flexible minority (Figure 6.2).

In contrast, if the text is attributed to two sources, influence is identical whether they are flexible or rigid. It is thus the unique, individualised character of the source which renders obstructive behaviours salient. Subjects attribute rigid minority positions to an excess of dogmatism; the image perceived comes to explain the minority's behaviour. By presenting two complementary texts derived from two independent sources, not only was perceived rigidity reduced, but it was less plausible to interpret the actions of two minorities in terms of individualised, dogmatic characteristics. Subjects focussed instead on the object of judgment, which appeared to have received two complementary and independent endorsements, instead of focussing on matters tending to define the minority argument as 'peculiar' or different and therefore inadmissible. Individualisation clearly leads the population to interpret oppositional minority positions as detached from an oppositional relationship; such interpretations are based instead on individual characteristics peculiar to the minority.

Psychologisation also deflects the minority's influence. This constituted the central feature of an experiment by Papastamou, Mugny and Kaiser (1982). The experimental manipulation ('psychologisation' versus 'content') was made prior to introducing the text on responsibility for

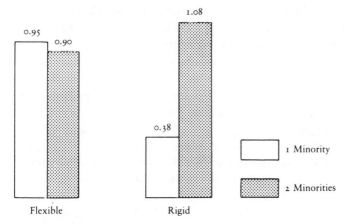

Figure 6.2. Mean influence (indirect items)

pollution. In the 'psychologisation' condition, subjects were informed that they would have to determine the personality traits of the author after reading the text. The instruction was: 'We are interested to know to what degree people manage correctly to evaluate someone's personality on the basis of what he has written.' In the 'content' condition, subjects were induced to focus their attention on the content of the text. The instruction here was: 'We are interested to know how, after reading a text, people manage to synthesise the content so as to summarise its essential elements.'

The experiment was successful in producing a psychologisation effect which suppressed adoption of the minority attitude.

Induction of psychologisation changes nothing in the influence processes set in motion by a rigid source; this tends to confirm that rigidity produces psychologisation in any case, whether or not this aspect is reinforced.

If subjects are led to attend to content, influence is substantially positive, whether with respect to direct or indirect items and whether the source is rigid or flexible. Directing subjects to the content inhibits categorisation of the source either in terms of rigid personality or in minority terms. Thus the act of categorisation leads subjects to reject minority influence.

Another experiment by Mugny and Papastamou (1980) confirms and elaborates on this observation. In this case, though, the pollution paradigm was not used. As in previous cases the experiment was conducted in Switzerland; the attitude questionnaire concerned evaluation of the Swiss national army. Initially the subjects, who were students, were rather unfavourable towards the army. In the first phase of the experiment, individual opinions about the army were evaluated. Then they were given an extreme left-wing tract to read, calling for a struggle 'in and against the army for the triumph of proletarian dictatorship'.

Having read the text but before responding to the attitude questionnaire again, subjects were asked to describe the supposed authors of the text. This description defined two experimental conditions: 'political' and 'psycho-political'. An evaluative adjective list, presented in the 'political' condition, included the following twelve adjectives: anarchist, apolitical, conservative, fascist, leftist, liberal, Marxist, nationalist, progressive, reactionary, reformist, revolutionary. In the 'psycho-political' condition, the experimenters presented the preceding list with the following twelve psychological adjectives added: arrogant, understandable, confused, effective, intolerant, irresponsible, lacking self-confidence, open, resolute, rigid, rigorous, simple.

For the analysis of results, the authors distinguished subjects moderately unfavourable towards the army from those extremely unfavourable towards the army. Given that the initial positions of the latter were already extreme, they could only change very little; minority influence tended in their direction. The results confirmed that an understanding of the influence agent in uniquely political terms brought about greater minority influence than an interpretation mixing psychological and political dimensions. In fact, there was no influence on the moderate subjects in the psycho-political condition, while a significant influence was exercised on these subjects in the political condition. Psychologisation constituted an ideological obstacle to minority influence and it was sufficient to inhibit this process to enhance the impact of the minority source.

Let us recapitulate. We now know that whether a position is minority or majority, it can be altered by inducing an image in terms of flexibility or rigidity. It is now evident that it is the perception of rigidity or flexibility rather than these two behavioural characteristics in themselves, which is decisive in the process of influence. If a minority's rigidity is made salient, perception of this rigidity dominates the way the minority is understood and its obstruction of negotiation becomes central. This in particular is what undermines the effectiveness of a consistent behavioural style.

Rigidity need not be an obstacle to minority influence if it is seen as a strategy in a conflict aimed at revealing and transforming social relationships. But if rigidity is individualised or naturalised, if it appears to be a consequence of the predispositions or personality traits of a minority individual, it becomes an obstacle to influence. This cognitive process, involving simplified traits that combine more diverse and subtle variations to create a more dramatic image, allows both an increase in discrimination and a reduction in the impact of the influence source which becomes an out-group of untouchables.

The introduction into the minority-power-population context of a political dimension which highlights conflict and social relations forms a part of the conditions for the exercise of influence by a minority. An experiment by Papastamou (1983) provides some confirmation of this. This experiment takes us back to the pollution paradigm, but with a variation: the opinion questionnaire is completed only once, after reading the minority text. Right at the beginning, subjects are asked to judge the texts, from which the slogans have been removed, in terms of one of two different dimensions which define the experimental conditions.

(1) They have to determine the degree to which the text is *politically* majority or minority. For example, they are informed that they can think in terms of the proportion of members of the government who share such an opinion. In this way the political dimension is rendered salient, together with the antagonistic relations it entails.

(2) Subjects are asked to decide to what extent the text is *numerically* majority or minority, by thinking in terms of the number of people who share such an opinion, as might for example be revealed in an opinion poll. To the degree that power relations are obscured here, the minority character should be less explicit.

The subjects are then presented with either the rigid or the flexible slogans and are required to judge their majority or minority character in the same manner, that is either in political or numerical terms.

The text is judged more minority in political terms than in numerical terms. In other words, obscuring power relations counteracts perception of the source's minority character. The rigid slogans are also judged more minority than the flexible slogans. In the situation requiring an evaluation in political terms, subjects are more influenced by the minority position. Evaluation in political terms reinforces the process of minority influence while evaluation in numerical terms only emphasises the deviant character of the rigid source and thus activates in the subjects a cognitive process of differentiation from the source.

Minority otherness

Rigidity in the minority behavioural styles defines the minority position very distinctly. Subjects perceive themselves as different from the minority group whether they consider themselves excluded from it or whether they lack any desire to be included. If the minority is emphasised in this way then this discrimination on the representational level will also entail behavioural and evaluative discrimination, especially as subjects will feel devalued and insecure as a consequence of the assurance shown by the minority. But this difference between subjects and minority can be reduced experimentally by suggesting that they share certain characteristics. This induces a more ready identification on the behavioural and judgmental level and thus facilitates the exercise of minority influence. The manipulation here involves blocking the process of psychological distancing which otherwise shields subjects from the reach of the minority (Mugny, 1982). Subjects were led to believe that they had either few or several category memberships in common with the influence source. One could hypothesise that the impact of a flexible minority would be little affected by this manipulation; flexibility directly excludes too strong a categorisation of the minority's position. In contrast, if subjects concede a community of membership with the rigid minority, the latter should be able to exert a stronger and more explicit influence.

The experiment, again using the pollution paradigm, was conducted in two parts, separated by an interval of one week. First, subjects' attitudes were measured using the standard questionnaire. One week later they were given the text to read, either with rigid or with flexible slogans, and they were informed that they either had few – one or two – or several – five or six – category memberships (sex, age, occupation, social background, etc.) in common with the influence source. Their task was to try and determine which were the categories (or category) that they shared with the influence agent.

For the analysis of results, the author introduced a distinction between subjects *proximate* to the influence source in terms of their intitial opinions, and subjects *distant* from the influence source.

It is important to establish first of all whether the subjects followed the instructions regarding choice of common category memberships. In the 'one or two categories' condition, the instructions were clearly followed; subjects chose on average 1.67 categories. In the other condition, subjects had greater difficulty choosing five or six categories, and on average chose only 3.85. This suggests that the experimental situation introduces a conflict, one which is especially strong for subjects with opinions more distant from those of the influence agent, subjects in other words who wish to distance themselves from the source. The results are particularly helpful with regard to the meaning of rigidity. They indicate that the 'shared membership' situation produces no direct influence, but indirect influence increases when the number of category memberships in common with the source is higher. One result in particular is remarkable; if the influence source is rigid, there is a negative influence on direct items for 'proximate' subjects in the condition of 'one common membership'. Thus a mechanism of active differentiation operates in this case, involving a search for difference and a rejection of identification.

This experiment thus confirms that one of the reasons why the minority encounters obstacles to its influence attempts, especially when it is rigid, is that subjects regard it as an out-group with which they have – or wish to have – nothing in common. And it is clearly this mechanism which is involved in negative categorisations like psychologisation.

The narcissism of minor differences

Let us return to the dissimilation shown by subjects who believe themselves to be part of a social world distinct from that of the influence source but who are nonetheless close in terms of their opinions. Paradoxically, it is for them that it is most important to be differentiated and not let themselves be influenced. But this paradox is only superficial. We touch here on the very foundations of an ideological mechanism of differentiation, the most developed form of which is racism. In effect, who do we wish to be most clearly distinguished from but those with whom we are most likely to be confused?

It comes down to an archaic fear of being engulfed and annihilated. Lack of differentiation signifies loss of identity and threatens our own integrity. Doubtless this is what underlies the expression 'they are everywhere', voiced for instance by anti-Semites when the 'rouelle' (a circle of coloured material worn by Jews in the Middle Ages) no longer enabled them to distinguish a Jew, at once so similar but so different. It is here that efforts at differentiation are at their strongest and almost any means may be used in pursuit of this end. It is here that myths about pollution, perversion, and danger are most excessive, giving rise to the most extravagant claims, such as the directive issued by Goebbels in February 1943: 'Be clear; if we lose the war we will not fall into the hands of some other state, we will all be annihilated by world Judaism. Judaism is absolutely committed to exterminating all Germans. International law and custom offers not the slightest protection against the Jewish desire for our total annihilation' (cited in Martens, 1982). Now this was in a Germany where the Jews were very little different from the rest of the population and actively laid claim to their German identity. It was here that anti-Semitism became most systematic and virulent, and with such horrific effects.

This issue of difference, it should be stressed, touches on a fundamental contradiction.

The paradox of the other, in effect, is that his difference first of all calls for a minimal degree of similarity, necessary if one is to be able to orient oneself in distinguishing oneself from him; in some fashion he fulfils the function of a negative guarantee; it is important therefore, if we are to be defended, that he remain 'in his place'... Identity is supported by a cluster of distinctive contrasts in which the positive is involved only superficially and as an after-thought. That is to say, *the other* is our safety net; if he should disappear by short-circuiting differences, then madness lies in wait for us, our bearings lost... There is nothing more reassuring to the identity of each person, in this perspective, than the exotic stranger examined *in situ*, and nothing less tolerable, in contrast, than this same person dressed up in our clothes and become a close neighbour, spreading in thousands of specimens to permeate our economy, to share our wives and our food, in brief 'assimilating' our life style, while challenging us by deliberately retaining a symbolic element of idiosyncrasy – folklore, cuisine, religion – which give the lie to any sincerity. From the point of view of psychic economy – and thus of anxiety – at this level it is as if the only acceptable thing in the end would be either *total* assimilation (which is a kind of disappearance) or excessive maintenance of distances. If one or the other means fails, if the stranger persists in becoming our neighbour, theoretically nothing remains but his elimination... (Martens, 1982, p. 98)

Discriminatory or racial distance is not to be taken for granted; it is an ideological construction, and increases in inverse proportion to distance from the discriminated group; the more we wish to mark ourselves off from those who are close to us, the more effort we must make to increase this demarcation. It is a process over which the subject has little control, of which he is not conscious, and which is socially pre-constructed; it is itself capable of defining an ideological mechanism. By a sleight of hand, refusal to communicate with the other or to take him into account is transformed into an externally imposed necessity attributed to the other's incapacity to communicate. This clearly is the ideological process which operates at the heart of naturalisation and psychologisation; indeed it is the basis of intolerance itself.

Contexts of social change

Originality
Individuals' resistance to influence is due to their refusal to be identified with the minority trying to persuade them. They wish to be neither seen nor categorised as deviants. Any ultimate consent puts their entire identity at risk. Because of the negative connotations of minority membership they are repelled by the idea of even considering the possibility that the

minority's point of view may be valid. Otherwise their faction would not have been chosen immediately nor imposed upon them by social practices of which they are as much the victims as the propagators.

There is nonetheless one way of distinguishing oneself which seems to be positive, namely in terms of originality. If the minority is perceived as original, it will certainly exercise influence, unless it is not perceived as original precisely because it is influential. Minority influence does not always get a bad press. These days, conformity is far less well received, at least overtly, than in the past. Originality is more attractive; it is synonymous with independence, creativity, and innovativeness. In a context where emphasis on the self is often taken to mean realising one's dreams and rejecting sheep-like habits, representation in terms of originality gives force and power to the attraction of minority behaviour. 'What is valued by three quarters of the French in the eighties is pursuit of their difference and of novelty rather than conformity' (from 'Quelles motivations au travail?', La Société Française de Psychologie du Travail, 1982, cited in *Le Monde*, 27 November 1983).

Who then will have influence? Those who howl with the wolves but an octave higher, or those who offer a different view? One does not need to be a great scholar to work out that a minority we think is original will be more influential; it offers new norms, new meanings, new rules of behaviour, another way of seeing and acting. It is in the context of this kind of regeneration of the social system that adepts are created.

If it is necessary to prove this yet again, we need only refer to an experiment by Nemeth and Wachtler (1973). They first showed subjects pairs of slides depicting paintings, one labelled 'Italian', the other 'German'. These labels were in fact assigned on a random basis. For each presentation, subjects had to indicate which of the two they preferred. Subjects participated in groups of five, one of whom was a confederate who displayed a consistent preference either for the Italian or for the German paintings. The experiment demonstrates that it is the confederate representing a different minority point of view who has the most impact on modification of aesthetic preferences.

If we take, as a starting point, the fact that the German position is a minority position in the classic sense while the Italian position is an extremisation of the majority viewpoints, we come to an interesting conclusion. A single confederate who takes a consistent minority position is effective in inducing the majority to change its judgments in the direction of the minority. However, if he overespouses the majority position or takes a position more extremely than does the majority itself, the effect is to polarise the subjects away from his position. He is still effecting a change, but in the opposite direction. It is possible that the deviate's taking a counterposition brings something new into the situation, causing subjects to consider aspects of reality which they had not previously considered. There is an element of courage in his behaviour. The deviate who overespouses the majority position, however, offers nothing new and his rigidity may cause polarisation from his position. (1973, p. 77)

Reappearances

Minority influence is enclosed within a set of meanings linked to ideological processes which are manifested by mechanisms of identification. These may often come to hinder its effects by displacing them from the public to the private sphere. The danger of these processes is that they deprive minority influence of its meaning or substance. The minority finds itself placed in an insoluble dilemma: either it exerts influence and loses its uniqueness or it remains different and so assumes the social costs of difference. But this perspective does not allow resolution of the enigma it poses: social change. To understand social change, one must assume the existence of overt, visible and effective minority influence; it cannot be entirely equated with any more servile process.

Some years ago, I carried out some research designed to identify the links existing between social contexts, minority influence and social change. It seemed to me essential to concentrate on the meaning of minority attitudes and their persuasive force in terms of more general historical changes.

At the end of the sixties, a fundamental development was taking shape through social action and a renewal of intellectual positions. This development concerned women, their place in society, their rights and privileges. Feminism was coming to the surface, struggling for rights which now seem to us obvious – contraception, abortion, and parental rights among others – but not without encountering fierce and sometimes psychologising opposition.

> One certainly tried to ridicule this movement. One looked for reassuring psychological explanations to dismiss this sudden social flare up against 'male society'. And one lapsed again into a well-worn determinism... If females were dissatisfied with their lot and dared to say so it was because they had attained neither sexual fulfilment nor maturity; these women should accept their femininity and reassume their passivity... What is interpreted in phallocentric terms as phallocentric claims can only be overcome by abandoning the regressive sexuality that lies behind all this peevishness and grumbling... What was disturbing in the

public demonstrations and protests by women, beyond the mere fact of their occurrence, was their total rejection of any compromise, which was regarded as a particularly 'feminine' attribute, and their generalised critique. They appeared to be dangerously accelerating an already existing process... Now this brutal acceleration of the process jerks people out of their complacency; it transforms the search for individual solutions, which is easily stifled, into collective claims which present much more of a problem. (Paicheler, 1974, pp. 16-17)

Multiplied interactions

If one considers the dominant attitudes towards women at the beginning of the seventies, they had moderated considerably in the feminist direction. In relation to these dominant attitudes one could distinguish two major poles of minority attitudes: the reactionary, anti-feminist pole which was therefore 'anti-normative', and the feminist pole, representing an avant-garde, innovative and 'normative' position stressing a general social tendency. The goal of my research was to compare the impact of the influence exercised by these two types of minority within the context of social interactions.

This contrast made it possible to examine phenomena of minority influence, not on the individual level alone but also considered as products of the confrontation between groups and social norms. It was possible to substitute an individualised approach with a more encompassing approach which treats the social actor as indissociable from his environment. Interaction, which was central in this study, operated simultaneously on two levels, first between group members as a function of the divergence of their opinions and second between the group and the meanings conveyed by norms defined at the level of society as a whole. These two levels were linked in the discussion and together enabled the operation of influence. The appearance and resolution of interindividual divergencies operated in parallel to adjustment to norms emerging in the group. Moreover, consistent behavioural style operated only as a function of the meaning attributed to it. It is, certainly, a major weapon of minorities, but not just of any minority and not just under any conditions.

We must regard the social actor as the node for two kinds of interaction; on the one hand a 'horizontal' interaction, that is to say between the individuals comprising a group; on the other hand, a 'vertical' interaction in the sense that reference to others is simultaneously reference to the social codes and norms to which our actor has access. (Paicheler, 1974, p. 180)

Reference to norms determines the relationship to the other. Interaction behaviours are signs devoid of meaning if they are not referred to the social principles according to which they are organised.

> The persuasive character of consistency is linked to its content. It is not extremism or implication in such a position which constitute the poles of influence, it is their social meaning which confers upon them their status. Consequently, one may see that an extreme behavioural style opposed to the norms will serve more to repel than to attract. Whatever form it takes, an extreme position illuminates the attitude field in a specific manner. However, at any given moment, the two contrasting extremes of an attitude will not have the same power of influence. The latter requires a more fine-grained analysis of the attitude and of the development of norms regulating it. One may also suppose that a consistent behavioural style will have a persuasive value to the degree that it is in accord with the development of norms, even if it is deviant or minority. Furthermore, it is perceived as minority and as a result has a specific attraction. On the other hand, if despite its internal coherence or the feeling of involvement it conveys, the behavioural style is expressed as a reaction to the development of norms, the influence it will exert, if not non-existent, will be more variable. (*Ibid.*, p. 205)

In the experiments which I will describe here, the confederate plays a central role. In the groups in which he is present, his behaviour, which is scripted in advance, is characterised principally by adoption of extreme positions. In the control groups, subjects discuss and decide on their shared position without the presence of a confederate. Let us define the role of the confederate. The extremity of positions, subjective confidence and certainty appear to be highly correlated and imply a resistance to change. This resistance to change, in so far as it characterises the subject and in so far as it is perceived by the group, has important consequences for the phenomenon of influence. The presence of extreme individuals in the group constitutes both a salient factor for the other members of the group and an important source of potential influence. One may suppose that subjects would immediately expect and demand less change by an extreme than by a moderate individual. But the manifestation of a radical position pushes the group members to abandon their own moderate, ambiguous or insignificant positions. It is in relation to or on the basis of extreme positions that each defines and clarifies his own position.

The *consistent* confederate adopts extreme, closed and internally coherent positions and never accedes to the attempts of other members of the group – the 'naive' subjects – to shift him towards their positions. His intransigence shows that his position is extremely important to him, and it gives a particular flavour to the interaction. A consensus being required at

Table 6.3. *Types of attitude change*

	Total disagreement								Total agreement
	−3	−2	−1	0	1	2	3	

1. After a day's work, it is for the wife to assume the household tasks, it is not the man's role.	−3	−2	−1	0	1	2	3
2. Unfaithfulness on the part of a woman is more serious than that by a man.	−3	−2	−1	0	1	2	3
3. Adolescents should be given information about contraception at school.	−3	−2	−1	0	1	2	3

the end of the discussion, the subjects have no other solution but to come to an agreement with him or, if agreement is impossible at the end of a defined period, they must admit failure.

In addition, the confederate, while adopting extreme and therefore deviant positions, locates these positions either *in the direction in which norms are changing*, or *against the current trend*. Thus, in terms of the themes taken up in the discussion, the confederate either displays normative positions – he is highly pro-feminism, or anti-normative – he is extremely anti-feminism.

These experiments were conducted in three phases, according to the classical design:

first phase: subjects individually fill in an attitude scale relating to women (see Table 6.3).

second phase (this is the interaction phase): subjects, in groups of four, discuss each item on the attitude scale until they reach consensus.
third phase: following the discussion, subjects again complete the attitude scale individually.

Let us now examine the results from the first experiment (Paicheler, 1976). First of all, in the control group subjects adopted more pro-feminist attitudes during and after group discussion. This effect was stable; it appeared during the search for consensus, and was maintained afterwards. Subjects changed their attitudes in the direction in which norms were evolving and avoided compromise agreements. This effect was also strong; in reaching consensus, 83% of subjects adopted positions which were more pro-feminist than at the beginning and, following the discussion, 79% of subjects remained more pro-feminist than they were at the outset. The collective situation and the interaction produced a polarisation in attitudes. It appears that group discussion leads to a radicalisation of attitudes and influence is exercised by reference to normative development (see Figure 6.3).

What happens when a confederate is present in the group? If the confederate is pro-feminist and consistent, his influence is very strong; in 95.4% of cases, subjects shifted to his extreme point of view. In only 4.6% of cases was the discussion suspended because of the impossibility of conformity to the confederate's attitude.

Each one then recorded his individual opinion, and in fact these were not very distant from that held by the confederate. Thus we have a demonstration of the strong potential influence of a pro-feminist confederate, representing, in the context of these experiments, an innovative norm. Change is thus very strong under the influence of an extremely pro-feminist individual who holds firmly to his position and who actualises the conflict arising from individual differences through his refusal to make any compromise. The strong influence exercised by this type of confederate needs to be related to the activation of norms resulting from his presence. In addition, the persuasive effect of norms must be related to their evolution in the context of society as a whole.

In groups where an extreme and consistent anti-feminist is present, counter-influence phenomena can be observed. The clarity, stability and coherence of a belief system are not sufficient in themselves. They play no part when the confederate stubbornly defends a counter-normative attitude. The processes activated by the presence of such a confederate are less clear than when he is pro-feminist and therefore normative.

Here it is worth noting first that the requirement to agree with the confederate was only rarely met, in fact in only 6.04% of cases. In the

Figure 6.3. Types of attitude change

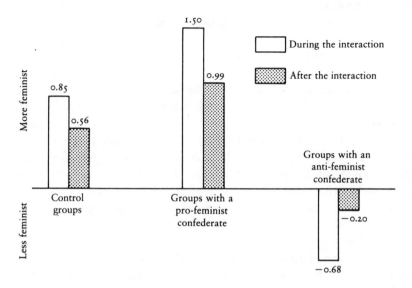

other 93.96% of cases, the subjects were not able to bring themselves to come to an agreement with the confederate and the discussions were terminated at the end of the time allowed. This inability to satisfy the experimental requirements was always experienced as highly frustrating by the subjects, a frustration exacerbated by the unconditional posture of the confederate which obstructed any negotiation in the groups.

Apparently, the presence in the groups of an anti-feminist confederate only affected each subject's attitudes slightly following the interaction. The constraint of agreement with him cannot be assumed but it nonetheless initiated a more ephemeral phenomenon: in the course of the discussion and even if there was no agreement with the confederate, subjects modified their attitude, tempering its feminist aspect a little. However, the effect of the interaction was that following the discussion each resumed his initial posture. One might have assumed that introduction of an anti-feminist into a discussion and decision-making group will only result in opposition or rejection, or in a ridiculing of his extremism and consistency. The phenomena revealed are much more subtle and benefit from closer study.

The most moderate subjects were the ones most inclined to change and to bend to the influence of the confederate. Although, over the three phases, there is only a slight difference in the frequency of the most feminist responses, and even an increase in these following the discussion, the intermediate responses do shift towards the negative pole, though remaining within a 'moderate' negative zone. This effect is slightly

197

accentuated following the group discussion. The presence of a resolutely anti-feminist individual splits the subjects into two antagonistic factions; one yields to his influence, the other resists. In the course of their search for consensus, a majority of subjects – 72.3% – are more or less influenced by the position adopted by the confederate. However, the constraint and frustration experienced during the interaction leads to a massive reaction against the confederate's attitude when the subjects find themselves in the individual situation. After the discussion, half of them react negatively to the confederate and polarise in the pro-feminist direction, while the other half move their positions closer to those of the confederate. Hence this experimental situation seems to be characterised by instability, with respect both to meanings and positions. Also, the way in which the confederate's behavioural style operates on the situation must, with respect to its content, be understood in terms of the social context itself.

Bipolarisation
The bipolarisation of attitudes in this experiment points to an obstruction of negotiation in the course of a conflict exacerbated as much by the appearance of differences as by the impossibility of resolving them. The result is a break-up of attitudes in the group, an indication of an irreducible ambiguity to the degree that a single meaning system which could organise the attitude field cannot be put into effect.

So as to study the bipolarisation in the groups with an anti-feminist confederate, and in order to compare this with the unexpected effects in the control groups and in those with a pro-feminist confederate, I divided the subjects into two equal groups. One consisted of those individuals with the highest attitude scores in the first phase and the other of those with the lowest scores, that is, those who were least pro-feminist. My aim was to compare changes during and following the group discussion (Paicheler, 1977). It is entirely reasonable to suppose that attitude change will operate differentially as a function of differing initial positions, in the case of one group more moderate and in that of the other more extreme.

In the control groups, those individuals who were least pro-feminist at the outset, who in effect expressed more moderate attitudes, changed their attitudes most in the pro-feminist direction. As for the most pro-feminist individuals, they changed very little. The group discussion only provided them with confirmation of their initial positions, something which allowed them to suppose that they were the true influence agents. The more moderate individuals shifted towards the norm which they exemplified (see Figure 6.4).

In the same way, in the experimental groups containing a pro-feminist

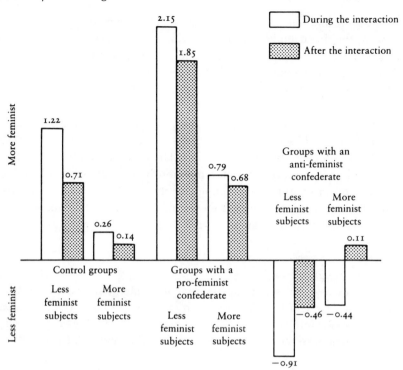

Figure 6.4. Types of attitude change

confederate, it was the most moderate individuals who yielded most to influence. The propensity for change is thus quite unequal from the very outset.

An extreme pro-feminist attitude, by virtue of the involvement it conveys and its concordance with the normative trend which it actualises in the group, represents an important point of reference for the subjects and particularly for the least feminist members of the group. For these latter the conflict in relation to this reminder of the norms is greater, and the greater the conflict, the stronger the influence.

Let us now consider how the groups react to the anti-feminist confederate. Here again, the subjects most liable to stable changes were those who initially display the least pro-feminist positions. Positions varied considerably according to whether the subjects were rather pro-feminist or rather anti-feminist before the experimental manipulation. The former resisted the confederate's influence in the long run, returning to their initial position after the interaction and indeed beyond it; they submitted in only the most transitory fashion to the requirement of consensus, though this was in fact rarely attained. The latter scorned the confederate's opinion

199

both during and following the interaction. Two contrary types of reaction coexist, the pro-feminist subjects drawing their power to resist from the fact that they know themselves to be in tune with the developing norms.

It is interesting to note that it is the same type of subject, the 'moderate', who is susceptible to change in either direction, liable to adopt a norm if it is presented to him in a determined fashion, whatever this norm may be. Nonetheless, there is no paradox in this. This experimental confirmation concurs with an observation which may be made currently in political life, for example, where political behaviour has become so variable as to be described as a 'morass'. We may mention here what is one of the best known and most dramatic examples of this in France: before and then after the Liberation of France from German occupation, the same equally dense and enthusiastic crowds greeted first the Nazi armies and then the allied forces.

Preventive change

Style of expression is not independent of content. In the course of an interaction, the conflict, the resolution of differences between individuals in order to achieve consensus, and behavioural styles all give meaning to the interaction, to the attitude object, to the other and to the experimental situation.

The active search for meanings clarifying the overall situation in which each is embedded can be more effectively understood by reference to another experiment comparing the reactions of homogeneous groups – all-male or all-female – with those of mixed groups – two males and two females – to the same situation (Paicheler, 1979). This will allow us to grasp more clearly how the representations brought into play by the experimental situation can transform the results of an experimental procedure built upon manipulation of the same variables.

First, we should note that we obtained the same effects in the homogeneous groups whether their composition was male or female. Things were quite different in the mixed groups where influence, by which we mean change towards the more feminist positions, was apparent as soon as the subjects were brought into one another's presence, during the pre-consensus stage and *before* any discussion had taken place between subjects. Sensitised at the outset to the conflict and changing norms by the attitude scale and the presence of individuals of different ('opposite') sexes, the subjects – males and females – are immediately led to shift towards what they suppose to be the 'appropriate' norm; this was indicated by the fact that in the mixed groups with a pro-feminist confederate, a female confederate exercised more influence during the discussions than a male confederate, while the latter produced more stable changes. When the confederate was anti-feminist, the confederate's influence differed according to gender. If female, she polarised the group against her, arousing an oppositional reaction. If male, the confederate exercised a slight influence, inducing slightly less feminist attitudes. His reactionary attitude is less surprising and it encounters less resistance.

Meaning and consensus

A further analysis of group discussions in the different experimental conditions, taking into account both the content and the outcome of interactions, confirmed the importance in the influence process of collective definitions of objects of judgment based on consensual meanings. Collective discussion serves the role of reducing uncertainty about the social environment. It provides each with information about the attitude object as much as about others' positions. But this information is not neutral. It conveys meanings at the same time as it is regulated by social norms. The emergence of meanings is going to occur in a preferential direction, reflecting social norms and their development. In the contrary case, it will have a destructive effect for the group, causing the emergence of differentiated positions, and creating an unbridgeable divide between them. Adherence to shared norms becomes impossible.

> Exchanges can only be ordered in a coherent fashion or one that is
> fertile for reaching an agreement if the group collectively redefines the
> attitude object, and this function is only filled if the commitments
> expressed are concordant with the norms which the collective situation
> activates. (Paicheler, 1974, p. 296)

This effect of norms was found in a similar fashion by Anne Maas in her study of what she called *Zeitgeist*, the spirit of the time or atmosphere of the period. This social climate causes particular attitudes and representations to stand out or emerge while undermining and causing the rejection of others. The 'Zeitgeist' is often surprising and unforeseeable. It might seem, for example, that a coherent attitude would lead individuals to accept abortion and reject the death penalty in the name of a concept of freedom which holds that one individual cannot take the place of another in decisions as serious as those concerning life and death. However, as the experiments by Maass *et al.* (1982) show, in the social climate in which we live, where the quest for sexual liberation, feelings of insecurity, and a subjective sense of increasing violence dominate, the same persons may at the same time be in favour of abortion and of the death penalty. In a single group discussion they will acquiesce to the influence of a confederate who defends abortion and then resist the same confederate's influence when he condemns the death penalty, *though his consistency is otherwise entirely equivalent,* for it is the same confederate who lends the same conviction to the defence of these attitudes.

The effect of minority influence must therefore be situated within an overall social context which takes account of the social codes and prescriptions in force in all their complexity and vitality. What also seems to be important is the innovative character of the minority behavioural style. If the minority fails to provide this feature of social regeneration its influence is considerably reduced and the active minority is transformed into the active deviant, all the more strongly rejected if it is opposed to functioning which is normal or consensual because habitual.

More generally, the entire phenomenon of social influence must be placed within the framework of social changes, movements, and historical contexts which make it possible by giving meaning to its expression. Social influence phenomena are linked to normative phenomena, and to evolving systems of representations themselves of greater or lesser duration. Minority influence is also involved in such evolution, both hastening its progress and acting as its catalyst.

The fact that languages, meanings, representations and practices operate effectively indicates that different kinds of influence process are so necessary as to appear self-evident. And indeed they often seem so natural to us that they cease to be visible at all. It is the paradox of influence that it is precisely when it is least visible that it is most effective.

Conclusion

My ambition at the outset was to examine an already well explored phenomenon, social influence, locating different explanatory theories in sequence. A historical analysis of this kind, uncommon in social psychology, makes it possible to organise conceptions and studies of this phenomenon in terms of their appropriate context so that they may be related to the particular view of the world which makes them possible. It also enables one to go beyond a level of investigation in which influence is conceived as a timeless, monolithic and immutable interindividual process, to move beyond an order of appearances and level of evidence that has been so misleading for the social sciences.

The axes around which I have organised my presentation of social influence refer simultaneously to breaches or ruptures in the sense that they contrast two contradictory positions, and to continuities because they reunite these same contrasting positions. The points of rupture require the successive presentation of multiple and varied influences. But continuity is interpreted in the use of a single term, influence, encompassing the two complementary aspects of a social relationship within the same fluid conceptual space. The unifying principle of this relationship is what we have to discover. By avoiding distinguishing between actor and target of influence our intention is to emphasise that it is the social relationship, and not the peculiarities of the individuals embedded in this relationship, that is primary.

Ruptures

In the end it is clear that the study of each new form of influence is erected upon a rupture with the one that precedes it.

The study of suggestion was one of the first occasions on which questions were raised about the complex relation between individual and society, a relationship fundamental to social psychology. From the beginning, the language of suggestion experienced a considerable success, albeit mixed with the sulphurous smell of its scandalous character. Sorcery, possession, magnetism and suggestion described the same order of phenomena under different names and in comparable manifestations. I have emphasised the connection of this incoercible form of influence with irrationalism, and thus its persistence. I have demonstrated its logic, its power and its violence. But I have perhaps not sufficiently stressed the sensual character of this influence, the dubious pleasure of no longer being responsible for oneself, of becoming the animate instrument of an external will, of allowing oneself to be subjugated, of being submerged in a relationship of extreme symbiosis and dependence to the point of absolute servitude, and of having all the rights at the same time as one is deprived of them, of having the feeling that all is possible while all scope for freedom is suppressed. This influence borders on weakness, madness, the stubborn forces of obscurantism. The link between this form of influence and the dark forces of Fascism creates a problem. One can, however, identify a homology between the social relations involved in suggestion and those in Fascism, as Thomas Mann's work illustrates.

As early as the 1920s, this anti-Fascist writer had understood and illustrated the links between, on the one hand, irrationality and its connotations – hypnosis, the occult, illusions – and on the other hand, the establishment of an absolute arbitrary power. During this period, in the Weimar Republic, all kinds of irrationalism burst out and at all levels including the most cultivated. It was a 'spiritual quagmire' in which the ferment of a radically anti-democratic ideology was to develop. In his diary for 1934, Thomas Mann 'presents occultism as the "necessary level" at which "swindles, sects, replacement religions, demi-sciences..." and everything "which determines the style of the epoch", flourishes' (Gisselbrecht, introduction to Mann, 1983). In *Mario and the Magician*, written in 1930, Mann describes the progressive submission of the population of a small Italian seaside town to the hypnotic magician, Cipolla: *prestidigitatore, illusionista* and *forzatore*; he was a fairground wrestler of a very unusual kind who, in a climate of mounting Fascism, imposed his will on the spectators, exerting a moral tyranny which evoked the political tyranny that made it possible. Hypnotism was both metaphor for and basis of an extreme authoritarianism. But it was simultaneously a 'scandalous pleasure', an 'infernal sensuality', ecstasy. The inevitable loss of critical perspective and self-control accompanied an increasing fascination on the part of the entire populace, the disappearance of laughter, jokes or doubts expressed in good-natured bantering, and in the end the elimination of all pockets of resistance. Punctuating his sordid desires with cracks of his leather whip, Cipolla subdued his public and reduced them to his mercy 'anche se non vuole', or 'whether you want to or not', as he says to a sceptic. The hypnotist fascinates, and is fascinated by the effect he has; he no longer recognises that he is going too far, until his own death finally confirms the transformation of this buffoonery into drama.

In this novel, as Gisselbrecht notes in his introduction, 'the central theme of hypnosis clearly reveals the limits of the liberal conscience, because it views Fascism as intimidation, as a frontal attack on liberal values – individual liberty, critical conscience and respect for culture' (*ibid.*, p. 25).

From this perspective one is better able to appreciate the scepticism and indeed the utter resistance of American theoreticians with respect to a concept which is so violently at odds with the fundamental values of their culture – individualism, free enterprise, free-will, self-control and personal responsibility. This reaction should be seen in the light of the opposition aroused by such violent social manifestations as possession or magnetism in enlightened circles in their day. In these two contexts, the ideology of the Enlightenment and American culture, this opposition marks the achievement of a process of rationalisation and individualisation of social influence phenomena. In addition, in the dialectic between rationality and irrationality which underlies it, the break with conformity and suggestion underlines the responsibility individuals have for their own development, opening the way to a psychology conceived as a science of consciousness, reason and self-control. This new-born intellectual discipline, based on individualisation, has gone on to *discipline* social life, regulating conduct and creating a radical separation of 'normal' life from all forms of deviance which are therefore pathological.

That conformity is a significant element of American life does not seem to be in doubt. It certainly had its moment of glory at the beginning of the 1950s.

Nonetheless, the values exalted under McCarthyism, so effective because they were shared by the majority, are far from extinct. The family, order, discipline, faith, free enterprise, individualism, all these still suffuse the American sensibility. And it is only possible to deviate if one creates a strong association within which one is still able to conform; marching to the sound of another drummer maybe but still marching in unison. The fundamental functions, the currents of influence which Tocqueville documented like some complacent entomologist, still flourish.

In a more recently published volume, Wrightsman (1972) considered the ubiquitous character of conformity in the American society of the time. He verified its degree of strength by reference to a Harris poll. Anti-Vietnam protesters were disapproved of by 68% of those questioned, 'unconventional' teachers by 58%. He even found 33% asserting that the wearing of bikinis 'is detrimental to the American way of life'. In this same period, according to the same author, the Department of Justice tightened up measures for fighting against dissidents of all kinds. In this they were doing no more than partaking of a long tradition of controls over freedom. Liberty, it should be understood, consists in desiring only what others wish one to desire. It originates in a basic consensus which itself is not free, as President Reagan affirmed in his address on the State of the Union in 1983: 'It is a matter...of extending the advantages of liberty *to all those who share our objectives*' (quoted in *Le Monde*, my italics).

Wrightsman also illustrates his view with the case of a child whose mother is dead and whose guardianship the Supreme Court of Iowa refuses to award to the father, described as 'an agnostic, atheist, Buddhist, unstable, unconventional, Bohemian artist', sending the child instead to the home of its grandmother, 'a respectable woman, a Sunday-school teacher at her church, stable, conventional, with a middle-class background in the Middle West', a worthy representative of the true America. The court concluded that 'security and stability is worth more' than the 'intellectual stimulation' which the child would gain from contact with its natural father. Every nook and cranny of his private life was brought up and subjected to scrutiny in pursuit of the slightest taint of dissidence. Certainly, everyone has the right to deviate. It is no longer forbidden to commit suicide, for as Tocqueville had already remarked, a life of dissidence is worse than death, as everybody knows. Thought comes to be gradually encircled because the very idea of difference is odious.

I have endeavoured to understand why America has produced such conformity, attempting a historical analysis and bringing to light the bases of an ideology which endures. The exploration of the precise composition of a set of historical, sociological and psychological mechanisms demonstrates how, so far as influence is concerned, their functioning converges on the necessity of conformity. This is not viewed in either a positive or a pejorative fashion; it is a matter of a form of influence necessarily involved in specific social conditions where it fulfils determined functions.

The problem posed by conformity is not its existence but the screen that it forms. It obscures other signs of influence which, from the perspective of a functionalist logic, can only be conceived as abnormal and rejected. It unites under its standard the good, the true and the meaningful and as a result occupies the entire explanatory spectrum.

For European social psychologists who, even if they have not been trained in American universities, have been nourished and indeed force-fed on their teachings, conformity has long been regarded as the only influence possible. Everything reinforced this assumption; most textbooks available to them were American and this is still the case. Most of the journals to which they had access were American and this also is still the case.

Through these textbooks and journals they were able to consume hundreds of articles on conformity. It is quite simple; in these works social influence is called *conformity* (see Kiesler & Kiesler, 1969). It is the only expression of influence worthy of consideration. On the basis of this fact, torrents of ink have flowed. More than an area of study, it has been regarded as a supreme value, a divinity to whom hundreds of experiments were ritually sacrificed, experiments to which the principle of conformity could still be applied because they all demonstrated – sometimes with considerable ingenuity – the same thing: the primacy of conformity in a tightly supervised climate of liberty.

To enlarge the study of social influence it was necessary to be able to analyse conformity not as a revealed truth but as a relative form, and then to be able to reveal the contradictory character of a number of well-established findings. It was necessary to be able to bring an external, independent perspective to bear on conformity, and this was made possible by adherence to a different system of values and by a specific historical context, that of the political ferment at the end of the sixties.

While the problematic of conformity went round and round, all the while murmuring the same soothing music to the tune of 'everyone is nice, everyone is similar', Moscovici broke new ground in his search for another form of influence, contrasting a genetic model of influence with the functionalist model in force at the time. He introduced the idea of minority or innovatory influence, perceiving it as ultimately capable of integrating the conflicts and explaining social change. The creation of a minority influence perspective at the end of the 1960s, has proved to be fruitful. It has had considerable heuristic value in attacking the routine functioning of research in which well-established findings had assumed the status of the self-evident. Despite the recurrent challenges to the legitimacy of his critique, the model of minority influence is now supported by a considerable number of studies conceived in a variety of forms.

Continuity

Although the study of a new form of influence has always marked a break with the previously dominant perspective, my objective has been to demonstrate that the principal forms of influence are not mutually exclusive but also that a continuity exists between them. The distinction between a public and a private level of influence is located at the juncture between a description in terms of discontinuity and one in terms of continuity. The existence of these two levels of influence obviously calls into question the universality of a form of influence within which it is possible to distinguish them. The contrast between a public and a private level implies conceptions of repression and secrecy.

If resistance to minority influence is always expressed in terms of a refusal to be influenced at the conscious level, it does not exclude the possibility that an apparently rejected minority opinion will exert influence at the unconscious level, or indeed that after a certain time there will occur a dissociation between the opinion and its minority identity. Thus differentiated influence effects appear even when individuals have no feeling of having been influenced. These are to be contrasted with cases in which individuals seem to yield to influence and 'do as everyone else' while resisting in their inner conscience and preserving their 'inner convictions'. What is revealed in these two contrasting instances is the common fear of appearing or being judged different and so being condemned by the group. Communal confirmation of error is frequently preferable to being right in isolation. Neutralising these self-censuring mechanisms can facilitate the exercise of minority influence.

Finally, the active preparation of individuals for influence is incorporated within a more general social discourse, and history reveals its persistence and manner of operation.

By locating the study of different forms of influence within a broader context of historical development, by seeking out their origins and the manner in which they endure, I have sought to stress the social meanings, the representations and mentalities they connote, the conditions which allow people to make sense of the world, such that at one extreme their thinking is based on the transparency of the evidence and at the other the impossibility of thought prevents recognition of any alternative social reality. It is in the over-abundance or emptiness of meaning that the organisation it produces in the social world is most clearly revealed.

Let us again emphasise that what makes influence possible, whatever it be, is a sharing of the same representations by both influencer and influenced – individual or group – and their reference to the same universe of meanings. Obviously this is not to say that they occupy the same position in this universe. The privileged and outcasts refer to the same semantic order, which reinforces their asymmetry and their disposition to exercise or yield to influence. Likewise with suggestion, there is no deceit or simulation. The influencer also participates in the collective illusion. He adheres as much as, if not more than, the others to the beliefs on which his arbitrary power depends.

The behavioural style of minorities, their coherence and autonomy, are important factors in their capacity to persuade. But these are not themselves sufficient; more critical than behavioural style itself is the manner in which it is interpreted. If it is interpreted negatively, as obstinacy or rigidity, minority influence is rejected. Conversely, when one wishes to reject minority influence one interprets minority behaviour as rigid. The process is circular and the defining characteristic in the two cases is the desire to deny influence. It creates a cleavage between belief and the desire to believe. This rejection of influence is linked to the threat contained in identification with or assimilation to the minority, to the dissident, the abnormal. This is why this effort at demarcation is all the more marked when the minority seems close and similar. Individuals have thoroughly integrated the ideological mechanisms of resistance to minority influence. By conforming to the majority norm, they provide concerted protection for the social order.

Minority influence must thus also rely upon a minimal sharing of meaning, for otherwise it remains impossible. An accelerator of the process of change, it sustains a critical, contradictory situation, depending on a more general evolution which renders it audible.

> The heretic's argument must not only contribute to a breaking of
> everyone's commitment to common sense by publicly announcing a
> break with the ordinary order, he must also produce a new common
> sense, invested with the legitimacy which public display and collective
> recognition confers, and introduce within it the tacit practices and
> experiences of an entire group. (Bourdieu, 1982, p. 151)

In achieving visibility minority action acquires both meaning and the possibility of conveying it. Similarly, from a dynamic perspective on social norms, the fact of being perceived as in the vanguard of a social change vastly increases a minority's persuasive force.

Interaction between individuals or groups is inseparable from the concomitant interaction between these individuals or groups and society as a whole; what is said between them makes sense in relation to what is said around and beyond them. To speak of the world is to describe it. Now, to describe the world, to classify it according to categories, implies a prescriptive power; to order *the* social world is tantamount to giving orders *to* the social world.

This is why the exercise of influence cannot be circumscribed within the interindividual sphere. On the contrary, intersubjectivity 'tends to cause us to perceive the construction of relations of meaning by and for individuals simultaneously, and brings about their inclusion within a social field with multiple dimensions and determinants' (Auge, 1979, p. 200). No one can regard themselves as shielded from influence by virtue of any 'natural' resistance and everyone is inclined to reproduce and so exercise influence. This may be understood in the fluid space of intersubjectivity, not in relation to more or less resistant personalities, but in relation to social positions connoting specific meanings. One of the fundamental questions in social psychology has concerned the meanings which actors give to their own actions, meanings influenced by numerous social determinants and which convey their own social locations, meanings located at the heart of the relationship between individual and society itself. More generally, this question of meaning is located at the epicentre of all activity in the social sciences, defining their point of mutual contact and their capacity for reciprocal fertilisation.

Bibliography

Aebischer, V., Hewstone, M. and Henderson, M. (1984). Social influence and musical preference: innovation by conversion not coercion. *European Journal of Social Psychology*, **14**, 23-33.

Allport, F. H. (1924). *Social psychology*. Boston: Houghton Mifflin.

Allport, G. (1968). The historical background of modern social psychology. In G. Lindzey & E. Aronson (eds.) *Handbook of social psychology*. Reading, Mass.: Addison-Wesley.

Andersen, H. C. (1962). *Contes*. Paris: Grund.

Asch, S. E. (1952). *Social psychology*. Englewood Cliffs, NJ: Prentice Hall.

(1959). A perspective on social psychology. In S. Koch (ed.) *Psychology, a study of a science*, vol.III. New York: McGraw Hill.

(1981). Independence and conformity in the Asch experiment as a reflexion of cultural and situational factors. *British Journal of Social Psychology*, **20**, 223.

Auge, M. (1979). *Symbole, fonction, histoire*. Paris: Hachette.

Babinsky, J. (1909). Demembrement de l'hystérie traditionnelle: piathiatisme. *Semaine Medicale* (Paris), **6** (1).

Baldwin, J. M. (1911). *The individual and society*. Boston: The Durham Press.

Baritz, L. (1965). *The servants of power: a history of the use of social science in American industry*. New York: Wiley.

Benedict, R. (1934). *Patterns of culture*. Boston: Houghton Mifflin.

Bernays, E. (1928). *Propaganda*. New York.

Binet, A. and Fere, C. (1885). La polarisation psychique. *Revue Philosophique*, **19**, 369-402.

Blake, R. K. and Mouton, J. S. (1961). Conformity, resistance and conversion. In A. Berg and B. Bass (eds.) *Conformity and deviation*. New York: Harper.

Bourdieu, P. (1982). *Ce que parler veut dire*. Paris: Fayard.

Brown, R. (1965). *Social psychology*. New York: Free Press.

Buss, A. R. (1976). Galton and the birth of differential psychology and eugenics: social, political and economic forces. *Journal of the History of Behavioral Sciences*, 12, 47-58.

Castel, F., Castel, R. and Lovell, A. (1979). *La société psychiatrique avancée*. Paris: Grasset.

Chase, A. (1977). *The legacy of Malthus: the social costs of the new scientific racism*. New York: Knopf.

Chertok, L. and de Saussure, R. (1973). *Naissance du psychanalyste: de Mesmer à Freud*. Paris: Payot.

Cohen, A. (1966). *Deviance and control*. Englewood Cliffs, NJ: Prentice Hall.

Cooley, C. H. (1902; 1964). *Human nature and social order*. New York: Charles Scribner's; reprinted, New York: Schocken Books.

Darnton, R. (1977). *Mesmerism and the end of Enlightenment in France*. Cambridge, Mass.: Harvard University Press.

Descombes, V. (1979). *Le même et l'autre*. Paris: Eds. de Minuit.

Deutsch, M. (1969). Conflicts productive and destructive. *Journal of Social Issues*, 25, 7-41.

    (1983). Qu'est-ce que la 'psychologie politique'? *Revue Internationale des Sciences Sociales*, 35, 245-265.

Deutsch, M. and Gerard, H. (1955). A study of normative and informational social influence upon individual judgment. *Journal of Abnormal and Social Psychology*, 51, 229-36.

Doise, W. and Moscovici, S. (1973). Les décisions collectives. In S. Moscovici (ed.) *Introduction de la psychologie sociale*. vol.II. Paris: Larousse.

Doms, M. and Van Avermaet, E. (1980). Majority influence, minority influence and conversion behaviour: a replication. *Journal of Experimental Social Psychology*, 16, 183-92.

Editorial Announcement. (1921). *Journal of Abnormal and Social Psychology*, 16, 4.

Ewen, S. (1977). *Captains of consciousness: advertising and the social roots of the consumer culture*. New York: McGraw Hill.

Exposé des recherches faites pour l'examen du magnétisme animal (presented at the Academy of Sciences by Bailly, Franklin, le Roy and Lavoisier, 4 September 1784). (1975). In *ORNICAR*, 4, 52-8.

Fanon, F. (1967). *Black skins, white masks*. New York: Grove.

Faucheux, C. and Moscovici, S. (1967). Le style de comportement d'une minorité et son influence sur les résponses d'une majorité. *Bulletin du CERP*, 16(4), 337-60.

    (1971). *Psychologie sociale, théorique et expérimentale*. Paris: Mouton.

Festinger, L. (1950). Informal social communication. *Psychological Review*, 57, 271-82.

(1953). An analysis of compliant behavior. In M. Sherif and M. O. Wilson (eds.) *Group relations at the cross-roads*. New York: Harper.

(1957). *A theory of cognitive dissonance*. New York: Harper and Row.

Festinger, L., Riecken, H. and Schachter, S. (1956). *When prophecy fails*. Minneapolis: University of Minnesota Press.

Foucault, M. (1977). *Discipline and punishment*. (Trans. Alan Sheridan.) London: Allen Lane.

Freud, S. (1955). Group psychology and the analysis of the ego. (Trans. J. Strachey.) London: Hogarth.

Furner, M. (1975). *Advocacy and objectivity: a crisis in the professionalisation of American social sciences, 1865-1905*. Lexington, Ky: University of Kentucky Press.

Godelier, M. (1983). *La production des grands hommes*. Paris: Fayard.

Gould, S. (1983). *The mismeasurement of man*. New York: Norton.

Guillaumin, C. (1972). *L'idéologie raciste: genèse et langage actuel*. Paris: Mouton.

Guillon, M. and Personnaz, B. (1983). Analyse des représentations des conflits minoritaires et majoritaires. *Cahiers de Psychologie*, 3(1), 65-87.

Haney, C., Banks, C. and Zimbardo, P. (1973). Interpersonal dynamics in a simulated prison. *International Journal of Penology*, 1(1), 69-97.

Haskell, T. L. (1976). *The emergence of professional social science: the American Social Science Association and the nineteenth century crisis of authority*. Urbana, Ill.: University of Illinois Press, 1976.

Hoffeld, D. R. (1980). Mesmer's failure: sex, politics, personality and Zeitgeist. *Journal of the History of Behavioral Sciences*, 16, 377-87.

Hollander, E. P. (1958). Conformity, status and idiosyncrasy credit. *Psychological Review*, 65, 117-27.

(1967). *Principles and methods of social psychology*. New York: Oxford University Press.

Jacquard, A. (1982). *Au péril de la science?* Paris: Seuil.

Jones, E. E. (1965). *Ingratiation: a social psychological analysis*. New York: Appleton Century Crofts.

Jones, E. E. & Gerard, H. B. (1967). *Foundations of social psychology*. New York: Wiley.

Kelman, H. C. (1958). Compliance, identification and internalization: three processes of attitude change. *Journal of Conflict Resolution*, 2, 51-60.

Kiesler, C. A. and Kiesler, C. B. (1969). *Conformity*. Reading, Mass.: Addison-Wesley.

Krantz, D. L. and Allen, D. (1976). The rise and fall of MacDougall's instinct doctrine. *Journal of the History of Behavioral Sciences*, 12, 347-53.

Kuna, D. (1976). The concept of suggestion in the early history of advertising psychology. *Journal of the History of the Behavioral Sciences*, 12, 347-53.

La Boétie, E. de. (1976). *Le discours de la servitude volontaire*. Paris: Payot.

Larsen, K. (1974). Conformity in the Asch experiment. *Journal of Social Psychology*, 94, 303-4.

Latane, B. and Wolf, S. (1981). The social impact of majorities and minorities. *Psychological Review*, 88, 438-53.

Le Bon, G. (1879). Recherches anatomiques et mathématiques sur les lois des variations du volume du cerveau et sur leurs relations avec l'intelligence. *Revue d'Anthropologie*, 2nd series, 2, 27-104.

(1894). *Les lois psychologiques de l'évolution des peuples*. Paris: Alcan.

(1896). *The crowd: a study of the popular mind*. London: Unwin.

Léonard, J. (1981). *La médecine entre les pouvoirs et les savoirs*. Paris: Aubier Montaigne.

Lewin, K. (1947). Group decisions and social change. In T. Newcomb and L. Hartley (eds.) *Readings in social psychology*. New York: Holt, Rinehart & Winston.

(1967). *Resolving social conflicts*. New York: Harper.

Maass, A., Clark, R. D. and Haberkorn, G. (1982). The effect of differential ascribed category membership and norms on minority influence. *European Journal of Social Psychology*, 12, 89-104.

MacDougall, W. (1908). *Introduction to social psychology*. London: Methuen.

Maire, C. L. (1981). *Les possédées de Morzine*. Lyons: Presses Universitaires de Lyon.

Mandrou, R. (1968). *Magistrats et sorciers en France au XVIIe siècle*. Paris: Plon.

Mann, T. (1971). *Mario and the magician*. In *Two stories*. Oxford: Blackwell.

Marienstras, E. (1976). *Les mythes fondateurs de la nation americaine*. Paris: Maspero.

Martens, F. (1982). Entre chiens et loups: le carré raciste. In *Le genre humain, no. 2, penser, classer*. Paris: Fayard.

Mauss, M. (1950; 1978). *Sociologie et anthropologie*. Reissued Paris: PUF.

Memmi, A. (1966). *Portrait d'un colonisé*. Paris: J. J. Pauvert.

Merton, R. K. (1961). *Social theory and social structure*. New York: Free Press.

Mesmer, F. A. (1971). *Le magnétisme animal*. Works published by R. Amadou. Paris: Payot.

Meyerson, R. (1979). Abundance reconsidered. In H. J. Gans, N. Glazer, J. R. Gusfield and C. Jencks (eds.) *On the making of Americans*. Philadelphia: University of Pennsylvania Press.

Milgram, S. (1964). Group pressure and action against a person. *Journal of Abnormal and Social Psychology*, **69**, 137-47.

(1974). *Obedience to authority*. New York: Harper and Row.

Milgram, S. and Toch, H. (1969). Collective behavior: crowds and social movements. In G. Lindzey and E. Aronson (eds.), *Handbook of social psychology*. Reading, Mass.: Addison-Wesley.

Mills, C. W. (1953). *White collar: the American middle class*. New York: Oxford University Press.

Moreno, J. L. (1934). *Who shall survive? A new approach in the problem of human relations*. Washington, DC: Nervous and Mental Diseases Publishing Co.

Moscovici, S. (1976). *Social influence and social change*. London: Academic Press.

(1979). *Psychologie des minorités actives*. Paris: PUF.

(1980). *A propos des recherches sur l'influence des minorités*. Conference on Minority Influence, Barcelona: Roneo.

(1985). *The age of the crowd*. Cambridge: Cambridge University Press.

Moscovici, S. and Doms, M. (1982). Compliance and conversion in a situation of sensory deprivation. *Basic and Applied Social Psychology*, **3**(2), 81-94.

Moscovici, S. and Lage, E. (1976). Studies in social influence: III. Majority versus minority influence in a group. *European Journal of Social Psychology*, **6**, 149-74.

Moscovici, S., Lage, E. and Naffrechoux, M. (1969). Influence of a consistent minority on the responses of a majority in a color perception task. *Sociometry*, **32**, 365-79.

Moscovici, S., Mugny, G. and Papastamou, S. (1981). 'Sleeper effect' ou effet minoritaire? Etude théorique et expérimentale de l'influence sociale à retardement. *Cahiers de Psychologie Cognitive*, **1**(2), 199-221.

Moscovici, S. and Neve, P. (1972). Studies in social influence: I. Those absent are in the right; convergence and polarization of answers in the course of social interaction. *European Journal of Social Psychology*, **2**, 201-14.

215

Moscovici, S. and Paicheler, G. (1978). Social comparison and social recognition: two complementary processes of identification. In H. Tajfel (ed.) *Differentiation between social groups*. London: Academic Press.

Moscovici, S. and Personnaz, B. (1980). Studies in social influence: V. Minority influence and conversion behaviour in a perceptual task. *Journal of Experimental Social Psychology*, **16**, 270-82.

Mugny, G. (1982). *The 'power' of minorities*. London: Academic Press.

Mugny, G. and Doise, W. (1979). Niveaux d'analyse dans l'étude ex-̄périmentale des processus d'influence sociale. *Social Science Information*, **18**, 819-76.

Mugny, G. and Papastamou, S. (1980). When rigidity does not fail: individualization and psychologization as resistances to the diffusion of innovations. *European Journal of Social Psychology*, **10**, 43-61.

Nemeth, C., Swedlund, H. and Kanki, B. (1974). Patterning of the minority's responses and their influence on the majority. *European Journal of Social Psychology*, **4**, 53-64.

Nemeth, C. and Wachtler, J. (1973). Consistency and modification of judgment. *Journal of Experimental Social Psychology*, **9**, 65-79.

(1983). Creative problem solving as a result of majority versus minority influence. *European Journal of Social Psychology*, **13**, 45-55.

Nuttin, J. M. (1972). Changement d'attitude et role-playing. In S. Moscovici (ed.) *Introduction à la psychologie sociale*, vol. I. Paris: Larousse.

ORNICAR. (1975) Revue de l'hypnotisme, in issue entitled *Sur l'hypnotisme*.

Orwell, G. (1949). *Nineteen eighty-four*. London: Secker and Warburg.

Paicheler, G. (1974). *Normes et changement d'attitudes de la modification des attitudes envers les femmes*. University thesis. Paris: Roneo.

(1976). Norms and attitude change: I. Polarization and styles of behaviour. *European Journal of Social Psychology*, **6**, 405-27.

(1977). Norms and attitude change: II. The phenomenon of bipolarisation. *European Journal of Social Psychology*, **17**, 5-14.

(1979). Polarization of attitudes in homogeneous and heterogeneous groups. *European Journal of Social Psychology*, **9**, 85-96.

Paicheler, G. and Bouchet, J. (1973). Attitude polarization, familiarization and group processes. *European Journal of Social Psychology*, **3**, 83-90.

Papastamou, S. (1983). Strategies of minority and majority influence. In W. Doise and S. Moscovici (eds.) *Current issues in European social psychology*, vol. I. Cambridge: Cambridge University Press.

Papastamou, S., Mugny, G. and Kaiser, C. (1982). Echec à l'influence minoritaire: la psychologisation. *Recherches de Psychologie Sociale,* 2, 41-56.

Perrin, S. and Spencer, C. (1981). Independence or conformity in the Asch experiment as a reflection of cultural and situational factors. *British Journal of Social Psychology,* 20, 205-9.

Personnaz, B. (1981). Study in social influence using the spectrometer method: dynamics of the phenomena of conversion and covertness in perceptual responses. *European Journal of Social Psychology,* 11, 431-8.

Plon, M. (1972). 'Jeux' et conflits. In S. Moscovici (ed.) *Introduction à la psychologie sociale.* Paris: Larousse.

Poitou, J. P. (1974). *La dissonance cognitive.* Paris: Armand Collin.

Poliakov, L. (1961). *Histoire de l'antisémitisme: de Mahomet aux Marranes.* Paris: Calmann-Levy.

Post, D. L. (1980). Floyd L. Allport and the launching of modern social psychology. *Journal of the History of Behavioral Sciences,* 16, 369-76.

Prigogine, I. and Stengers, I. (1979). *La nouvelle alliance.* Paris: NRF, Editions Gallimard.

Rapport secret sur le mesmerisme ou magnétisme animal. (1975). Presented by Bailly and signed by Franklin, Bory, Lavoisier, Bailly, d'Arcet, Guillotin, Leroy (1784). In *ORNICAR,* 4, 59-63.

Reiss, A. (ed.) (1968). *Cooley and sociological analysis.* Ann Arbor, Michigan: University of Michigan Press.

Ricateau, P. (1970). Processus de catégorisation d'autrui et les mecanismes d'influence sociale. *Bulletin de Psychologie,* 71, 989-91.

Ross, E. A. (1896). Social control. *American Journal of Sociology,* vol. 1. (1908; 1974). *Social psychology.* New York: Macmillan; reissued, Arno Press Inc.

Samelson, F. (1977). World War I intelligence testing and the development of psychology. *Journal of the History of Behavioral Sciences,* 13, 274-82.

Satariano, W. A. (1979). Immigration and the popularization of social science: 1920 to 1930. *Journal of the History of Behavioral Sciences,* 15, 310-20.

Schachter, S. (1951). Deviation, rejection and communication. *Journal of Abnormal and Social Psychology,* 46, 190-207.

Schachter, S. and Singer, J. (1962). Cognitive, social and physiological determinants of emotional state. *Psychological Review,* 69, 379-400.

Secord, P. F. and Backman, C. W. (1964). *Social psychology.* New York: McGraw Hill.

Sennett, R. (1970). *The uses of disorder.* New York: Knopf.

(1979). What Tocqueville feared. In H. J. Gans, N. Glazer, J. R. Gusfield, and C. Jencks (eds.), *On the making of Americans.* Philadelphia: University of Pennsylvania Press.

Sherif, C. W. and Sherif, M. (1968). *Attitude, ego involvement and change.* New York: Wiley.

Sherif, M. (1936). *The psychology of social norms.* New York: Harper.

(1965). Influences du groupe sur la formation des normes et des attitudes. In A. Lévy (ed.) *Psychologie sociale: textes fondamentaux.* Paris: Dunod.

Sherif, M. and Sherif, C. W. (1969). *Social psychology.* New York: Harper and Row.

Sills, D. (ed.) (1968). *International encyclopedia of the social sciences.* New York: Macmillan.

Simmel, G. (1955). *Conflict: the web of group affiliation.* New York: Free Press.

Sokal, M. M. (1981). The origins of the Psychological Corporation. *Journal of the History of Behavioral Sciences,* 17, 54-67.

Stark, D. (1980). Class struggle and the transformation of the labor process. *Theory and Society,* 9, 89-130.

Steiner, I. D. (1966). Personality and the resolution of interpersonal disagreements. In B. A. Maher (ed.) *Progress in experimental personality research,* vol. III. New York: Academic Press.

Sternhell, Z. (1978). *La droite revolutionnaire. 1885-1914. Les origines française du fascisme.* Paris: Seuil.

Tajfel, H. (1972). Experiments in a vacuum. In H. Tajfel and J. Israel (eds.) *The context of social psychology: a critical assessment.* London: Academic Press.

Tajfel, H., Flament, C., Billig, M. and Bundy, R. P. (1971). Social categorisation and intergroup behaviour. *European Journal of Social Psychology,* 1, 149-78.

Tarde, G. de. (1890; 3rd. edn, 1900). *Les lois de l'imitation.* Paris: Alcan.

Thibaut, J. and Strickland, L. M. (1956). Psychological set and social conformity. *Journal of Personality,* 25, 115-29.

Thuillier, J. (1982). *Le paria du Danube.* Paris: Ballard.

Tocqueville, A. de. (1961). *Democracy in America* Vols. I and II. New York: Schocken Books.

Tort, P. (1983). *La pensée hiérarchique et l'évolution.* Paris: Aubier.

Tristan, A. and de Pisan, A. (1977). *Histoire du MLF.* Paris: Calmann-Levy.

Veith, I. (1973). *Histoire de l'hystérie.* Paris: Seghers.

Bibliography

Walker, C. R. and Heyns, R. W. (1967). *An anatomy for conformity.* Belmont, Calif.: Brooks/Cole.

Weber, M. (1930). *The protestant ethic and the spirit of capitalism.* London: Unwin.

(1964). *L'éthique protestante et l'espirit du capitalisme.* Paris: Plon.

Weisberger, D. A. (1969). *The new industrial society.* New York: Wiley.

Wrightsman, L. (1972). *Social psychology in the seventies.* Monterey, Calif.: Brooks/Cole.

Youmans, E. L. (1875). Under false colors. *Popular Science Monthly,* 7, 365-6.

Author index

Subject index